WITHDRAWN

WRITING ENGLISHNESS
1900–1950

The period 1900–1950 witnessed fierce debate over what constituted Englishness. Two world wars drew sharp attention to concepts of national identity, whilst the economic crises of the 1920s and 1930s suggested an England in which many were dispossessed and excluded as a result of poverty and unemployment

The writings included in *Writing Englishness* invite the question 'What does it mean to say I am English?' Gathered from a wide range of sources such as letters, diaries, journalism, fiction, poems, parliamentary speeches and governmental reports, it provides a wealth of fascinating material exploring the meanings of Englishness.

Helpful and informative critical commentary, a chronological table, an annotated bibliography and suggested activities make *Writing Englishness* not only an invaluable source of primary material but also an indispensable study tool. It is also fascinating reading for anyone who has ever asked what nationality means.

Judy Giles is Senior Lecturer in Women's Studies, Cultural Studies and Literature at the University College of Ripon & York St John. She is the author of *Women, Identity and Private Life in Britain 1900–1950* (1995).

Tim Middleton is Senior Lecturer in Literary and Cultural Studies and Head of the English Studies programme at the University College of Ripon & York St John.

WRITING ENGLISHNESS 1900–1950

An introductory sourcebook on national identity

Edited by Judy Giles and Tim Middleton

London and New York

First published 1995
by Routledge
11 New Fetter Lane, London EC4P 4EE

Simultaneously published in the USA and Canada
by Routledge
29 West 35th Street, New York, NY 10001

Editorial material © 1995 Judy Giles and Tim Middleton

Typeset in Garamond by Solidus (Bristol) Limited

Printed and bound in Great Britain by Biddles Ltd,
Guildford and King's Lynn

British Library Cataloguing in Publication Data
A catalogue record for this book is available from the British Library

Library of Congress Cataloguing in Publication Data
A catalogue record for this book has been requested

ISBN 0-415-11441-1 (hbk)
ISBN 0-415-11442-X (pbk)

CONTENTS

CONTENTS

CONTENTS

CONTENTS

ACKNOWLEDGEMENTS

We are grateful to the following for permission to include extracted material from the titles stated: Oxford University Press for *The Character of England* ed. Sir Ernest Barker; A. P. Watt Ltd on behalf of Mme V. Eldin for *The Old Wives' Tale* by Arnold Bennett; Routledge for 'The Tendencies of Modern Art' by James Bone; the Estate of the late W. H. Davies and Jonathan Cape for 'England'; Faber & Faber Ltd for *Notes Towards the Definition of Culture* by T. S. Eliot; David Higham Associates Ltd for *The Spirit of the People* by Ford Madox Ford; King's College, Cambridge and the Society of Authors as the literary representatives of the E. M. Forster Estate for *Howards End*; Martin Gibbs for *England Speaks* by Philip Gibbs; Faber & Faber Ltd for *Girls Growing Up* by Pearl Jephcott; Collins for *Progress at Pelvis Bay* by Osbert Lancaster; the Estate of the late Frieda Lawrence Ravagli and Viking Penguin for 'Nottingham and the Mining Countryside' by D. H. Lawrence; Hodder & Stoughton for *Looking Ahead: Wartime Speeches by the Right Hon. Herbert Morrison*; Reed Consumer Books for *In Search of England* by H. V. Morton and *English Journey* by J. B. Priestley; HMSO for *The Teaching of English in England* (the Newbolt Committee) and Ministry of Information, *Documentary Newsletter*; the Estate of the late Sonia Brownell Orwell and Martin Secker & Warburg for 'Boys' Weeklies' by George Orwell; the Trustees of the Mass-Observation Archive at the University of Sussex, reproduced by permission of Curtis Brown Group Ltd, London; George T. Sassoon for 'Memorial Tablet' by Siegfried Sassoon; the *Lancet* for 'The Suburban Neurosis' by Stephen Taylor; the Estate of the late Virginia Woolf and the Hogarth Press for *Three Guineas*.

We have tried to contact all copyright holders but if there are any whom we have been unable to trace we invite them to contact the publisher, Routledge, in the first instance.

INTRODUCTION

This book is about the construction of national identity, and one specific identity across a particular historical period: Englishness 1900 to 1950. It provides a sequence of extracts which – when viewed together – make it possible to explore some of the competing accounts of Englishness produced by writers, politicians, doctors, social-historians, journalists and ordinary people during the first half of the twentieth century. We have chosen to focus on the main ways in which English people thought about their nation and its culture during this period, and have concentrated upon a version of Englishness written by the English about England. We offer material on what might be called the 'common myths and historical memories' (Smith 1991: 14) which contributed to the construction and maintenance of accounts of what it might mean to be 'English'. These myths, memories and other representations can never be divorced from the economies, geographical territories or social and legal structures which helped to produce them, since 'national identity is fundamentally multi-dimensional; it can never be reduced to a single element, even by particular factions of nationalists, nor can it be easily or swiftly induced in a population by artificial means' (ibid.).

The writings you will find in this book come from a variety of genres and modes – journalism, poetry, popular fiction, letters, literary fiction, speeches, educational and political writing. They should be read not simply as discrete texts but as part of a wider debate about England and Englishness, a debate which is located in specific historical circumstances and influenced by particular social structures and economic relations. Throughout the collection we use the short introductions to the various chapters to draw attention to the wider context in which these writings can be profitably read (see also the chronology). We hope that this collection is seen not simply as presenting readings from across a range of disciplines, but also as a means of demonstrating the fruitful potential of interdisciplinary work to produce understandings of what E. P. Thompson has called 'cultural and moral mediations'; that is, 'the way... material experiences are handled... in cultural ways' (cited in Hunt 1989: 4).

Our aims for this introductory sourcebook are firstly to facilitate discussion about the ways in which cultural constructions of a specific national identity function; secondly to offer extracts which enable the diversity of discourses of Englishness in the period 1900–1950 to be encountered and set in the context of the general history of the period, as well as in relation to the canonical literary history of those years; and thirdly to provide a framework for seminar or individual study which we hope will enable you to go beyond the primary sources collected here (see the appendix). We should say at the outset that the extracts we have included in this collection are, of necessity, highly selective. We make no claim for inclusivity or representativeness and remain aware that another, equally valid collection of sources for studying Englishness could have been chosen from the volume of material available. In line with our stated aims we have tried to include material which is not readily accessible in other forms and/or remains generally unstudied on traditional under-graduate programmes. Throughout we have tried to suggest ways in which sources may be set in dialogue with each other and with more familiar literary and historical material from the period. Our hope is that you will bring to this book your own interests in the period and so find yourself noticing connections and productive juxtapositions beyond those we have suggested.

We are aware of the omission of non-English writings on the English and we recognise that this collection represents a specific and (it might be argued) narrow view of Englishness. The book's apparent narrowness is intentional: the versions of Englishness to be found in our selection are those dominant in England in the period under scrutiny. It is precisely their exclusivity which we hope will be noted and discussed. The versions of Englishness we re-present in this introductory sourcebook are fragments from a wider picture that it would be difficult to reproduce meaningfully in a work of this scope. Those versions of Englishness we have foregrounded are, we believe, precisely those which were to the fore in the debates and discussions of national identity in the period under investigation. That they offer a narrowly defined sense of what it means to be English is not the issue; rather we would want to stress that the narrowness of the versions of Englishness this book seeks to evoke is contingent upon the very restricted sense of English identity being articulated in the period. To include those attempts to rework the English's versions of what it means to be English, or to offer those perspectives on England generated in the Commonwealth and other foreign contexts, would be to give weight to perspectives which, in the period, lacked any real impact on the dominant sense of what it meant to be English.

Why Englishness?

We should also at this point explain our usage of the terms 'English' and 'England'. We remain aware that to use the term 'English' may appear to marginalise those from Scotland, Wales or Northern Ireland, and that it has frequently been used to subsume those who perceive their national identity as other than 'English'. We recognise also that the term 'British' may be equally problematic in its assumption of a common identity amongst a nation which comprises such heterogeneous nationalities as Welsh, Irish, Scottish and English.

We have used 'England' when we mean the geographical territory, but also when we mean the culturally constructed idea of an 'England' which serves certain ideological purposes in the period's debates about the characteristics of national identity. As this book addresses itself to dominant articulations of national identity it inevitably replicates the period's exclusion of Scots, Irish and Welsh perspectives. In doing this our intention is neither to subsume other identities nor to exclude them, but to draw attention to the signifiers 'English' and 'England' which were (and are) used by commentators to invoke a specific set of interrelated ideas, images and values. Hence where contemporary accounts use the terms 'English' and 'England' we too have used these in the full knowledge of the problems they give rise to. Our intention is to problematise such exclusive accounts of national identity, and our hope is that you will explore closely the negations and meanings carried by terms such as 'English' or 'British' as they recur across the extracts which make up this collection. You might also consider the legacy of such accounts in relation to current debates about national identity.

The construction of national identities is a highly relevant topic to the

1990s. Across the world, old and once seemingly stable national boundaries have been dissolved in the name of nationalist politics, and these
new states can be the site of often bloody struggles as newly resurgent
national identities clash. Nearer to home, European federalism and Irish
nationalism have raised questions about national identities located in
ideas of a 'Great Britain' or a 'United Kingdom'. The assertions 'I'm
Basque', 'I'm Irish', or 'I'm English' depend for their meanings on the
negation as well as the assertion of a particular set of national characteristics: thus to identify yourself as Scottish means, in part at least, 'I'm not
English', and, as we have seen in the case of the former Yugoslavia or in
the case of Ireland, such negations may lead to conflict and terrible war.
Nor should we deny the positives: a consciousness of national identity
offers opportunities for collective cultures and thus for the development
of a sense of community and belonging. Any history of a nation reveals
how profoundly the process of social change is intricately embedded in
shifting sets of ideas and beliefs about national identity: being 'British'
today means something very different from being 'British' in the mid-
nineteenth century and the changes which have occurred are deeply linked
to political and economic factors such as Britain's position in the world
economy and the break-up of the British Empire and, latterly, the British
Commonwealth.

In selecting as our focus the period 1900–1950, we have been
influenced by the richness of this period's debates about the nature of
England and English identity: debates which in part were given impetus by
the momentous events of the two world wars, both of which contributed
to the radical transformation of English society. Our interest in the
period's social and cultural history also derives from our sense of its
centrality to debates about the transformation of social structures such
as those of gender or class, and in its equally significant contribution to
the (rather less seismic) shifts in the modes of, approaches to, and sense
of the functions for art, architecture, music and literature.

What is Englishness?

Debates over what constitutes the essence of Englishness have raged
throughout English history. Images of the English have included the beef-
eating, ale-swilling John Bull of the eighteenth century; the philistine,
public-school educated 'new gentleman' of the nineteenth century;

INTRODUCTION

J. B. Priestley's 'little Englanders' of the mid-1930s; Churchill's cheerful Cockneys of 1940 who survived the Blitz by 'smilin' through'; or the stiff-upper-lipped repressiveness of the middle-class women who refused to 'make a fuss', memorably represented by Celia Johnson in the 1945 film, *Brief Encounter.* In more recent years it is harder to identify an image of Englishness which is not in some way negative: we have the football 'hooligan'; the 'enemy within' conjured up by Margaret Thatcher during the 1984 miners' strike; the 'lager lout' and 'yob culture' bemoaned by middle-England's Tory tabloids the *Daily Mail* and *Daily Express*; 'our lads' in the Falklands or the Gulf War as celebrated by the *Star,* the *Mirror* and the *Sun.* In the 1990s the attempt to pin down some essence of English national character continues despite (perhaps because of) our experience as a multicultural society. In this context, John Major's 1993 evocation of a seemingly exclusively white, quasi-rural middle England of village cricket, bicycling spinsters and warm beer can be seen as simply another attempt to put a version of Englishness to work in the service of political aims.

Nationalism and concepts of national identity are, of course, not unique to England. They are a means of collective and individual self-definition which can be seen as part of a broader process in which economic, social and historical forces interact with cultural processes to produce a range of identities which may be taken up, rejected, opposed, or adapted for individual or group need. Englishness is not simply about something called 'the national character' but has to be seen as a nexus of values, beliefs and attitudes which are offered as unique to England and to those who identify as, or wish to identify as, English. In other words Englishness is a state of mind: a belief in a national identity which is part and parcel of one's sense of self. However, a given version of what it means to be English can frequently be traced to a particular social group, and as such can suggest or confirm our understanding of the social dynamics operating at a specific time. For example, the notion of fair play is often yoked with Englishness, yet this supposedly national characteristic can be traced back only so far as the late nineteenth century and its origins in the public-school code (see the section on Sport and National Identity in chapter 4). In context this notion of English character can be seen as the expression of a particular social group who sought to define the national character in their own, exclusive, terms.

To identify as English in 1900 or 1949 was to draw upon a complex set of images, myths, collective memories and beliefs. These were made available through a range of media and social practices – visual representations, religious and community practices and writing in a variety of forms and genres. This book is about the ways in which certain dominant versions of Englishness were constructed and articulated in writing at specific moments in the first four decades of this century. It is also about the ways in which the ideas that informed the dominant conceptions of what was involved in 'being English' changed over the period.

To identify oneself as English in, say, 1939 meant at least tacit acceptance of a significantly different set of values and beliefs than those which would have been called upon to define Englishness in 1900. Moreover to lay claim to 'being English' was easier for some social groups than others. Women, the working classes or ethnic groups might find themselves excluded from dominant or prevailing versions of Englishness. The England of Rupert Brooke's poem, 'The Old Vicarage, Grantchester', in which there will always be honey for tea, evokes a set of social relations which would have meant something very different to the female domestic servant who might have supplied the tea to a male Cambridge undergraduate (see chapter 5, Domestic and Urban Englands, for the text of Brooke's poem). Brooke's England as a place where 'men with Splendid Hearts may go' quite deliberately excludes women; and the tea-table loaded with honey is reliant upon the invisible work of servant hands.

The construction of a monolithic national identity is never complete: it is constantly disrupted by supplementary, competing or radically alternative versions of Englishness. These may simply be assimilated by the dominant discourse; some may become oppositional and others may occasion adaptation in the prevailing versions of a given year. This collection offers a range of material from which you may begin to develop a sense of some of the more influential competing discourses of Englishness from the period 1900–1950. As has been suggested, debates over national identity have been conducted more or less fiercely at different times; we have chosen the period 1900–1950 because during these years the debates were particularly fierce. Two world wars drew sharp attention to concepts of nationalism, for in both cases the belief that war was being waged to preserve a specifically English set of values against attack from foreign competition underpinned the morale-boosting speeches of politicians and other public figures, and sought to ensure that the nation rallied to the calls of patriotism (see chapter 3, War and National Identity).

Whilst patriotic nationalism fostered identification with national aspirations during times of crisis, in post-war contexts the failure to deliver on the promises made in the interests of morale and national unity led to a growing disillusionment in many sectors of society. Post-First World War disillusionment becomes an important factor in the changing accounts of Englishness produced in the 1930s. In *Three Guineas* Virginia Woolf concluded that the daughters of educated men have 'very little to thank England for in the present' (Woolf 1938: 124) whilst George Orwell's *The Road to Wigan Pier* (1936), along with the numerous social surveys of the period, suggests an England in which many were dispossessed and excluded as a result of unemployment and poverty. Meanwhile Graham Greene, in his novel *England Made Me* (1935), expresses a sense of moral bankruptcy allied to an English middle-class upbringing. These writers would not and could not accept the unquestioned assumptions of Englishness which pre-First World War writers such as Rupert Brooke had drawn upon (see Brooke's 'The Soldier', in chapter 3, War and National Identity). Resistance to the ideals of a patriotic blood-sacrifice, so potently popular in 1914, were not confined to writers and intellectuals as the Mass Observation accounts of conscripts' attitudes to the Second World War suggest (see chapter 3). Popular writers such as Agatha Christie or Jan Struther created fictions which tapped the shift in national self-conceptions: fictions in which robust common sense and brisk cheerfulness are substituted for the Victorian legacy of high melodrama or excessive sentimentality, and which articulated the values of reserve and self-restraint as being peculiarly English.

The disillusioned mood of post-First World War England thus produced a cultural climate which, by the late 1930s, meant that expressions of national identity could no longer take the form of patriotic heroism or celebrations of the nation's progress. Optimistic assertions of England's imperial greatness or economic progress were impossible to sustain in the aftermath of an imperialist war or the grinding depression which followed. When these broad influences are coupled with such factors as the growth of suburbia, the emergence of 'mass' culture, the increased opportunities for the entry of women into civil and political life and the development of new technologies, we can begin to piece together the various facets which contributed to a sustained questioning of the viability and validity of the pre-war versions of Englishness.

The titles published during these years which suggest such a questioning are legion. *In Search of England; England's Green and Pleasant Land; England, My England; Tell England; England Made Me; The Heart of England*: these are only a small selection; any literature search of the period will reveal many more. The advent of 'mass' democracy and the emergence of a 'mass' culture raised questions about 'whose England?' and these were no longer answerable by reference to a mythic agrarian and hierarchical England in which Squire and labourer existed in respectful harmony, although many, as will become apparent, continued to valorise such versions of 'Merrie England' (see chapter 1, the Ideas and Ideals of Englishness, and chapter 2, Versions of Rural England, for some of the debates around these issues).

In this period there was considerable interaction between the discourses of exclusivity – which promoted the idea that the essential English qualities remained the property of the 'civilised' upper middle classes – and those which sought to incorporate the 'ordinary man' as the 'backbone' of England. Both projections tended to be wary of 'the masses'; of women other than 'the English gentlewoman'; of regionality beyond the Tory shires of Middle England or the Home Counties; and of immigrants from anywhere (see, in particular, chapter 1, the Ideas and Ideals of Englishness, for examples of this). It is important to remember that accounts of national identity are rooted in political motivation as much as they are in social and economic circumstances. Attempts to rewrite Englishness were thus often attempts to empower a hitherto marginalised group. Walter Greenwood, in *Love on the Dole* (1933), for example, writes of an England which was normally hidden from the South and the middle classes. Equally, organisations like the Ramblers' Association or the Clarion Cycling Club were attempts to reclaim rural England for the urban worker. One might also note that for many colonial immigrants England was 'the Motherland', often imagined as a site of opportunity and security. However, it must be stressed that the linking of specific political positions with versions of Englishness is notoriously difficult – discourses of a bygone pastoral are not the monopoly of conservatism, nor are those discourses which include women necessarily progressive or feminist.

By 1940 the tensions and oppositions which we have suggested were called into question once more – if not held in abeyance – by the impact of war upon national life. Right-wing nationalism and left-wing socialism joined forces in order to appeal to 'commonly held' notions of national identity and to a set of English values threatened by the forces of totalitarianism and Nazism (see chapter 3, War and National Identity). By 1950 a 'people's war' and the 'people's peace' of the welfare state had transformed the meanings of England and Englishness generated by the disillusioned 1930s. In fact the versions of Englishness occasioned by the Second World War have remained potent tools in more recent accounts of the 'English character' in *extremis*: thus during the Falklands War in 1982 it was 1940 and Dunkirk rather than 1914 which was re-invoked to capture the spirit of England. We may, however, have seen a shift in attitude in the 1990s if a 1994 trailer for the BBC's *Sportsnight*'s coverage of a European cup-tie is anything to go by. This featured the usual fast-moving sequences of football footage and contemporary music but was voiced-over by a reading from Churchill's 'You ask, what is our aim? I can answer in one word: Victory...' (see chapter 3 for Churchill's speech).

How to use this book

In compiling this book we have not assumed a detailed knowledge of either the historical period, its literary history, canonical texts or the sociological theories of gender, class and culture one might use to examine them. We have provided brief head-notes to most extracts which should allow you to place the writer and text in the period.[1] We have also provided a chronology, but this, like all chronologies, cannot pretend to be exhaustive. It can, however, act as a framework and provide the necessary footholds in order to trace continuity and change across time. For detailed explorations of the period's cultural and economic history we would refer you to the various historical surveys cited in the bibliography under the heading 'Other works'. We hope that you will feel able to follow up particular areas of interest from these sources as well as those specifically suggested as appropriate further reading for each chapter in the appendix.

Our aim, as mentioned, has been to make available material which is not usually included in the literary canon for the period. Canonical literary material is readily available, and further documentary material on particular topics may be obtained from other published sources (see, for example, Longmate 1981). In addition, where period texts have been reprinted or are widely used in histories and studies of the period's culture we have tended to cross-reference rather than reprint extracts here: hence, for example, we have chosen to include H. V. Morton's 1927 account of Wigan rather than George Orwell's better known *The Road to Wigan Pier* (1937) which is widely available in a Penguin Classics paperback edition. In the interests of clarity of layout we do not give source-text details in the head-notes to each extract but, of course, list all these sources in the bibliography. In addition we have listed a range of period works which we did not have the space to include but which represent readily available sources for further work on topics and issues raised through the material represented here.

We have divided the book into five chapters, with subsections to suggest more specific topics. It is possible to focus on one section and to use the extracts and suggested activities and further reading as sources for an in-depth study of a particular topic and its relation to concepts of national identity. However, potentially more innovative work could be produced by exploring the ways in which topics intermesh and link. Thus ideas of the urban rely heavily on the opposition with ideas of the rural; war propaganda often drew upon the idea of a threatened rural way of life; and the greatest figure in the construction of the canon of English literature (Shakespeare) is closely allied to the beauties of the Warwickshire countryside. In fact, rural England is so pervasive in accounts of national identity in the period that we have deliberately kept the chapter on Versions of Rural England concise.

At times we have sought to raise potentially interesting questions by establishing unusual juxtapositions. For example, placing Rupert Brooke's 'The Old Vicarage, Grantchester' under Domestic and Urban Englands requires that it be read, not, as is more usual, as a celebration of a disappearing rural England, but as an articulation of the tension inscribed in the opposition exile/home. Equally, approaching du Maurier's *Rebecca* as an expression of national identity, written at a specific historical moment, might produce very different readings from those previously ascribed to the novel. Similarly, to read our extracts from Jan Struther's *Mrs. Miniver* alongside Ernest Raymond's *Tell England*, and both in parallel with Woolf's *Three Guineas*, is to raise questions about class, gender, national identity and war which are potentially productive. Hence we urge you to read not only for discrete topics but also to read across the chapters and across the genres represented here, and in doing so to juxtapose and combine the methodologies of different disciplines.

INTRODUCTION

The introductory material which precedes each chapter is not intended to provide an exhaustive overview but rather serves as a springboard for further exploration and discussion. One of our aims is to encourage you to follow up for yourself the ideas and material which interest you. To facilitate this we suggest further reading which will elaborate, in far greater detail, the topics touched upon in the introductory material to each chapter. Most of the books and articles we suggest are readily available in most academic libraries and can often be found in public libraries as well; we hope that you will feel encouraged to seek out the further knowledge you need or desire. We have not provided detailed references for names, quotations and allusions in the extracts as all of the extracts can be read without the need to look up sources for quotes and allusions; but you may find it helpful to use basic information sources such as CD-ROM multimedia encyclopaedias and copies of national news-papers, as well as print-based resources such as general histories, dictionaries of biography, companions to literature and other reference books to provide your own notes for a particular extract.

We should stress that there is a wealth of visual and audio material relevant both to the period and to the construction of national identity within it. This could not be readily included in a conventional book format so we have made a number of suggestions for further reading on these aspects of the culture of the period and would encourage you to incorporate this material in any investigation of the construction of national identity in the period. The 1930s were, of course, the heyday of the cinema, and whilst we have suggested some films which we feel are of particular interest, there are many more. Equally, painting and archi-tecture were frequently expressions of what it meant to be English – the vernacular Tudorbethan of countless suburban homes testifies to 'a spirit of England' located in the 'Merrie England' of the sixteenth century. You will have many examples of your own and could fruitfully consider these alongside the extracts in this collection.

Finally, we would urge you to use the book as its title suggests: as a practical, introductory sourcebook for work on national identity. We believe we have offered a useful source of new material and suggestions for work on writing and Englishness, and hope that it will stimulate further thoughts and ideas on the subject which are truly interdisciplinary.

INTRODUCTION

Note

1   Only the first extract from a writer whose work appears more than once contains a biographical head-note.

1900–1950: A CHRONOLOGY

	EVENTS	*TEXTS*
1900	Planck announces quantum theory Marconi broadcasts radio 　　message across Atlantic Labour Party founded Oscar Wilde dies Nietzsche dies	Conrad *Lord Jim* Dreiser *Sister Carrie* Saintsbury *History of Criticism* Nietzsche *Ecce Homo* Freud *Interpretation of Dreams* Yeats 'The symbolism of poetry'
1901	Death of Victoria: accession of 　　Edward VII	Chekhov *Three Sisters* Raleigh *Style*
1902	Boer War ends	Bennett *Anna of the Five Towns* Conrad *Youth: A Narrative: and Two 　　Other Stories* Hobson *Imperialism* Howard *Garden Cities of Tomorrow*
1903	Wright Brothers fly Lenin and Bolsheviks split from 　　Russian SDP George Gissing dies *Daily Mirror* launched	Butler *The Way of all Flesh* Conrad *Typhoon* James *The Ambassadors*
1904		Weber *The Protestant Ethic and 　　the Spirit of Capitalism* Symons *Studies in Prose and 　　Verse* Conrad *Nostromo*
1905	Foundation of Sinn Fein Einstein: Special Theory of 　　Relativity Attempted revolution in Russia: 　　Tsar makes concessions to 　　remain in power	Forster *Where Angels Fear to 　　Tread* Wells *Kipps* Synge *Riders to the Sea* Wharton *House of Mirth*

EVENTS	TEXTS
1906 Labour Party makes significant electoral gains Start of suffragette campaign	Galsworthy *A Man of Property* (first volume of *The Forsyte Saga*) Thomas *The Heart of England*
1907 Hampstead Garden Suburb created Boy Scout Movement founded by Baden Powell	Conrad *Secret Agent* Gosse *Father and Son* Joyce *Chamber Music* Synge *Playboy of the Western World* Ford *The Spirit of the People*
1908 Ford Madox Hueffer founds *English Review* Old Age Pensions introduced Ford: Model T ushers in modern factory working methods Cubist exhibition in Paris	Bennett *The Old Wives' Tale* Forster *A Room with a View* Stein *Three Lives* Yeats *Collected Works I and II* Grahame *Wind in the Willows* Mee *The Children's Encyclopaedia*
1909 Bleriot flies Channel Housing and Town Planning Act Labour Exchanges Act Lloyd George's People's Budget	Wells *Tono Bungay* Marinetti *Manifeste du futurisme* Masterman *The Condition of England*
1910 Post-Impressionist exhibition, London Edward VII dies: George V succeeds	Forster *Howards End* Yeats *Poems II*
1911 Increased suffragette activity Agadir Crisis National Insurance Act	Brooke *Poems* Conrad *Under Western Eyes* Lawrence *The White Peacock* Pound *Canzoni* S. and B. Webb *Poverty*
1912 Futurist exhibition, Paris Home Rule voted by Commons Serious strikes and unrest (1912–1913) Loss of *Titanic*	de la Mare *The Listeners* Lawrence *The Trespasser* Wells *Marriage* Pound *Ripostes* Freud *Totem and Taboo* Hulme's poems appear in *New Age*

EVENTS	TEXTS
1913 Balkan Wars	Lawrence *Sons and Lovers, Love Poems*
1914 Wyndham Lewis founds Vorticist movement *Blast* begins publication (until 1915) *Egoist* begins publication Trades Union Triple Alliance Threat of Civil War in Ireland Germany invades Belgium: Britain joins the war	Conrad *Chance* Joyce *Dubliners* Lawrence *The Prussian Officer* Pound (ed.) *Des Imagistes* Buchan *The Thirty-Nine Steps*
1915 Battles at Ypres and Loos Gallipoli landings Coalition Government Shop-stewards movement	Brooke *1914 and other poems* Conrad *Victory* Ford *The Good Soldier* Lawrence *The Rainbow* Pound *Cathay*
1916 Battle of the Somme: 400,000 British casualties: 60,000 on the first day Conscription introduced Easter Rising Dada launched in Zurich with Cabaret Voltaire	Joyce *A Portrait of the Artist…* Lawrence *Twilight in Italy* Quiller-Couch *On the Art of Writing* H. D. *Sea Garden*
1917 Russian Revolution (Bolshevik Revolution) USA enters war	Eliot *Prufrock* Lawrence *Look! We have Come Through* Thomas *Poems* Yeats *The Wild Swans at Coole*
1918 Armistice ends war Representation of the People Act: all adult men given vote; women over 30 enfranchised	Joyce *Exiles* Lawrence *New Poems* Lewis *Tarr* Strachey *Eminent Victorians*

EVENTS	TEXTS
1919 Treaty of Versailles formally ends war	Anderson *Winesburg, Ohio*
League of Nations founded	Conrad *The Arrow of Gold*
Widespread strikes and rioting: 'Red Clydeside': troops and tanks used to break up demonstrations	Woolf *Night and Day*
Continuing Civil War in Russia: Allied intervention	Keynes *The Economic Consequences of the Peace*
Alcock and Brown's transatlantic flight	Eliot *Poems*
Rutherford's research in physics	Sassoon *War Poems*
The Bauhaus founded	
1920 End of Civil War in Russia	Eliot *The Sacred Wood*
Independence and Partition of Ireland	Pound *Hugh Selwyn Mauberley*
Dada 'exhibition', Cologne: shut by police	Weston *From Ritual to Romance*
Prohibition in USA	Mansfield *Bliss*
	Jung *Psychological Types*
	Ford *Thus to Revisit*
1921 Economic crisis: 2 million unemployed	Lawrence *Women in Love, Sea and Sardinia, Tortoises*
Communist Party of Great Britain founded	Lubbock *The Craft of Fiction*
Peace between Ireland and Britain	Mencken *Prejudices*
Newbolt Report: *Teaching of English in England*	Pirandello *Six Characters in Search of an Author*
	Moore *Poems*
1922 Mussolini forms fascist government in Italy	Eliot *The Waste Land*
Ghandi imprisoned	Galsworthy *The Forsyte Saga*
Irish Civil War	Joyce *Ulysses* (published in Paris)
	Lawrence *Fantasia of the Unconscious*
	Mansfield *The Garden Party*
	Raymond *Tell England*
1923 End of Irish Civil War	Lawrence *Birds, Beasts and Flowers, Studies in Classic American Literature, Kangaroo*
USSR established	Wodehouse *The Inimitable Jeeves*
Yeats awarded Nobel Prize	Raleigh *Some Authors*

EVENTS	TEXTS
1924 January–October: first Labour Government Death of Lenin Foundation of Imperial Airways	Forster *A Passage to India* Lawrence *England my England* Hemingway *In Our Time* Woolf 'Mr Bennett and Mrs Brown' Richards *Principles of Literary Criticism*
1925 Baird displays the first television Locarno Pact Shaw wins Nobel Prize	Dreiser *An American Tragedy* Eliot *Poems 1905–25* Woolf *Mrs Dalloway, The Common Reader* Webb *Precious Bane* Yeats *A Vision* Hitler *Mein Kampf (Vol. I)* Kafka *The Trial* (posthumous) Robertson-Scott *England's Green and Pleasant Land*
1926 General Strike Germany joins League of Nations	Hemingway *The Sun Also Rises* Lawrence *The Plumed Serpent* Pound *Personae* Milne *Winnie-the-Pooh* Ford *A Man Could Stand Up* Baldwin *On England* Lewis *The Art of Being Ruled*
1927 First 'talkie' Financial collapse of Germany	Forster *Aspects of the Novel* Joyce *Pomes Penyeach* Woolf *To the Lighthouse* Morton *In Search of England*
1928 Votes for women at 21 Fleming discovers penicillin	Joyce *Anna Livia Plurabelle* Lawrence *Lady Chatterley's Lover*, 'Dull London' Woolf *Orlando* Yeats *The Tower* Lewis *Tarr* (revised edition)
1929 Second Labour Government Collapse of US Stock Exchange	Faulkner *The Sound and the Fury* Hemingway *A Farewell to Arms* Lawrence *Pansies* Woolf *A Room of One's Own* Yeats *The Winding Stair* Richards *Practical Criticism* Joyce *Tales Told of Shem and Shaun* Priestley *The Good Companions*

EVENTS	TEXTS
1930 Rise of fascism in Austria	Auden *Poems* Eliot *Ash Wednesday* Empson *Seven Types of Ambiguity* Faulkner *As I Lay Dying* Ford *The English Novel*
1931 Mass unemployment National Government formed by MacDonald Independence granted to Dominions	Woolf *The Waves* Sassoon *Memoirs of an Infantry Officer* Cardus *Good Days*
1932 Ghandi arrested Heisenberg awarded Nobel Prize for Physics *Scrutiny* founded Hunger March to London Shakespeare Memorial Theatre opened	Greene *Stamboul Train* Huxley *Brave New World* Thomas *The South Country* Blunden *The Face of England*
1933 Hitler becomes Chancellor of Germany	Wells *The Shape of Things to Come* Orwell *Down and Out in Paris and London* Greenwood *Love on the Dole* Spender *Poems* Yeats *The Winding Stair*
1934 'Night of the Long Knives', Germany	Auden *Poems* Waugh *A Handful of Dust* Thomas *Eighteen Poems* Orwell *Burmese Days* Priestley *English Journey*
1935 Italy invades Abyssinia Baldwin succeeds MacDonald First National Park: Snowdonia	Greene *England Made Me* Isherwood *Mr Norris Changes Trains* Gibbs *England Speaks* Swinnerton *The Georgian Literary Scene*

18

EVENTS	TEXTS
1936 Death of George V: Edward VIII accedes then abdicates; succeeded by George VI Penguin Books founded Keynes: *The General Theory of Unemployment* Spanish Civil War Stalin's purges, USSR Germany occupies Rhineland Rome–Berlin Axis	Huxley *Eyeless in Gaza* Eliot *Collected Poems* Cary *The African Witch* Orwell *Keep the Aspidistra Flying* Roberts *FaberBookOfModern Verse* Yeats (ed.) *OxfordBookofModern Verse* Lancaster *Progress at Pelvis Bay* Lawrence *Phoenix* (posthumous) (includes 'Nottingham and the Mining Country') Holtby *South Riding*
1937 Chamberlain succeeds Baldwin Picasso's *Guernica* First jet engine	Woolf *The Years* Compton Burnett *Revenge for Love* Tolkien *The Hobbit*
1938 Germany annexes Austria	Greene *Brighton Rock* Orwell *Homage to Catalonia* Isherwood *Goodbye to Berlin* White *The Sword in the Stone* Woolf *Three Guineas* du Maurier *Rebecca*
1939 End of Spanish Civil War Outbreak of Second World War	Thompson *Lark Rise* Joyce *Finnegans Wake* Orwell *Coming up for Air* Struther *Mrs Miniver* Lewis *The Hitler Cult* Massingham (ed.) *The English Countryside*
1940 Churchill forms National Government Berkeley cyclotron built Development of penicillin by Florey and others Dunkirk evacuation Battle of Britain Trotsky assassinated	Greene *The Power and the Glory* Snow *Strangers and Brothers* Orwell 'Boys' Weeklies' in *Inside the Whale*
1941 Hitler invades Russia Atlantic Charter signed USSR joins war	Eliot *Dry Salvages* Churchill *Into Battle: War Speeches*

EVENTS	TEXTS
1942 Montgomery's North African campaign: El Alamein Fall of Singapore Beveridge Report	Eliot *Little Gidding* C. S. Lewis *Screwtape Letters*
1943 German surrender at Stalingrad Battle of the Atlantic Italian Campaign	Morrison *Looking Ahead: Wartime Speeches* Jephcott *Girls Growing Up*
1944 Invasion of Normandy Butler Education Act	Carey *The Horse's Mouth* Eliot *Four Quartets*
1945 Defeat of Germany Yalta Conference Labour Election victory (Atlee PM) Family Allowance Act Atomic Bombs dropped on Japan	Orwell *Animal Farm* David Lean (dir.) *Brief Encounter* Evelyn Waugh *Brideshead Revisited* Churchill *Victory: War Speeches* ...
1946 Nationalisation of Bank of England and mines Creation of New Towns National Insurance Act Creation of Arts Council Nuremberg War Trials BBC inaugurates Third Programme	Peake *Titus Groan* Dylan Thomas *Deaths and Embraces*
1947 Nationalisation of railways Indian Independence Cold War begins Nuclear reactor built at Harwell	Lowry *Under the Volcano* Barker (ed.) *The Character of England*
1948 Ghandi assassinated National Health Service established Poor Law ends Marshall Plan (USA) World Council of Churches formed Russian blockade of Berlin: allies air-lift	Auden *The Age of Anxiety* Greene *The Heart of the Matter* Eliot *Notes Towards the Definition of Culture*
1949 Devaluation of the pound North Atlantic Treaty Ireland Act Russian nuclear testing	Orwell *1984* Bowen *The Heat of the Day* Eliot *The Cocktail Party*
1950 Labour Government re-elected (no overall majority) Korean War Guerrilla War in Malaya	C. S. Lewis *The Lion, the Witch, and the Wardrobe* Peake *Gormenghast*

1

THE IDEAS AND IDEALS OF ENGLISHNESS

INTRODUCTION

The extracts in this chapter all refer, often quite explicitly, to a common idea of what it means to be English or to an idea of what England is – even if, as in the letters by D. H. Lawrence, that idea is perceived as tarnished or in danger of collapsing. Each extract is the (sometimes idiosyncratic) view of the individual writer; yet taken together the extracts do suggest several common themes, patterns and ideas which come together to constitute key ideas about, and ideals of, Englishness.

The writers, despite their disparate views and the differing purposes of their writing, draw from a common stock of images, ideas and beliefs which you will find repeated, adapted and reworked throughout the writings in this book. These images and ideas constitute what we might call a cultural storehouse from which writers draw material (not always consciously) in order to construct their version of what it means to be English.

The cultural material available at any given moment from which writers generate ideas of national identity is specific to that historical period. Thus in his 1910 novel *Howards End*, E. M. Forster uses certain cultural stereotypes of German identity which might be used very differently in 1940 (see, for example, Churchill's speeches in chapter 3, War and National Identity).

J. B. Priestley's celebration of the little Englander is both produced from the social conditions created by the anti-heroic and cosy domesticity of middle England in the 1930s and itself contributes to the cultural construction of a certain version of Englishness specific to that period: an Englishness legitimated by the political rhetoric of Prime Minister Stanley

Baldwin (see chapter 2, Versions of Rural England).

James Thomas, a trade unionist and Labour MP, locates his vision of a socialist Britain in an 'England of tomorrow' within which the (differing and conflicting) interests of Scotland, Wales and Ireland become subsumed to an apparent common interest, figured as 'England'. Cultural images, stereotypes and ideals reproduce ideas and are themselves reproduced in relation to the social, historical and economic circumstances in which they occur. In relation to this you might note, for example, how D. H. Lawrence's sense of England is reworked in the two letters from 1913 and 1915, or the differences in the way James Thomas and Phillip Gibbs view the future.

History, in the sense of England's past or England's traditions, is evoked by all the writers and would appear to be an important way in which national identity is conceptualised and reconceptualised in this period. Certain aspects of English history are, you will find, drawn upon more than others: for example, neither the Peasant's Revolt of the fourteenth century nor, in more recent times, the Dockers' strike victory of 1889 or the victories of the suffragette movement are evoked as moments of England's greatness (see the chronology). Evoking an apparently common past and a common culture is one of the ways in which a sense of national identity is promoted. In this context you might like to note, throughout the extracts in this book, the frequent allusions to Shakespeare, to the Tudor period, to the defeat of the Spanish Armada and to the civilisations of Ancient Rome and Greece, and consider how and why they are used by the writers concerned.

Another commonly recurring trope is that of an idealised rural landscape in which England is figured as a pastoral Eden (for further coverage see chapter 2, Versions of Rural England). The idealisation of rural life is central to the romanticisation of the tramp or vagrant who, certainly in the Edwardian and inter-war period, was often figured as representing the freedom and adventure of a life on the open road. The poet W. H. Davies, with his youthful wanderings, his lost leg and his life in the doss-houses of London, offered, both in his life and in his poetry, that nature worship which was, for many people, the essence of Englishness (on the tramp and Englishness also see material from H. V. Morton and Edward Thomas in chapter 2).

You might also consider the ways in which the national origins of the writers impact upon their perception of Englishness: T. S. Eliot, for example, was born in the USA, and in later sections of this book you will come across writings by John Buchan (Scottish) and Edward Thomas (Welsh). It was never only the English who were concerned to define and redefine Englishness: 'Rule Britannia', for example, was written by the Scottish James Thomson. Non-English writers not only contributed to the construction of a mythology of England but often modified an existing set of myths to allow a place for that which had been previously excluded. In the period we are studying, this might include not only the Welsh, the Scottish and the Irish, but also 'Northerners', the working classes and women.[1] This is not to deny, of course, that many non-English writers and commentators preferred to construct alternative national identities, often defined in opposition to the discourses of Englishness – as we shall see in the case of Virginia Woolf, who challenged the concept of national identity as offering any cultural space for women in her *Three Guineas* (see chapter 3, War and National Identity).

Our coverage of the ideas and ideals of Englishness concludes with a series of extracts concerned with two key issues for the period's debates about national identity: firstly, what characterises the English as a race of people, and secondly, what constitutes the nation as a whole, both in its relation to the individuals that constitute it and in its relation to the world beyond its boundaries. In the years leading up to the First World War the politics of national identity were shaped and influenced by a host of external and internal factors: the resurgence of Irish nationalism; economic and political competition on the world stage from Germany and the USA; imperialism; and the aftermath of the Boer War are just some of the issues which impacted upon ongoing debates about national identity in this period.

Whilst Germany and the USA may have increasingly threatened the world dominance of English trade and commerce, English good manners remained a highly exportable commodity in many middle-class accounts of Englishness. Commentators on this era such as Ford Madox Ford and Charles Masterman are concerned to establish 'Englishness' as a specific, benign, and frequently superior form of national identity. Ford cites an American commentating on the perfect manners of the English middle-class gentleman as evidence of the superiority of certain kinds of behaviour.

In 1947 Ernest Barker comments approvingly on what he perceives to be the significant attributes of the 'English character' – social harmony, amateurism, the idea of the gentleman, eccentricity, and what he calls 'the voluntary habit'. It is not, of course, coincidental that such praiseworthy evaluations and re-evaluations of a supposed national character emerge at moments of national crisis, pride or celebration. Barker is writing just after the end of the Second World War; Ford celebrates English manners (though, it should be noted, not unambiguously) at the apogee of British imperialism – although his attitude to this is not straightforward, as his reference to the scandal of the Belgian Congo suggests.

Masterman, writing at the same historical moment as Ford, is concerned to identify 'the temper, mettle, response ... [and] character of an island race at a particular period of its "supremacy"'. He writes *The Condition of England* not simply in order to celebrate this 'supremacy' but rather to understand and confront the challenges to the dominant versions of national identity brought about by rapid social change. Masterman alludes to the 'problem' of Ireland, to economic competition from other nations, but above all to what he calls 'the Deluge' – the attainment of political, cultural and economic power by the working classes. He is concerned, as were other commentators of the period, that the spread of mass culture and mass democracy would fatally undermine the 'true spirit' of England. Phillip Gibbs, in his essay on the occasion of George V's Jubilee, gives voice to some of those who constituted Masterman's 'Populace': indeed Gibbs identifies the 'authentic voice of England', which Masterman had sought in the upper middle classes, as belonging to 'the ordinary citizen in small shops and third-class railway carriages'. Gibbs's essay seeks to represent English society as an harmonious whole united by the symbolic appeal of the monarchy: an appeal which, in Gibbs's account, spreads beyond the boundaries of Great Britain to include Germany and America.

Masterman's and Gibbs's concern for domestic social harmony – an England in which the social classes exist in equilibrium – is echoed less subtly in the extract from Arthur Mee's *Children's Encyclopaedia*. Here the nation is imaged as a living body with every organism playing its part in keeping the whole healthy. In this formulation any attempt to disturb the 'natural' workings of the body politic via the conflicts of class and, particularly in this version, gender, is to endanger the 'health' of the body politic.

Wyndham Lewis's polemic in favour of federalism from *The Hitler Cult* resonates in the light of recent movements towards European unity.

Lewis, unlike the other writers, is less concerned to foster English independence from other nations, but he too continues to celebrate 'the soul' of a nation which is somehow, in his formulation, distinct from the economic and political aspects of nationhood. For Lewis, a federal Europe would bring together the best of each nation's 'soul' and mitigate its worst aspects. Above all, Lewis favours internationalism as a means of preventing nationalist wars. This international theme is taken up in a very different vein by Jan Struther's *Mrs. Miniver*, written in 1939 on the eve of the Second World War.

Mrs. Miniver exhibits all the complacency of the English middle classes. She believes that peace between nations would be assured if everybody recognised the common interests of a world-wide humanity, imaged as a family of young boys who hate cleaning their teeth and eating vegetables. Nonetheless, despite its note of middle-class smugness, Mrs. Miniver's voice, with its insistence on the domestic and the familial and its celebration of the maternal, is a female voice to set against the other accounts of national identity in which to be English is always to be an English*man*. Struther, rather than seeking to identify a distinctive English-ness either for better or for worse, either male or female, repudiates such distinctions altogether and suggests that identity is constituted along lines which cross national boundaries – such as occupation, youth, age, or disability. Although Struther does not explicitly add gender to this list, her argument creates a space in which women might be perceived not only as having common interests which cut across particular national identities (in this instance, maternal), but also, therefore, as being outside the prevailing constructs of what constituted 'Englishness'. Although Struther's Mrs. Miniver remains ultimately a non-feminist and conservative voice, nonetheless her impulse towards internationalism raises, if never realising, the possibility of a feminist analysis of nationalism.

Note

1   For coverage of these groupings see the essays in Samuel 1989a. Also see Mackay and Thane 1986 (pp.191–229) and Boyce 1986 (pp.230–253).

1 J. B. PRIESTLEY
'Little Englanders'

From *English Journey* (1934)

J. B. Priestley (1894–1984) was born in Bradford, served in the First World War, and went to Trinity Hall, Cambridge, in 1919. During the 1930s and 1940s he secured a reputation as an essayist and critic, as well as writing novels and plays. His novels include *The Good Companions* and *Angel Pavement*, and he achieved an international reputation with plays such as *An Inspector Calls* and *Dangerous Corner*. During the Second World War he broadcast regularly for the BBC, and one of these broadcasts is included in chapter 3, War and National Identity. *English Journey*, published in 1934, was the result of Priestley's journey through England in the autumn of 1933, and we have included a number of extracts from this key text. *English Journey* follows in the tradition of writers such as William Cobbett in the nineteenth century, and in part parallels George Orwell's slightly better-known *The Road to Wigan Pier*, which offers an account of a journey to the depressed areas of the North of England in 1936.

I thought about patriotism. I wished I had been born early enough to have been called a Little Englander. It was a term of sneering abuse, but I should be delighted to accept it as a description of myself. That *little* sounds the right note of affection. It is little England I love. And I considered how much I disliked Big Englanders, whom I saw as red-faced, staring, loud-voiced fellows, wanting to go and boss everybody about all over the world, and being surprised and pained and saying, 'Bad show!' if some blighters refused to
10 fag for them. They are patriots to a man. I wish their patriotism began at home, so that they would say – as I believe most of them would, if they only took the trouble to go and look – 'Bad show!' to Jarrow and Hebburn.

After all, I thought, I am a bit of a patriot too. I shall never be one of those grand cosmopolitan authors who have to do three chapters in a special village in Southern Spain and then the next three in another special place in the neighbourhood of Vienna. Not until I am safely back in England do I ever feel that the world is quite sane. (Though
20 I am not always sure even then.) Never once have I arrived in a foreign country and cried, 'This is the place for me.' I would rather spend a holiday in Tuscany than in the Black

Country, but if I were compelled to choose between living in West Bromwich or Florence, I should make straight for West Bromwich. One of my small daughters, bewildered, once said to us: 'But French people *aren't true*, are they?' I knew exactly how she felt. It is incredible that all this foreignness should be true. I am probably bursting with blatant patriotism. It does not prevent me from behaving to
30 foreigners as if they felt perfectly real to themselves, as I suspect they do, just like us. And my patriotism, I assured myself, does begin at home. There is a lot of pride in it. Ours is a country that has given the world something more than millions of yards of calico and thousands of steam engines. If we are a nation of shopkeepers, then what a shop! There is Shakespeare in the window, to begin with; and the whole establishment is blazing with geniuses. Why, these little countries of ours have known so many great men and great ideas that one's mind is dazzled by their riches. We stagger
40 beneath our inheritance. But let us burn every book, tear down every memorial, turn every cathedral and college into an engineering shop, rather than grow cold and petrify, rather than forget that inner glowing tradition of the English spirit. Make it, if you like, a matter of pride. Let us be too proud, my mind shouted, to refuse shelter to exiled foreigners, too proud to do dirty little tricks because other people can stoop to them, too proud to lose an inch of our freedom, too proud, even if it beggars us, to tolerate social injustice here, too proud to suffer anywhere in this country
50 an ugly mean way of living. We have led the world, many a time before to-day, on good expeditions and bad ones, on piratical raids and on quests for the Hesperides. We can lead it again. We headed the procession when it took what we see now to be the wrong turning, down into the dark bog of greedy industrialism, where money and machines are of more importance than men and women. It is for us to find the way out again, into the sunlight. We may have to risk a great deal, perhaps our very existence. But rather than live on meanly and savagely, I concluded, it would be better to
60 perish as the last of the civilised peoples.

2 E. M. FORSTER
'If one wanted to show a foreigner England ...'

From *Howards End* (1910)

E. M. Forster (1879–1970) was educated at public school and King's College, Cambridge. A member of the Cambridge Apostles and later of the Bloomsbury group, his credo centred on the importance of personal relationships and the necessity for free intellectual discussion. *Howards End* (1910) and *A Passage to India* (1922–1924) are his most well-known novels in which his concern for individual relations, captured in the epigraph to *Howards End*, 'Only connect', is located in and frequently conflicts with the wider forces of politics and history. Forster was always interested in the position of the outsider: in *Maurice*, published posthumously, he explores the loneliness of homosexuality in a dominantly heterosexual world. Forster also wrote biography and literary criticism, as well as essays, *Abinger Harvest* and *Two Cheers for Democracy*, which expressed his concerns about modern life. *Howards End* was concerned with the tension between intellectualism and enterprise and the erosion of nineteenth-century liberal values by the demands and necessities of mass democracy and mass culture.

If one wanted to show a foreigner England, perhaps the wisest course would be to take him to the final section of the Purbeck hills, and stand him on their summit, a few miles to the east of Corfe. Then system after system of our island roll together under his feet. Beneath him is the valley of the Frome, and all the wild lands that come tossing down from Dorchester, black and gold, to mirror their gorse in the expanses of Poole. The valley of the Stour is beyond, unaccountable stream, dirty at Blandford, pure at Wim-
10 borne – the Stour, sliding out of fat fields, to marry the Avon beneath the tower of Christchurch. The valley of the Avon – invisible, but far to the north the trained eye may see Clearbury Ring that guards it, and the imagination may leap beyond that onto Salisbury Plain itself, and beyond the Plain to all the glorious downs of central England. Nor is suburbia absent. Bournemouth's ignoble coast cowers to the right, heralding the pine trees that mean, for all their beauty, red houses, and the Stock Exchange, and extend to the gates of London itself. So tremendous is the City's trail!
20 But the cliffs of Freshwater it shall never touch, and the island will guard the Island's purity till the end of time. Seen

from the west, the Wight is beautiful beyond all laws of beauty. It is as if a fragment of England floated forward to greet the foreigner – chalk of our chalk, turf of our turf, epitome of what will follow. And behind the fragment lie Southampton, hostess to the nations, and Portsmouth, a latent fire, and all around it, with double and treble collision of tides, swirls the sea. How many villages appear in this view. How many castles! How many churches, vanquished

30 or triumphant! How many ships, railways and roads! What incredible variety of men working beneath that lucent sky to what final end! The reason fails, like a wave on the Swanage beach; the imagination swells, spreads and deepens, until it becomes geographic and encircles England.

So Frieda Mosebach, now Frau Architect Liesecke, and mother to her husband's baby, was brought up to these heights to be impressed, and, after a prolonged gaze, she said that the hills were more swelling here than in Pomerania, which was true, but did not seem to Mrs Munt

40 apposite. Poole harbour was dry, which led her to praise the absence of muddy foreshore at Friedrich Wilhelms Bad, Rügen, where beech trees hang over the tideless Baltic, and cows may contemplate the brine. Rather unhealthy Mrs Munt thought this would be, water being safer when it moved about.

'And your English lakes – Vindermere, Grasmere – are they then unhealthy?'

'No, Frau Liesecke; but that is because they are fresh water, and different. Salt water ought to have tides, and go

50 up and down a great deal, or else it smells. Look, for instance, at an aquarium.'

'An aquarium! Oh, *Meesis* Munt, you mean to tell me that fresh aquariums stink less than salt? Why, when Victor, my brother-in-law, collected many tadpoles –'

'You are not to say "stink", interrupted Helen; 'at least, you may say it, but you must pretend you are being funny when you say it.'

'Then "smell". And the mud of your Pool down there – does it not smell, or may I say "stink, ha, ha"?'

60   'There always has been mud in Poole harbour,' said Mrs
     Munt, with a slight frown. 'The rivers bring it down, and a
     most valuable oyster fishery depends upon it.'
        'Yes, that is so,' conceded Frieda; and another inter-
     national incident was closed.

3 W. H. DAVIES
'England'

From *Our Nation's Heritage*, ed. J. B. Priestley (1939)

William Henry Davies (1871–1940) spent his youth in America, seeking his
fortune in the Klondike, where he lost a leg. In 1908 he published his
Autobiography of a Super-Tramp, which recorded his experiences on the road.
In 1905 he published his first volume of poems, which express his particularly
individual response to the natural world. He was greatly encouraged at the
start of his career by George Bernard Shaw and later by Edward Thomas. His
tramp persona was attractive to certain sectors of the literary establishment which celebrated the values of the simple, rural life of an England which
was felt to be rapidly disappearing. In this context see Edward Thomas's
evocation of the tramp in the later extract from *The Heart of England* (see
chapter 2, Versions of Rural England). Davies's *Complete Poems* were
published posthumously in 1963 with an introduction by Osbert Sitwell.

England

We have no grass locked up in ice so fast
That cattle cut their faces and at last,
When it is reached, must lie them down and starve,
With bleeding mouths that freeze too hard to move.
We have not that delirious state of cold
That makes men warm and sing when in Death's hold.
We have no roaring floods whose angry shocks
Can kill the fishes dashed against their rocks.
We have no winds that cut down street by street
10   As easy as our scythes can cut down wheat.
No mountains here to spew their burning hearts
Into the valleys, on our human parts.
No earthquakes here, that ring church bells afar,
A hundred miles from where those earthquakes are.
We have no cause to set our dreaming eyes,

Like Arabs, on fresh streams in Paradise.
We have no wilds to harbour men that tell
More murders than they can remember well.
No woman here shall wake from her night's rest,
20 To find a snake is sucking at her breast.
Though I have travelled many and many a mile,
And had a man to clean my boots and smile
With teeth that had less bone in them than gold –
Give me this England now for all my world.

4 D. H. LAWRENCE
'I don't like England very much, but ...'

From *The Letters of D. H. Lawrence* (1932)

David Herbert Lawrence (1885–1930) was one of five children of a Nottinghamshire miner and a schoolteacher. He was educated at Nottingham High School which he left at the age of 15 to work in a surgical goods factory. In 1906 he managed the fee which allowed him to enrol at Nottingham University College for a teacher's certificate. In 1912 Lawrence eloped with Frieda Weekly: they spent the years of the First World War in Cornwall and thereafter lived a nomadic life, travelling to Italy, Australia, Ceylon, America and Mexico. He died of tuberculosis in 1930. Lawrence wrote numerous novels, travel books, poems and short stories, together with much literary criticism; his novels, as in the most famous example, *Lady Chatterley's Lover*, were frequently received with outrage and condemned for obscenity. His is a particularly idiosyncratic view of England and the English. The following letters, written between 1913 and 1915, suggest the ambivalence and fluidity of his changing views, as well as his frequently misogynistic view of women.

To Ernest Collings, 22 July 1913

I don't like England very much, but the English *do* seem rather lovable people. They have such a lot of gentleness. There seems to be a big change in England, even in a year: such a dissolving down of old barriers and prejudices. But I look at the young women, and they all seem such sensationalists, with half a desire to expose themselves. Good God, where is there a woman for a really decent earnest man to marry? They don't want husbands and marriage any more – only sensation.

To Lady Cynthia Asquith
Garsington Manor, Oxford, 9 November 1915

When I drive across this country, with autumn falling and rustling to pieces, I am so sad, for my country, for this great wave of civilisation, 2000 years, which is now collapsing, that it is hard to live. So much beauty and pathos of old things passing away and no new things coming: this house – it is England – my God, it breaks my soul – their England, these shafted windows, the elm-trees, the blue distance – the past, the great past, crumbling down, breaking down, not under the force of the coming birds, but under the weight

10 of many exhausted lovely yellow leaves, that drift over the lawn, and over the pond, like the soldiers, passing away, into winter and the darkness of winter – no, I can't bear it. For the winter stretches ahead, where all vision is lost and all memory dies out.

It has been 2000 years, the spring and summer of our era. What, then, will the winter be? No, I can't bear it, I can't let it go. Yet who can stop the autumn from falling to pieces, when November has come in? It is almost better to be dead, than to see this awful process finally strangling us to

20 oblivion, like the leaves off the trees.

I want to go to America, to Florida, as soon as I can: as soon as I have enough money to cross with Frieda. My life is ended here. I must go as a seed that falls into new ground. But this, this England, these elm-trees, the grey wind with yellow leaves – it is so awful, the being gone from it altogether, one must be blind henceforth. But better leave a quick of hope in the soul, than all the beauty that fills the eyes.

It sounds very rhapsodic: it is this old house, the

30 beautiful shafted windows, the grey gate-pillars under the elm trees: really I can't bear it: the past, the past, the falling, perishing, crumbling past, so great, so magnificent.

5 E. M. FORSTER
'Middle-class people smell'

From *Selected Letters of E. M. Forster: Volume 1: 1879-1920*

For a biographical note on Forster, see p.28.

To Goldsworthy Lowes Dickinson, 25 June 1917

You can remain a patriot if you will become a snob. Realise that the lower class, not the middle, is the typical Englishman, and you can love our race without difficulty. Officers, stock-brokers, politicians, grocers – they run us, but they are not England numerically, and their self-righteousness is not our national characteristic. Shuttleworth and I have decided to be snobs. We shrink, consciously, from such people, just as they shrink unconsciously from the lower class whom we love. We used to pretend we shrank from no one. But it's no good. Middle-class people smell.

6 PHILLIP GIBBS
'Here, then, is something of England ...'

From *England Speaks* (1935)

Phillip Gibbs (1877–1962) became literary editor of the *Daily Mail*, the *Daily Chronicle* and the *Tribune* in 1902. During the First World War he was a distinguished war correspondent, receiving the Chevalier de la Légion d'Honneur in 1919 and a knighthood in 1920. Between 1920 and his death in 1962 he published over ninety books, including histories, essay collections, novels and autobiographies. *England Speaks* was published to celebrate the Silver Jubilee of George V in 1935. The book's subtitle reads: 'Being Talks with Roadsweepers, Barbers, Statesmen, Lords and Ladies, Beggars, Farming Folk, Actors, Artists, Literary Gentlemen, Tramps, Down-and-outs, Miners, Steelworkers, Blacksmiths, The-Man-in-the-Street, Highbrows, Lowbrows, and all manner of folk of humble and exalted rank. With a panorama of the English scene in this year of grace, 1935.'

Here, then, is something of England. ... We are still a nation of individualists, and I think that comes out in this book in which I have given a portrait gallery of people not yet standardised by the mass production of thought and charac-ter. In this machine age, which is killing some of our

character and some of our beauty every day, England is still beautiful where one slips away from the roar of traffic and the blight of industrialism; and in these quiet places where there are still English meadows not yet taped out by the
10 jerry builder, and trees not yet marked for the axe, and old houses with old timbers, there are, as I have shown, men and women still living very deep in tradition.

The two worlds live side by side – the old-world England hardly touched by the increasing rhythm of the speed mania which is called Progress, hardly affected by the trash of the mind, the jazzing up of life, the restlessness, the triviality, which goes by the name of the Modern Spirit. Yet in this other world of bricks and mortar, of picture palaces, of factories and flats, and electric trams and chain stores, there
20 is something still very traditional in the crowds that pass, and in the individuals who make up the crowd. All this modernisation is, I find, very superficial. I mean, it has not yet bitten into the soul of England or poisoned its brain.

7 J. H. THOMAS
'I do foresee a far happier England . . .'

From *When Labour Rules* (1920)

James Henry Thomas (1874–1949) was Labour MP for Derby from 1910 to 1936, holding several ministerial posts (unemployment, colonial secretary, Dominions secretary). Thomas was also general secretary of the National Union of Railwaymen (1918–1931). He was expelled from the Labour Party and the NUR for staying with Ramsay MacDonald in the 1931 National Government crisis.

There is nothing Utopian in my vision of the England of To-morrow; I am not one of those confident and optimistic people who imagine that once Labour comes into power all will be well with the world; nevertheless, I do foresee a far happier England than any historian has yet been in a position to describe.

Utopia, as I understand it, is a place which cannot be improved upon; a State in which the social and political
10 conditions have reached a standard which cannot be excel-

led; a State of ideal perfection. I cannot conceive England or any other country reaching the summit of such an ambition in a thousand tomorrows, but I can and do conceive an England which by to-morrow will have made greater strides towards perfection than our grandfathers would have believed to be possible within hundreds of years.

It may safely be assumed, however, that whatever progress to-morrow may be able to look back upon it will find human nature still very much what it is to-day; there will still be jealousies and bickerings and disputes and dis-
20 content – above all, there will be discontent, and were this not to be I, for one, would have little hope of the future; but the discontent of to-morrow will differ fundamentally from the discontent of the past, inasmuch as it will not be based upon a sense of injustice and will not be received in a spirit of hostility.

Furthermore, the grounds for discontent will be considerably fewer. The holiday-maker will still have the weather to grumble about; the dyspeptic will continue to complain of his breakfast, and the farmer will still find a
30 grievance in the state of his crops, but no man will have occasion to protest against the conditions under which he is expected to live; no man will be able to state that some one else is living on his sweated labour; and no man will be able to proclaim that he lacks the opportunity to improve his lot if he wishes to do so.

There will be no profiteers, no unemployment, no slums, no hungry children. No man will be expected to work an excessive number of hours, and no man who is fit for work will be permitted to shirk it; the right to live upon the
40 accumulated wealth of another will no longer exist; the right to the best and highest education the country can afford will no longer be the exclusive privilege of a favoured class, but will be open to all whose talents show that they will benefit by receiving it: the only qualifications for the higher civil service will be character and ability.

8 ARNOLD BENNETT
'An honest and naïve goodwill ... in the very air of England'

From *The Old Wives' Tale* (1908)

Arnold Bennett (1867–1931) was born in the Pottery town of Hanley in Staffordshire. His major novels used the Potteries of his childhood as a setting in which to explore the lives of ordinary people in relationship to time and history. Arnold Bennett also wrote plays, two volumes of short stories and numerous articles on general subjects. *The Old Wives' Tale* tells the story of two sisters whose lives diverge when Sophia elopes to France in an attempt to escape the stifling codes of their Victorian upbringing. The extract here narrates the meeting of the two sisters after thirty years; Sophia has been deserted and Constance widowed.

Certainly she could not claim to have 'added up' Constance yet. She considered that her sister was in some respects utterly provincial – what they used to call in the Five Towns a 'body'. Somewhat too diffident, not assertive enough, not erect enough; with curious provincial pronunciations, accents, gestures, mannerisms, and inarticulate ejaculations; with a curious narrowness of outlook! But at the same time Constance was very shrewd, and she was often proving by some bit of a remark that she knew what was what, despite
10 her provinciality. In judgements upon human nature they undoubtedly thought alike, and there was a strong natural general sympathy between them. And at the bottom of Constance was something fine. At intervals Sophia discovered herself secretly patronizing Constance, but reflection would always cause her to cease from patronage and to examine her own defences. Constance, besides being the essence of kindness, was no fool. Constance could see through a pretence, an absurdity, as quickly as anyone. Constance did honestly appear to Sophia to be superior to
20 any Frenchwoman that she had ever encountered. She saw supreme in Constance that quality which she had recognized in the porters at Newhaven on landing – the quality of an honest and naïve goodwill, of powerful simplicity. That quality presented itself to her as the greatest in the world, and it seemed to be in the very air of England.

9 E. M. FORSTER
'Why has not England a great mythology?'

From *Howards End* (1910)

In this extract Margaret, the novel's major protagonist, visiting rural Hertford-
shire, contemplates the traditions of English culture and its roots, as she
perceives it, in folklore and a classic pastoralism. She believes 'the spirit' of
rural England has yet to be captured in poetry and literature.

For a biographical note on Forster, see p.28.

Walking straight up from the station, she crossed the village
green and entered the long chestnut avenue that connects it
with the church. The church itself stood in the village once.
But it there attracted so many worshippers that the Devil,
in a pet, snatched it from its foundations, and poised it on
an inconvenient knoll, three-quarters of a mile away. If this
story is true, the chestnut avenue must have been planted by
the angels. No more tempting approach could be imagined
for the lukewarm Christian, and if he still finds the walk too
10 long the Devil is defeated all the same, Science having built
Holy Trinity, a Chapel of Ease, near the Charleses, and
roofed it with tin.

Up the avenue Margaret strolled slowly, stopping to
watch the sky that gleamed through the upper branches of
the chestnuts, or to finger the little horseshoes on the lower
branches. Why has not England a great mythology? Our
folklore has never advanced beyond daintiness, and the
great melodies about our countryside have all issued
through the pipes of Greece. Deep and true as the native
20 imagination can be, it seems to have failed here. It has
stopped with the witches and the fairies. It cannot vivify one
fraction of a summer field, or give names to half a dozen
stars. England still waits for the supreme moment of her
literature – for the great poet who shall voice her, or, better
still, for the thousand little poets whose voices shall pass
into our common talk.

10 T. S. ELIOT
'What is part of our culture is also part of our lived religion'

From *Notes Towards the Definition of Culture* (1948)

Thomas Stearns Eliot (1888–1965) was born in America, and educated at Harvard, the Sorbonne and Oxford University. He settled in England just prior to the First World War, and in 1927 became a British subject. Eliot's poetry of the 1920s and 1930s established him as one of the major poets of the modernist movement in England (the key work here is *The Waste Land* (1922)). Both his poetry and his influential critical works secured him a reputation as the foremost cultural critic of the first half of the twentieth century. *The Oxford Companion to English Literature* suggests Eliot 'may be called the M. Arnold of the 20th century' (p.312), and in this short extract from *Notes Towards the Definition of Culture* the concern with culture as part of national identity and social cohesiveness echoes Arnold's concerns in the nineteenth century.

Taking now the point of view of identification, the reader must remind himself as the author has constantly to do, of how much is here embraced by the term *culture*. It includes all the characteristic activities and interests of a people: Derby Day, Henley Regatta, Cowes, the twelfth of August, a cup final, the dog races, the pin table, the dart board, Wensleydale cheese, boiled cabbage cut into sections, beetroot in vinegar, nineteenth-century Gothic churches and the music of Elgar. The reader can make his own list. And then we have to face the strange idea that what is part of our
10   culture is also a part of our *lived* religion.

11 C. F. G. MASTERMAN
'We cannot help being interested in ourselves'

From *The Condition of England* (1909)

Charles Frederick Gurney Masterman (1874–1927) was an author, journalist and Liberal politician. His writings are infused with apprehension and nostalgia as he surveys the changing social conditions in England prior to the First World War. He wrote about slum life, the ravages, as he perceived them, of urbanisation, and the lack of an energising spiritual life with which to meet the rapid social changes of his time. He was perhaps less successful as a practical politician than as an imaginative writer. *The Condition of England*, from which this extract is taken, expresses Masterman's fears for an England lacking spiritual commitment.

'Contemporary England' – its origin, its varying elements of good and evil, its purposes, its future drift – is a study demanding a lifetime's investigation by a man of genius. But every tiny effort, if sincerely undertaken, may stimulate discussion of a problem which cannot be discussed too widely. It will study the most sincere of the popular writers of fiction, especially those who from a direct experience of some particular class of society – the industrial peoples, the tramp, the village life, the shop assistant, the country house

10   – can provide under the form of fiction something in the nature of a personal testimony. It is assisted by those who to-day see instinctively the first tentative effort towards the construction of a sociology-investigation into the lives and wages, social character, beliefs and prejudices of various selected classes and localities. Biography is not without its contribution, especially the biography of typical men – a labour-leader who reveals himself as a conspicuous member of a labouring class at the base, or a politician who voices the scepticisms, manners, fascinations, and prejudices of a

20   cultured, leisured society at the summit of the social order. The satirist and the moralist, if the grimace in the case of the one be not too obviously forced and bitter, and the revolt in the case of the other not too exacting and scornful, may also exhibit the tendencies of an age. And there is always much to be learned from those alien observers, each of whom, entering into our midst a stranger, has set down his impression of the life of our own people with something of the freshness and curiosity of a child on a first visit to Wonderland.

30   And here indeed it is largely upon foreign criticism that we have to depend. We are familiar with the 'composite photograph' in which thousands of superimposed like-nesses result in the elimination of personal variants, the production of a norm or type. We seek a kind of mental or moral 'composite photograph' showing the average senti-ment, the average emotion, the average religion. And this is a method of investigation far more familiar to Europe, where introspection is regarded as a duty, than to England,

where introspection is regarded as a disease. Most modern
40 attempts at the analysis of the English character have come
from the European resident or visitor. In books translated
from the French, like that of M. Boutmy, or from the
German, like that of Dr. Karl Peters, the Englishman learns
with amazement that he presents this aspect to one observer,
that to another. His sentiments are like that of the savage
who is suddenly confronted with the looking-glass; or,
rather (since he is convinced that all these impressions are
distorted or prejudiced), like the crowd which constantly
gathers before the shop windows which present convex or
50 concave mirrors – for the pleasure of seeing their natural
faces weirdly elongated or foreshortened. Yet we are
compelled to read such books. We are compelled to read all
such books. Even as a result of such unfair description we
acknowledge the stimulus and challenge which such
description affords. We cannot help being interested in
ourselves. Sometimes, indeed, these impartial minds are able
to sting us into anxiety by their agitation over things which
we generally accept as normal. Again and again the foreigner and the colonial, entering this rich land with too
60 exuberant ideals of its wealth and comfort, have broken into
cries of pain and wonder at the revelation of the life of
poverty festering round the pillars which support the
material greatness of England. A picture to which we have
become accustomed, which we endure as best we may,
seems to them a picture of horror and desolation. Again and
again we have found our material splendours and extrava-
gances which have developed by almost inconspicuous
gradations year by year and generation by generation, set
out for surprise or condemnation, by those who had
70 maintained a tradition of simplicity, even of austerity, in
England's social life. Again and again a revisit, after prolonged absence, has exhibited some transformation of
things of which those who have been living in the current
are hardly themselves conscious – a transformation effected
by no man's definite desires.

All such observations, however, are faced with some

fundamental difficulties. One of these is the difficulty of ascertaining where the essential nation resides: what spirit and temper, in what particular class or locality, will stand to
80 the future for twentieth-century England. A few generations ago that difficulty did not exist. England was the population of the English countryside: the 'rich man in his castle', the 'Poor man at his gate'; the feudal society of country house, country village, and little country town, in a land whose immense wealth still slept undisturbed. But no one to-day would seek in the ruined villages and dwindling population of the countryside the spirit of an 'England' four-fifths of whose people have now crowded into the cities. The little red-roofed towns and hamlets, the labourer
90 in the fields at noontide or evening, the old English service in the old English village church, now stand but as the historical survival of a once great and splendid past. Is 'England' then to be discovered in the feverish industrial energy of the manufacturing cities? In the vast welter and chaos of the capital of Empire? Amongst the new Plutocracy? The middle classes? The artisan populations? The broken poor? All contribute their quota to the stream of the national life. All have replies to give the interrogator of their customs and beliefs and varying ideals. All together make
100 up a picture of a 'roaring reach of death and life' in a world where the one single system of a traditional hierarchy has fissured into a thousand diversified channels, with eddies and breakwaters, whirlpools and sullen marshes, and every variety of vigour, somnolence, and decay.

Again, no living observer has ever seen England in adversity: beaten to the knees, to the ground. No one can foresee what spirit – either of resistance or acquiescence – latent in this kindly, lazy, good-natured people might be evoked by so elemental a challenge. England is often
110 sharply contrasted with Ireland, and the Irish with the English people. What spirit would be manifest amongst the English people to-day if they had been subjugated by an alien conqueror, with their lands dispossessed, their religion penalised, their national ideals everywhere faced with

opposition and disdain? Such an experience might have been stamped upon history if the Armada had reached these shores; it might have 'staggered humanity' with unforgettable memories. Would an invaded England offer the resistance of an invaded Germany, or of an invaded Spain,
120 in the Napoleonic Wars? How would we actually treat our 'Communists' if they seized London after a time of national disaster and established a 'Social' Republic? No one can tell what a man will do in such a shock as the Messina earthquake, or when the shells of the invader, without warning, crash through the ruins of his home. And no one can foresee what a nation will do in adversity which has never seen itself compelled to face the end of its customary world.

Again, we know little or nothing to-day of the great
130 multitude of the people who inhabit these islands. They produce no authors. They edit no newspapers. They find no vocal expression for their sentiments and desires. Their leaders are either chosen from another class, or, from the very fact of leadership, sharply distinguished from the members of their own. They are never articulate except in times of exceptional excitement; in depression, when trade is bad; in exuberance, when, as on the 'Mafeking' nights, they suddenly appear from nowhere to take possession of the city. England, for the nation or foreign observer, is the
140 tone and temper which the ideals and determinations of the middle class have stamped upon the vision of an astonished Europe. It is the middle class which stands for England in most modern analyses. It is the middle class which is losing its religion; which is slowly or suddenly discovering that it no longer believes in the existence of the God of its fathers, or a life beyond the grave. It is the middle class whose inexhaustible patience fills the observer with admiration and amazement as he beholds it waiting in the fog at a London terminus for three hours beyond the advertised
150 time, and then raising a cheer, half joyful, half ironical, when the melancholy train at last emerges from the darkness. And it is the middle class which has preserved under all its

security and prosperity that elemental unrest which this
same observer has identified as an inheritance from an
ancestry of criminals and adventurers: which drives it out
from many a quiet vicarage and rose garden into a journey
far beyond the skyline, to become the 'frontiersmen of all
the world'.[1]

But below this large kingdom, which for more than half
160 a century has stood for 'England', stretches a huge and
unexplored region which seems destined in the next half-
century to progress towards articulate voice, and to demand
an increasing power. It is the class of which Matthew
Arnold, with the agreeable insolence of his habitual attitude, declared himself to be the discoverer, and to which he
gave the name of the 'Populace'. 'That vast portion of the
working-class', he defined it, nearly forty years ago, 'which,
raw and half-developed, has long been half hidden amid its
poverty and squalor, and is now issuing from its hiding-
170 place to assert an Englishman's heaven-born privilege of
doing as he likes, and is beginning to perplex us by
marching where it likes, meeting where it likes, bending
what it likes, breaking what it likes'. 'To this vast residuum',
he adds, 'we may with great propriety give the name of
Populace'. To most observers from the classes above, this is
the Deluge; and its attainment of power – if such attainment
ever were realised – the coming of the twilight of the gods.
They see our civilisation as a little patch of redeemed land
in the wilderness; preserved as by a miracle from one decade
180 to another. They behold the influx, as the rush of a bank-
holiday crowd upon some tranquil garden: tearing up the
flowers by the roots, reeling in drunken merriment on the
grass plots, strewing the pleasant landscape with torn paper
and broken bottles. This class – in the cities – cannot be
accused of losing its religion. It is not losing its religion,
because it had never gained a religion. In the industrial
centres of England, since the city first was, the old inherited
faiths have never been anything but the carefully preserved
treasure of a tiny minority. It is a class full of sentiment
190 which the foreigner is apt to condemn as sentimentality.

Amusing examples are familiar of its uncalculating kindliness. An immense traffic is held up for considerable time because a sheep – on its way to immediate slaughter – is entangled between two tramcars. The whole populace cheerfully submit to this inconvenience, sooner than consummate the decease of the unfortunate animal. In a certain pottery manufactory, the apparatus has been arranged for the baking process, and the fires are about to be lighted, when the mewing of a cat is heard from inside the kiln. The
200 men refuse to proceed with the work. A whole day is spent in an endeavour to entice the cat out again; and, on this proving fruitless, in the unloading of the kiln, in order to rescue the creature. When it is liberated, it is immediately hurled – with objurgations – into the river. The men were exasperated with the trouble which had been caused and the time wasted; but they could not allow the cat to be roasted alive.

Next to this 'sentimentality', so astonishing to Europe – because so irrational – comes the invincible patience of the
210 English workman. He will endure almost anything – in silence – until it becomes unendurable. When he is vocal, it is pretty certain that things *have* become unendurable. I once had occasion to visit a family whose two sons were working on the railway when the dispute between directors and the union leaders threatened a universal disturbance. I inquired about the strike. There was an awkward pause in the conversation. 'Jim won't have to come out,' said the mother, 'because he isn't on the regular staff.' 'Of course Jim will come out,' said the father firmly, 'if the others come
220 out.' 'The fact is,' they explained, after further silence, 'we don't talk about the strike here; we try to forget that there ever may be one.' It was the experience of a thousand homes. There was no recognised or felt grievance. There was no clear understanding of the purpose and meaning of it all. But there were firmly planted in the mind two bedrock facts: the one, the tragedy that the strike would mean in this particular household; the other, the complete impossibility of any other choice but of the boys standing

44

with their comrades in the day of decision. And this is
230 England; an England which has learnt more than all other
peoples the secret of acquiescence, of toleration, of settling
down and making the best of things in a world on the whole
desirable; but an England also of a determination unshaken
by the vicissitudes of purpose and time, with a certain
ruthlessness about the means when it has accepted the end,
and with a patience which is perhaps more terrible in its
silence than the violence of a conspicuous despair.

These and other qualities form an absorbing subject of
study. A figure emerges from it all. It is the figure of an
240 average from which all its great men are definitely variants.
No body of men have ever been so 'un-English' as the great
Englishmen, Nelson, Shelley, Gladstone: supreme in war, in
literature, in practical affairs; yet with no single evidence in
the characteristics of their energy that they possess any of
the qualities of the English blood. But in submitting to the
leadership of such perplexing variations from the common
stock, the Englishman is merely exhibiting his general
capacity for accepting the universe, rather than for rebelling
against it. His idea of its origin or of its goal has become
250 vague and cloudy; definite statements of the average belief,
set out in black and white by the average congregation,
would astonish the average preacher. But he drives ahead
along the day's work: in pursuing his own business,
conquering great empires: gaining them by his power of
energy and honesty, jeopardising them by his stiffness and
lack of sympathy and inability to learn. So he will continue
to the end; occupying, not in Mr. Pinero's bitter gibe the
'suburb of the Universe'; but rather that locality whose
jolly, stupid, brave denizens may be utilised for every kind
260 of hazardous and unimaginable enterprise; fulfilling the
work of another, content to know nothing of the reason of
it all; journeying always, like Columbus, 'to new Americas,
or whither God wills'.

Note

1 F. M. Hueffer in 'The Spirit of the People,' a clever and suggestive analysis of Middle-Class England.

12 FORD MADOX FORD
'The Englishman feels very deeply and reasons very little'

From *The Spirit of the People* (1907)

Ford Madox Ford (1873–1939) published over eighty books in a career which included editing the *English Review*, journalism, essay writing, fiction, poetry, autobiography and literary criticism. He was invalided home from France in 1917 and in 1918 wrote a volume of poems inspired by his war experience. He was a close friend of C. F. G. Masterman (see above) and wrote a number of articles for him. Between 1898 and 1904 Ford became a friend and collaborator of the writer Joseph Conrad. They produced two novels (*The Inheritors* (1901) and *Romance* (1903)) but Ford also carried out a great deal of unacknowledged work as co-author at a time when Conrad's physical and mental health prevented him from writing. Ford's poetry was highly regarded by Ezra Pound, but he is better known today for his novels *The Good Soldier* (1914) (echoes of which are to be found in the extract which follows) and the four-volume *Parade's End* (1924–1928). This excerpt from chapter V, 'Conduct', is taken from the American edition of *England and the English* (1907), which combined three volumes published separately in England: *The Soul of London* (1905), *The Heart of the Country* (1906) and *The Spirit of the People* (1907).

The defects of the Englishman's qualities are strange in practice, but obvious enough when we consider the root fact from which they spring. And that root fact is simply that the Englishman feels very deeply and reasons very little. It might be argued, superficially, that because he has done little to remedy the state of things on the Congo, that he is lacking in feeling. But, as a matter of fact, it is really because he is aware – subconsciously if you will – of the depth of his capacity to feel, that the Englishman takes
10 refuge in his particular official optimism. He hides from himself the fact that there are in the world greed, poverty, hunger, lust or evil passions, simply because he knows that if he comes to think of them at all they will move him beyond bearing. He prefers, therefore, to say – and to hypnotize himself into believing – that the world is a very

good – an all-good – place. He would prefer to believe that such people as the officials of the Congo Free State do not really exist in the modern world. People, he will say, do not do such things.

20   As quite a boy I was very intimate with a family that I should say was very typically English of the middle classes. I spent a great part of my summer holidays with them and most of my week-ends from school. Lady C–, a practical, comfortable, spectacled lady, was accustomed to call herself my second mother, and indeed, at odd moments, she mothered me very kindly, so that I owe to her the recollection of many pleasant, slumberous and long sum-mer days, such as now the world no longer seems to contain. One day I rowed one of the daughters up a little

30 stream from the sea, and halting under the shade of a bridge where the waters lapped deliciously, and swallows flitted so low as to brush our heads, I began to talk to the fair, large, somnolent girl of some problem or other – I think of poor umbrella-tassel menders and sweated industries that at that time interested me a great deal. Miss C– was interested or not interested in my discourse; I don't know. In white frock she lay back among the cushions and dabbled her hands in the water, looking fair and cool, and saying very little. But next morning Lady C– took me into the rose garden, and,

40 having qualified her remarks with: 'Look here. You're a very good boy, and I like you very much,' forbade me peremptorily to talk to Beatrice about 'things'.

It bewildered me a little at the time because, I suppose, not being to the English manner born, I did not know just what 'things' were. And it harassed me a little for the future, because I did not know at the time, so it appeared to me, what else to talk about but 'things'. Nowadays I know very well what 'things' are; they include, in fact, religious topics, questions of the relations of the sexes; the conditions of

50 poverty-stricken districts – every subject from which one can digress into anything moving. That, in fact, is the crux, the Rubicon that one must never cross. And that is what makes English conversation so profoundly, so portentously,

troublesome to maintain. It is a question of a very fine game, the rules of which you must observe. It is as if one were set on making oneself interesting with the left hand tied behind one's back. And, if one protests against the inconveniences attendant upon the performance of this prime conjuring trick, one is met by the universal; 'Oh, well; it's the law!'

60   The ramifications of this characteristic are so infinite that it would be hopeless to attempt to exhaust them. And the looking out for them leads one into situations of the most bizarre. Thus, I was talking about a certain book that was hardly more than mildly 'shocking' to a man whose conversation among men is singularly salacious, and whose life was notoriously not clean. Yet of this particular book he said, in a manner that was genuinely shocked:

'It's a thing that the law ought to have powers to suppress.' There was no doubt that he meant what he said.

70   Yet he could recount with approval and with gusto incidents that rendered pale and ineffectual the naïve passions depicted in the work in question. But Mr N–'s position was plainly enough defined and sufficiently comprehensible; it said in effect: 'These things are natural processes which must exist. But it is indelicate to mention them.' And you may set it down that 'delicacy' is the note of the English character – a delicacy that is almost the only really ferocious note that remains in the gamut. It is retained at the risk of honour, self-sacrifice, at the cost of sufferings that may be

80   life-long; so that we are presented with the spectacle of a whole nation that permits the appearance of being extraordinarily tongue-tied, and extraordinarily unable to repress its emotions.

I have assisted at two scenes that in my life have most profoundly impressed me with those characteristics of my countrymen. In the one case I was at a railway station awaiting the arrival of a train of troops from the front. I happened to see upon the platform an old man, a member of my club, a retired major. He, too, was awaiting the train;

90   it was to bring back to him his son, a young man who had gone out to the war as of extraordinary promise. He had,

the son, fulfilled this promise in an extraordinary degree; he was the only son, and, as it were, the sole hope for the perpetuation of an ancient family – a family of whose traditions old Major H– was singularly aware and singularly fond. But, at the attack upon a kopje of ill-fated memory, the young man, by the explosion of some shell, had had an arm, one leg, and one side of his face completely blown away. Yet, upon that railway platform I and the old

100 man chatted away very pleasantly. We talked of the weather, of the crops, of the lateness of the train, and kept, as it were, both our minds studiously averted from the subject that continuously was present in both our minds. And, when at last, the crippled form of the son let itself down from the train, all that happened was the odd, unembarrassing clutch of left hand to extended right – a hurried, shuffling shake, and Major H– said:

'Hullo, Bob!' his son: 'Hullo, Governor!' – And nothing more. It was a thing that must have happened, day in day

110 out, all over these wonderful islands; but that a race should have trained itself to such a Spartan repression is none the less worthy of wonder.

I stayed, too, at the house of a married couple one summer. Husband and wife were both extremely nice people – 'good people', as the English phrase is. There was also living in the house a young girl, the ward of the husband, and between him and her – in another of those singularly expressive phrases – an attachment had grown up. P– had not merely never 'spoken to' his ward; but his

120 ward, I fancy, had spoken to Mrs. P–. At any rate, the situation had grown impossible, and it was arranged that Miss W– should take a trip round the world in company with some friends who were making the excursion. It was all done with the nicest tranquillity. Miss W–'s luggage had been sent on in advance; P– was to drive her to the station himself in the dog-cart. The only betrayal of any kind of suspicion that things were not of their ordinary train was that the night before the parting P– had said to me; 'I wish you'd drive to the station with us tomorrow

130 morning.' He was, in short, afraid of a 'scene'.

Nevertheless, I think he need have feared nothing. We drove the seven miles in the clear weather, I sitting in the little, uncomfortable, hind seat of the dog-cart. They talked in ordinary voices – of the places she would see, of how long the posts took, of where were the foreign banks at which she had credits. He flicked his whip with the finest show of unconcern – pointed at the church steeple on the horizon, said that it would be a long time before she would see that again – and then gulped hastily and said that Fanny ought 140 to have gone to be shod that day, only she always ran a little lame in new shoes, so he had kept her back because Miss W– liked to ride behind Fanny.

I won't say that I felt very emotional myself, for what of the spectacle I could see from my back seat was too interesting. But the parting at the station was too surprising, too really superhuman not to give one, as the saying is, the jumps. For P– never even shook her by the hand; touching the flap of his cloth cap sufficed for leave-taking. Probably he was choking too badly to say even 'Good-bye' – and she 150 did not seem to ask it. And, indeed, as the train drew out of the station P– turned suddenly on his heels, went through the booking-office to pick up a parcel of fish that was needed for lunch, got into his trap and drove off. He had forgotten me – but he had kept his end up.

Now, in its particular way, this was a very fine achievement; it was playing the game to the bitter end. It was, indeed, very much the bitter end, since Miss W– died at Brindisi on the voyage out, and P– spent the next three years at various places on the Continent where nerve cures 160 are attempted. That I think proved that they 'cared' – but what was most impressive in the otherwise commonplace affair, was the silence of the parting. I am not concerned to discuss the essential ethics of such positions, but it seems to me that at that moment of separation a word or two might have saved the girl's life and the man's misery without infringing eternal verities. It may have been desirable, in the face of the eternal verities – the verities that bind and gather

all nations and all creeds – that the parting should have been complete and decently arranged. But a silence so utter: a so
170 demonstrative lack of tenderness, seems to me to be a manifestation of a national characteristic that is almost appalling.

Nevertheless, to quote another of the English sayings, hard cases make bad law, and the especial province of the English nation is the evolution of a standard of manners. For that is what it comes to when one says that the province of the English is to solve the problem of how men may live together. And that, upon the whole, they are on the road to the solution of that problem few people would care to deny.
180 I was talking in Germany last year to a much travelled American, and he said to me that it might be taken for granted that English manners were the best in the world. In Turks, in Greeks, in Americans, in Germans, in French, or in Redskins certain differing points were considered to distinguish the respective aristocracies – morals, quiet cordiality, softness of voice, independence of opinion and readiness of quiet apprehension – each of these things were found in one or the other nations separately and were regarded as the height of manners. And all these things were
190 to be found united in the Englishman.

Personally, I think that the American was right; but I do not wish to elevate the theory into a dogma. And against it, if it be acknowledged, we must set the fact that to the attaining of this standard the Englishman has sacrificed the arts – which are concerned with expression of emotions – and his knowledge of life; which cannot be attained to by a man who sees the world as all good – and much of his motive-power as a world force which can only be attained to by a people ready to employ to its uttermost the human–
200 divine quality of discontent.

It is true that in repressing its emotions this people, so adventurous and so restless, has discovered the secret of living. For not the railway stations alone, these scenes of so many tragedies of meeting and parting, but every street and every office would be uninhabitable to a people could they

see the tragedies that underlie life and voice the full of their emotions. Therefore, this people which has so high a mission in the world has invented a saving phrase which, upon all occasions, unuttered and perhaps unthought,
210 dominates the situation. For, if in England we seldom think it and still more seldom say it, we nevertheless feel very intimately as a set rule of conduct, whenever we meet a man, whenever we talk with a woman: 'You will play the game.' That an observer, ready and even eager to set down the worst defects of the qualities in a people, should have this to say of them is a singular and precious thing – for that observer at least. It means that he is able to go about the world in the confidence that he can return to a restful place where, if the best is still to be attained to, the worst is
220 nevertheless known – where, if you cannot expect the next man in the street to possess that dispassionate, that critical, that steady view of life that in other peoples is at times so salutary, so exhilarating and so absolutely necessary, he may be sure that his neighbour, temperamentally and, to all human instincts, will respect the law that is written and try very conscientiously to behave in accordance with that more vital law which is called Good Conduct. It means that there is in the world a place to which to return.

13 PHILLIP GIBBS
'The soul of England spoke again . . .'

From *England Speaks* (1935)

For a note on Gibbs and *England Speaks*, see p.33.

This extract celebrates the first radio broadcast to the nation by the monarch. It was the occasion of George V's Silver Jubilee in 1935 and was the forerunner of the annual Christmas broadcasts by the reigning monarch. Edward VIII broadcast his abdication speech to the nation in 1936. These broadcasts prefigured the extensive use of the radio in the Second World War to broadcast morale-boosting propaganda – see, for example, the extracts here from Churchill's speeches and the extract from one of J. B. Priestley's wartime broadcasts (both in chapter 3, War and National Identity). The radio broadcast was one of the most significant media for creating a sense of national identity, particularly during the war, but also in peacetime – the tradition by which the monarch speaks to 'the people' at times of crisis or celebration has continued into the present with the Queen's annual Christmas message, relayed by both television and radio.

Something happened on the night of the King's jubilee which had never happened before in the history of mankind. A human voice – the King's – spoke to the whole world. Hundreds of millions of people, thousands of miles away from where he sat in a quiet room, listened to his words, clearly and finely spoken with an undertone of real emotion. He was speaking to the peoples of the British Empire as the Father of the Family, and these sincere and simple words were heard by men and women of every creed
10 and colour, eager to show their allegiance to the British Crown and their affectionate loyalty to the man who wore it. But they were heard by people who serve under other flags and have other loyalties. The United States listened and were moved by emotion, as American citizens have told me. Germany listened . . . .

It was perhaps a portent – this one human voice talking to all the world. One day a man may say something to all the world which may change its destiny.

That night in England, in thousands of villages far from
20 the glare and traffic of London, surrounded by quiet fields and woodlands, the rural folk gathered and tramped to their hillsides to see the lighting of bonfires which made a chain from peak to peak, not only in England but from Wales to the north of Scotland, as when the beacons were lit in the days of Elizabeth when the Armada was sighted. The soul of England spoke again that night, and these rustic folk remembered the war in which many of them had served, and were glad of peace and proud, I know, of a country which, with all its faults and troubles and injustice here and
30 there, stands still, they think, for liberty. . . .

I noticed at this time that the ordinary citizen in small shops and third-class railway carriages and other places where one hears the authentic voice of England, was for once self-conscious about the spirit of his own country. This Jubilee demonstration of good will and good order –

this sense of happiness among the people – had surprised him, and even made him talkative on the subject.

The man from whom I often buy an evening paper when I am in town, is often critical of public men and public affairs. He has a grouse against the Government for not dealing more efficiently with the problem of unemployment. He is a bit of a Socialist, he tells me, and hates anything like privilege or class benefit. He has hard things to say sometimes while handing out his papers to his clients in a London square. But on one of these evenings after the first Jubilee night he stared at me with the blue eyes of a naval man and spoke emotionally.

'This is a country and a half. Not a sign of Communism in spite of unemployment and all that. Well, I admit it's wonderful. It's a tribute to the King, but more than all it's a sign to the outside world that England is going strong and stands united, and won't stand for any monkey tricks. Well, I'm a bit of a Socialist and I don't deny it. But I'm not against Royalty and I'm not against decency. Take the Prince of Wales. What's wrong with him? I've respected him since a night he came to Homerton and sat down among our club fellows without any fuss or any side. A man and a brother. A leader of the younger crowd who would do well to follow him. Anyhow this jubilee show won't pass unnoticed in foreign countries. I can't see anything wrong with it. Why, the crowds were as peaceable and law-abiding and decent and good-natured as a school treat in a country park. I'm proud of England, and I don't mind saying so.'

I liked to hear him say so, because it was a pride in our decent qualities and in human liberty and order. Among all the voices in the crowd during this time of jubilation I heard words of good humour. It was not all loyalty or King-worship. Those young boys and girls who danced their shoes off were having a great circus. They passed the word along, 'It's amusing to see the dawn over London. We're having some good fun down our way. Come and join in!' A lot of that, no doubt. But there were other instincts stirred. England had been through a time of trouble. Now the tide

seemed to have turned a little. The cuts had been restored from clipped wages in a time of economy when England had gone off the gold standard. There had been threats and fears of wars, making people anxious. Well, England was all right. The winter had been long and dark. Now the fine weather had come and the pipes of Pan were calling even
80 down mean streets. England is still a little pagan when the cuckoo shouts its first note, when the first gleam of spring falls aslant factory walls, or creeps into slum courtyards. Other nations had dictatorships, tyrannies, denial of free speech and liberties. But after all the English air is good to breathe for men who like their freedom. So I heard the voices in the crowd.

14 SIR ERNEST BARKER
'Some Constants of the English Character'

From *The Character of England* (1947)

Sir Ernest Barker (1874–1960) was a political scientist, from humble beginnings – his father was a farm worker, his mother, the farmer's daughter. Barker had a high-flying academic career culminating in the Professorship of Political Science at Cambridge. He was knighted in 1944. *The Character of England* is one of a number of books on the national character (see also *The National Character* (1927), *Britain and the British People* (1942) and *Traditions of Civility* (1948)).

Perhaps enough homage has been paid to change (though even in speaking of change we have seen that the more the Englishman changes, the more he remains the same); and we may now turn back to some constants. It may not be foolish to list some half dozen (rather as examples than as a complete list), and, in doing so, to give each of them some single name.

1. The name of the first (one might wish that it were simpler) is *social homogeneity*. England has had little class-feeling – and that though, down to our own days, it has had,
10 and has even cherished, a whole ladder of class-differences. The habitat has somehow produced understanding and even fusion. One reflects on the difference between Norman and

Saxon, after 1066; and then one remembers that a sober treasury official could write, within a century of 1066, that, 'with Saxons and Normans living together (*cohabitantibus*) and intermarrying, the stocks are so mixed that you can hardly distinguish to-day who is Saxon, and who Norman, by birth'. Or again one reflects on the difference between
20 the feudal noble and the man of business in the age of medieval chivalry: and then one reflects that the noble's younger sons become commoners by English usage, and that in English practice Michael atte Pool, the son of a merchant of Hull, could become de la Pole and first Earl of Suffolk as early as the reign of Richard II. So it has gone through the centuries – the blood and the profits of business families flowing into the families of the land, and enabling them to keep their landed estates; the blood and the brains of the younger sons of the families of the land running into
30 trade, overseas commerce, adventure, and settlement. But this tendency to social homogeneity is qualified by, or combined with, an English doctrine and practice of what may be called 'position'. England has always been full of positions, or what Shakespeare calls 'degrees' and the Catechism calls 'states of life'. She has run through the ages into a graded hierarchy, with men taking positions, and holding stations, on this rung and that of a very long ladder. But there has always been a mutual respect between different positions; and the ladder has always been a ladder
40 of possible ascent.... It is in this way that English life has long been a pageant of positions – positions based on capacity – with men respecting positions because they respect capacity. There is no reason in the nature of things why this fashion of life should alter. In a new age of equality it may well become more elastic and fluid. If it does so, it will still remain the same, and even more the same. A system of positions based on capacities, if it has grown under individualism, may also grow, and grow even higher, under socialism.
50   At the same time a system of positions, even if the positions are mutually respected and even if they become

56

increasingly fluid, has its motes and shadows. One of these
shadows is snobbery. Snobbery is an appetite for false
position: it is the desire to enjoy in the estimation of others
a position which is not enjoyed in fact. At its best it may be,
as a friendly critic has called it, 'an honest expression of
social idealism': a longing to rise and to be translated, in a
friendly society which is none the less a society of degrees,
to a higher range and an ampler air. From that point of view
60 we may regard it as a tension, or rather the result of a
tension – a tension between the two poles of a sense of social
homogeneity and a sense of the difference of social positions. But this is perhaps only a gloss; and snobbery in
general, as the same friendly critic has also said, 'is really a
vice: it tempts us to neglect and despise our proper virtues
in aping those of other people'. Is it a modern English vice,
and was it the invention, or discovery, of Thackeray; or is
it an ancient English sin, as ancient as Ancient Pistol? At
any rate it is there, an offence against honesty and a breach
70 of the commandment, 'To thine own self be true'. The pity
is that it is not the only offence against honesty. Snobbery
has a companion, of even greater dimensions, which goes by
the name of hypocrisy; and indeed it may even be said that
snobbery is only a form or species of the genus hypocrisy.
The English hypocrite cannot be said to have been invented
or discovered by Dickens. He is the creature of a disjunction to which our stock seems sadly prone – the disjunction
between profession and practice. We may seek to explain
the disjunction historically as another form or expression of
80 tension – the tension, in this case, between the exuberant
Elizabethan, still within us, with all his full-blooded activity, and the grey inhibited Puritan, still present too with his
brooding sense of duty.... But the reproach remains. Not in
vain, and not without reason, have other nations made the
reproach, looking particularly at our public professions of
policy and the practice we actually follow. The Puritan
within us will not leave us; but he is not the only thing
within us. And we have anyhow something of a tendency to
live in a make-believe world. The very continuity of our

90 constitutional development, preserving antiquities which have become formalities, encourages the tendency. When you preserve so much of the past in the present you are apt to get mixed between shadow and substance.

2. Another constant in the character of England is the vogue of the *amateur*. Here again a paradox emerges. England is the home of professions – organized professions; barristers, doctors, architects, teachers, civil servants, and the rest – and she may even be said to have built up, during the nineteenth century, a new 'professional aristocracy' 100 which is an even greater power in the land than the old aristocracy. But England is also anti-professional. She has always cultivated an amateur quality – in sports; in politics; in the management of agriculture; and even in the private and family concerns which are still a large part of her industry. This amateur quality has its defects; and the defects become all the more apparent as the world grows more aggregated and complicated. But it has also its merits. It prevents life from being too hugely serious, leaving a space for the fun (the humours and even the whims) which 110 the boy in most Englishmen craves. It also fosters a multiplication of free individual initiatives: it takes away strain, and distributes the demands upon nervous energy. A society with an amateur quality is a society with a good circulation, less liable to clots and seizures ... and whatever his merits or defects, the amateur has long been with us, and is likely to remain. Raleigh and Sidney were of that strain: Cromwell was an amateur who learned as he went, in war and politics: the eighteenth century was an age of amateurs *domi atque militiae*; even Bentham, in his own field of law, 120 belongs to the company. Our very statesmen have often been amateurs of scholarship (as well as of politics): Mr. Gladstone and Lord Derby both surrendered their affections to Homer; and Mr. Winston Churchill – amateur in many fields, full of the amateur's defects and merits, and a professional only in the rare and generous profession of patriotism – has been a notable amateur of history. It may be a pity that we have not offered a greater sacrifice on the

altar of competence and efficiency. But it is perhaps a true
economy of effort which has inspired us to be the lovers of
130 activity (for the amateur is by definition a lover) rather than
its servants.

3. Another constant in English character is the figure
and idea of the *gentleman*. The idea of the gentleman is
not a class idea (it was ceasing to be that even in the
sixteenth century): it is the idea of a type of character. It
is an idea which has had its mutations. In the eighteenth
century a gentleman knew his tenants, his fields, and his
foxes: he helped to govern his country, and might sit in
parliament at Westminster; he might even be interested in
140 architecture and painting, and indulge himself in music. He
was an amateur furnished with ability – the apotheosis of
the amateur. But the essence was a code of conduct – good
form: the not doing of the things which are not done:
reserve: a habit of understatement. The code became
disengaged, and explicit, with the spread of boarding or
'public' schools during the nineteenth century. It was in
many ways a curious code. It was hardly based on religion,
though it might be instilled in sermons: it was a mixture
of stoicism with medieval lay chivalry, and of both with
150 unconscious national ideals half Puritan and half secular.
Yet if it contained such national ideals, it was not a national
code, in the sense that it embraced the nation: it was
the code of an *élite* (from whatever classes the *élite* was
drawn) rather than a code of the nation at large. On the other
hand *élites* will always count; and 'social idealism', or
snobbery at its best, made the code of the gentleman
pervasive. It is impossible to think of the character of England
without thinking also of the character of the gentleman. But it
is also impossible to think of the character of the gentle-
160 man clearly. It has an English haze. The gentleman is shy,
yet also self-confident. He is the refinement of manliness;
but the manliness is sometimes more obvious than the
refinement.... Yet a pattern of behaviour, however hazy,
remains a pattern; and whether you love it or laugh at it,
this English pattern spreads more and more as more and

59

more schools set themselves to the work of forming and strengthening character. The Englishman's clothes – like English sport (or at any rate English football) – are something of a general mode. His pattern of behaviour 170 matters as much or even more.

4. Another of the constants in this summary list is the *voluntary habit*. It is an old tradition of Englishmen to do things for themselves, on a voluntary basis, in free association with others; not to expect all things from 'the State', or remit all things to the government. It has shown itself in many fields – education; the service of health in hospitals; the improvement of the condition of the working classes by their own Trade Unions; missionary societies, Bible societies; societies for the protection of aborigines. It has created 180 a general distinction, in our thinking and our action, between state and society.... But the distinction is far from absolute: the two elements interact, and they may even at times co-operate in an amicable dyarchy. We developed, for instance, three centuries ago, a system of political parties – voluntary 'clubs' or associations – which have somehow got into the state and affect the government. We have kept party and government together, and yet kept each in its place – a delicate operation; indeed the most delicate and difficult of all operations in politics. It's so easy to let party become a 190 devouring monster of totalitarianism: it is so easy, at the other end, to cry, 'a plague upon parties: let us all be for the state'. In a blended country of compromise – compromise and imprecision – we have hitherto managed to make the best of both worlds and to keep both balls in the air.... It may be that things are changing: that we are beginning to be all for the state – and to give all things to the state. But perhaps it is at least as likely that old ways and habits of thought will show a persistent tenacity, and the submerged part of the iceberg will still float under the water. There is 200 still a good deal in our life – Trade Unions, for instance – which belong to the sphere of society. England will not very readily say, *L'état, c'est moi*! The *moi* is something larger.

5. Another constant which foreign observers have

generally noted in the character of England is *eccentricity*.
They have spoken of 'mad dogs and Englishmen'. One
observer, speaking more gently, has said that the Englishman is governed by 'the weather in his soul'. Among
ourselves we should hardly notice this idiosyncrasy, or
detect much difference of the weather in our souls; but if all
210 are eccentric, eccentricity will be so normal that it is
commonplace. Far from noticing it ourselves, we may even
be puzzled to find it noticed by others: and we may think
it astonishing that men who have a horror of publicity, who
like old grey clothes and dislike their houses or anything
that is theirs to be conspicuous, who tune down their
discourse and cultivate the idea of a level equanimity, should
ever be thought to be curious. Yet there are men we know
who seem to us 'characters' (though we generally lament
that they are disappearing – and not least from our
220 Universities, where they once had a way of flourishing):
there are even some whom we are apt to call 'cranks'....
There must be a certain truth behind this general rumour of
English eccentricity. Are we a country of humours, and of
every man in his humour? Is our worship of form only a
sort of insurance of an inner vitality, which can bubble all
the more freely because it is thus insured and protected? Or
may we say, less subtly, that most of us are mixtures,
unreconciled mixtures, and that elements of freakishness,
disconcertingly mixed with the element of form, can make
230 disconcerting appearances? May it also be said of us that we
have a would-be self-sufficiency, an individualism in the
grain, which makes our eccentricity the assertion of a real,
if often unconscious, egocentricity? It can hardly all be a
myth. But it remains a puzzle to most of us that the country
of 'good form' and plodding habit should also be counted
a country of rebellion against conventions and canons.

    6. A last constant which may be noted is the constant of
youthfulness. This, as has already been mentioned, is a trait
which the English share with the ancient Greeks. But their
240 youthfulness has a quality of its own. They begin with a
protracted period of growing up, and a deferred maturity,

which is perhaps a good insurance for a later and longer development. Inured to sport, and practising a creed of keeping fit, they join in games and practise the play of the muscles till the evening of their days; and they may be seen engaged in lawn tennis, or golf, or even hunting, when they are septuagenarians. In this way they keep themselves young in spirit; and this, in turn, ensures an easy communication between the generations. Age escapes being
250 crabbed, and can live with youth: the torch of tradition can be handed on readily to young colleagues and friends – in politics, or in scholarship, or in business. There is a general interest of the old in the young, with little trace of superiority or patronage: the generations are friendly, and equal. This may explain why there are English books which can be read by readers of the age of seven and readers of the age of seventy: it may explain the peculiar character of the English 'children's books' – *Alice in Wonderland*, *Wind in the Willows*, the books of Beatrix Potter, and many more –
260 which unite the generations.... Youthfulness has its companion in a general love of what we call 'nonsense': the worshipper of common sense is also a worshipper of the nonsense of limericks, clerihews, and the general play of the joke, 'practical' as well as verbal. At its best and purest the love of nonsense has no admixture of malice: it is simple play, even if the play is often clumsy and sometimes degenerates into horseplay. Often, it is true, the joke is mixed with a grumble; and this is that mixture of the comic and the tragic which has already been noticed. Alike in the
270 north and the south this mixture of grumbling and joking is characteristic – wittier, perhaps, in the south, and in the quick quips of the Londoner; more humorous, perhaps, in the north. Sometimes, again, the joke is in the nature of chaffing; and this too is a general habit, sometimes with a dangerous edge, but more generally like the play of young animals tumbling and rolling one another over. It makes a sort of freemasonry: it is a habit of friends who know one another by sign and countersign. But generally the love of nonsense is a simple and unmixed play of the mind, free

62

280 from the shadow of grumble and even from the thistledown
of chaff. This is the essence of Edward Lear's *Book of
Nonsense*. It is still the essence today of *1066 and All That*
– the Englishman laughing at his own history.

15 ARTHUR MEE
'The nation is a living body'

From *The Children's Encyclopaedia*

Arthur Henry Mee (1875–1943), journalist and writer, is best known for two enterprises: *The Children's Encyclopaedia*, which he began publishing in 1908 in fortnightly parts, and *The King's England*, a 41-volume account of the counties of England, largely based upon his personal visits. This extract is from Volume 9 of *The Children's Encyclopaedia*, from the 'Ourselves' section, subtitled 'The Wonderful House We Live In, and Our Place in the World'.

Ourselves and the Nation

However far back we go in the history of thought we find
it recognised that man is, as Aristotle called him, a social
animal. 'None of us liveth to himself, and no man dieth to
himself.' We are members one of another. No one knows
what a solitary human being would be like, for the best of
all good reasons, which is that there could not be a solitary
human being. Each of us is part of a great whole.

... We are so made that it is quite impossible for a human
10 being to exist at all apart from the influence of other human
beings over him. We come into the world helpless, less able
to take care of ourselves than any other creature, animal
or vegetable, and we remain helpless for a longer period
than any other creature. From our first hour we are
dependent on others who influence us from the cradle to
the grave, so that every one of us is, in some degree, a social
product.

... If we were to take a grown-up, healthy, sane,
intelligent human being, and separate him entirely from the
20 company of all other men, he would lose his reason and
become less than human. The solitary man becomes insane.
All this might be proved and discussed at any length, for it

is one of the most important facts in the world. We are in very truth members one of another. . . .

The Great Truth that a Nation is like a Living Body

We can see that this must be so if every individual is, in part, a product of all other individuals, and helps to produce the others by direct and indirect influences on them. So we have many phrases to express the idea that, in a sense, a nation is
30 like a great living creature. We call it the body politic, or the social organism, and sometimes figure it as a noble woman, Britannia, for example. This comparison of a nation with the body of a living individual is a very valuable one.

Elsewhere in this book we read, that though an atom is a whole, it is made up of parts called electrons, and we have only learned to understand the atom because the key to every fact about it lies in the nature of the electrons that make it. On a higher plane we learn that the living body, though it is a whole, is made up of parts called cells, which
40 are themselves alive; and we have only begun to understand the living body since we learned something about the nature of the cells which make it up.

How Our Own Body Helps Us to Study the Life of a Nation

So, also, we may imagine that the nation is a living body, but we shall never really understand the life of a nation till we understand the nature of the persons who make it up. That is the great key which governs all true thinking about a nation; and that is why we have been very carefully
50 studying the lives, the bodies and the minds of ourselves, so as to lead up to the study of the nation of which each one of us, young or old, is a part. . . .

The Life of the Body and the Life of the Nation

Now, with this key we can begin to understand many things. A nation has to live just as the body has to live; it has to have men to guide it, and the men who guide a nation

correspond to the nerve-cells of the brain. It has to have men who make special things for the nation, and the manufacturers correspond to the gland-cells of the body. It
60 has to have people like soldiers, scavengers, doctors, and nurses to protect it from enemies inside and outside; and the bodies of these protectors correspond to the white cells of the blood, which kill microbes, remove dirt from the air-passages, and carry medicine and food to the parts of the body that have been injured.

The body could not exist without the division of labour; and the division of labour could not be carried on as it is unless the cells of the body were different. A nerve-cell cannot do the work of a red blood-cell, nor a red blood-cell
70 that of a nerve-cell; and neither of them can do the work of a muscle-cell; and any of the three would make a very poor cell to cover the outside of our teeth. So we might go on endlessly. Now, the point is that this is precisely true of a nation. If all the cells of the body were born the same it could never be a body at all; and if all men were born the same they could never make a nation. . . .

The First and Greatest Division of Labour that Must Endure for Ever

Ages ago, in rude and savage tribes, though there always
80 was division of labour, there was not nearly so much as there is now. The first and greatest and most eternal division of labour, which is that between men and women, is as old as mankind and must endure for ever.

There was also a certain amount of division of labour between young and old, between the skilful and the strong, between the enterprising and the stay-at-homes. But, just as the difference between a low form of animal and a high form of animal is to be found in the greater division of labour in the higher animal, in the same way we find that high nations
90 cannot exist without increasing division of labour. . . .

There is a famous Roman story of a revolt in the body, when the other parts of it said that the stomach did no part of the work but got all the food. Of course, we see that that would be a very foolish thing for the body.

What Would Happen If the Parts of Our Bodies Quarrelled

It would be just as bad for the body if the stomach revolted and said it would keep all the food it received. The stomach would get indigestion and the rest of the body would starve.
100 That is exactly what would happen if rich men were to seize all the wealth and refuse to use it for the rest of the community; and so we learn that one part of the body and one kind of cell must not be at enmity with another part of the body and another kind of cell. A house divided against itself cannot stand. Doctors know that perfect health is perfect harmony. It means that every part of the body, like every part of a wonderful machine, is serving all the rest and is being served by all the rest, because it is doing its own work rightly in beautiful harmony with all the others.
110 The great truth we learn from this is that he is an enemy of the nation who stands for any part of it against the others, unless, of course, the others are in the first place injuring it. It must be an injury to the social body to set religion against religion, or class against class, or school against school.

In some future day, the dawn of which can only be seen by the prophet's eye, the eye of faith and hope, men will realise that what is true of one nation is true also of the whole of the nations which we call mankind. They will understand that, as to oppose one part of the body against
120 another is to injure it or to destroy it, as strikes or labour wars injure the social body, so wars between nations injure that mightiest body of all, the living body which we call humanity.

16 WYNDHAM LEWIS
'Dear old Great Britain has to take in partners'

From *The Hitler Cult* (1939)

Percy Wyndham Lewis (1882–1957) was born in Canada, and studied at the

Slade School of Art. Lewis became a leading figure in the Vorticist movement of 1912–1915: a literary and artistic movement which celebrated mechanisation, modernisation and violence, and condemned the emotionalism and sentimentality of nineteenth-century art. In the 1920s and 1930s Lewis continued to challenge what he perceived as the hollowness of twentieth-century culture and civilisation, particularly in his attacks on the Bloomsbury Group. His associations with Fascism and his support of Hitler in the 1930s further alienated him from the literary world. As well as essays and criticism, he wrote a number of novels of which *Tarr* (1918) is probably the best known.

Wherever I go to-day I hear people talking about a Federal scheme, the object of which is to induce the great democratic states of the West, especially Great Britain and America, to abandon their national sovereignty, pool their resources, have a common Parliament and armies under one direction. The establishment of something that would resemble the British Commonwealth of Nations, but more centripetal, is, I suppose, the idea.

    Let me say at once that I am in favour of such a scheme:
10 and if France, Spain, Portugal, and the Scandinavian countries would join it so much the better. Let me also say that I have not always been in favour of arrangements of this order, I have tended to advocate individualist political structures: small units as against big ones. And I will explain why....

    Here then is the case against the surrender of sovereign rights, and against a great merger of this kind. The main argument runs on the same lines as that used against any monopoly or trust: namely, it would be too big, and the
20 interests of the individual would suffer accordingly.

    As recently as two or three years ago I favoured that small unit – the nation. 'For years to come the whole world will be busy answering the question: "Are you for the super-state of internationalism, or for the sovereign state of non-international politics?"' So I wrote in 1936. And my answer then was that I preferred the sovereign state – preferred decentralized government to centralized government. Or, as I put it, I was for *the part*, rather than for *the whole*. I was for 'those who wish to retain the maximum
30 freedom for *the parts*: and to withhold unreasonable and

too oppressive power from *the whole*. For *the whole* would be only a verbal figment,' I added. 'It would mean government by a handful of individuals.'

'The part' seems to me at present just as much a 'verbal figment' as 'the whole.' It also means government by a handful of individuals, and by no means the most representative. Whether the unit thus *mis*-represented comprises forty million or four hundred million souls makes little difference.

40   When I stated that, should we follow the Geneva road of the League of Nations Union, then 'the destiny of England, perhaps, for centuries to come, is to be decided in a Swiss City by a motley collection of gentlemen whose names most of us are unable to pronounce,' I was overlooking the fact that the Parliament that sits in London is so peculiarly unrepresentative of the real interest of England that 'a motley collection of gentlemen' in Geneva could not be any worse, and, in spite of their unpronounceable names, might be considerably better.

50   It is a very powerful argument in favour of retaining sovereignty and independence, that 'out of sight is out of mind,' and that power ought to be vested in the hands of people who are in daily contact with those they are to rule. Even such a short way away from the Scottish Border as is London, it is far enough for a Parliament sitting in London to forget or overlook the peculiar needs and problems of Scotland. That is a very powerful argument. But how much more valid it would be if the Parliament sitting at Westminster did not forget and overlook just as much the
60   peculiar needs and problems *of Londoners*, who are right there under its nose!

I have had my eyes fixed upon the political scene now for six years without intermission. My conclusions to-day differ, not unnaturally, from those arrived at earlier. More every day I am convinced that to isolate any part of that Whole is impracticable. We should let the whole thing rip. Our instincts as men born to a great tradition of human freedom is to hold back what we can from the political

merger. The monster business concern is 'soulless,' we say;
70 the monster state must be the same. But monstrous and
'soulless' wars to stop the merger – to stop *Earth Limited*
coming into being – are no solution. Such wars, in any case,
can only be undertaken by mergers. (Grossdeutschland is a
merger.) One monopoly is much the same as another:
though if I have to be part of a vast concern I prefer it
should be a trust that has swallowed up the English. I want
to be with them, wherever I am, on a *my country submerged
or afloat* principle!

Some years ago I hoped to be *only* with the English – for
80 us to be distinct. Now, after a great deal of close observation, I see that is impossible. I have to have my England
diluted, or mixed. Dear old Great Britain has to take in
partners. I believe if we could all of us have made up our
minds to that earlier we could have avoided a general war.
No one would have taken on *all* the Anglo-Saxons and their
satellites.

But the most compelling argument of all in favour of the
great international merger is that it has already occurred.
That surely should be an argument to put a stop to all
90 argument. Even the anarchists, for all their rigid isolationism, are a part of the system they oppose. And as for us,
have not we taken to barter?

What I mean is that whether nations merge politically or
not, they cannot keep out the *Zeitgeist* or isolate themselves
from the spirit of their neighbours. Ideas pay no attention
to frontiers; they slip in and out like elves. But since it is
only the soul of a nation that is worth preserving, once we
recognize that that long ago has *merged*, however exclusive
it may have desired to be, the political and economic side of
100 it is unimportant. It is not worth having great nationalist
wars if there are no true nations left to fight about.

... The individual national systems as typified by their
governments, are in every case too corrupt, too stagnate,
and in some cases even too ludicrous, to make any intelligent European observer feel over-conservative. If France,
Italy, Spain, and England joined up, the resultant state,

when it brought forth its composite executive – sitting in Paris, of course – could scarcely prove to be less good than are the individual governments as they exist to-day. The
110 insularity of the English would be modified, the French receive an access of 'steadiness', the Spaniards lose some of their *grandeeism*, and the Italians lose Mussolini (with about as much regret as a man loses a stiff neck).

How greatly some federal scheme for the Western democracies would appeal to me is obvious from what I have said. But we must be realist, and we have to ask ourselves if it is likely to happen.

Were you to propose to-morrow to the French and English nations that they should amalgamate, even the
120 majority, their respective 'publics', quite apart from the wealthy and influential minorities, would be stunned at the idea. They would receive your proposal at first with incredulity, ridicule, and distrust.

Should you propose to either, on the other hand, that they should *attack* and destroy the other, they would understand that at once. Owing to the *Entente Cordiale* they would be a little astonished at first; but in a very short time they would come to see that their neighbours were a lot of treacherous blackguards, and the sooner they were
130 pushed off the earth the better.

The prospective federalist will find it none too easy to reverse what for so long these unfortunate people have been encouraged to think. The Government and the Press of all countries have exploited national sentiment too thoroughly for it to be possible, without long preparation, to bring them to take seriously such a merger. And the people of the United States have been taught to regard Europe as a backward, impoverished, quarrelsome, and unscrupulous part of the world ever since 1920. That cannot be undone in a day.

140 However that may be, the effort should be made. The more 'sovereign states' that cease to be sovereign the better for all of us. And it is not perhaps too much to hope that the fact of a common tongue, English, will start the rot; disintegrate these stupid barriers.

17 JAN STRUTHER
'Back from Abroad'

From *Mrs. Miniver* (1939)

Joyce Anstruther (Jan Struther) (1901–1953) wrote a column for *The Times*, in which her fictional creation 'Mrs. Miniver' recounted the day-to-day events of a middle-class family shortly before the Second World War. The 'Mrs. Miniver' columns were published in book form in 1939 and *Mrs. Miniver* went on to become a successful MGM film, starring Greer Garson. Mrs. Miniver's brand of homespun philosophy was usually developed from some insight or anecdote taken from the daily events of her upper-middle-class family life. This extract is taken from Mrs. Miniver's account of her return from a trip to Switzerland, accompanying her niece who is spending six months with a Swiss family. Toby is her youngest son.

... But that moment, for Mrs. Miniver, was still far ahead. She had not even quite detached herself yet from the place she had just left. Like the earth-bound spirit of one who has recently died, she still thought in terms of the life she had been leading. Glancing up at the clock of the dining-car, she reflected: 'Hansi's mother will just be tying the napkin round his neck; and he will be saying "*Bit*-te, Mama, *keinen* Blumen-kolh."' The first time she had heard him say this she had caught his mother's eye and smiled: for the tone and
10   the sentiment were so exactly Toby's. She had smiled, too, when she overheard at breakfast the so familiar question: 'Aber du, Hansi, hast du dir die Zähne gut geputzt?' But she had done more than smile when Hansi, after a day or two's distant politeness, had taken her by the hand and led her to a row of curiously-shaped pebbles in a secret hiding-place between the wood-stacks.

'Meine Sammlung,' he said briefly. 'My c'lection,' echoed Toby's voice in her memory. Her heart turned over: how could there be this ridiculous talk of war, when little boys
20   in all countries collected stones, dodged cleaning their teeth, and hated cauliflower?

Indeed, what always struck her when she went abroad was how much stronger the links are between people of the same calling than between people of the same race; especially if it is a calling which has more truck with the laws of

71

nature than with the laws of man. The children of the world are one nation; the very old, another; the blind, a third: (for childhood, age and blindness are all callings, and hard ones at that). A man who works with wood, a man who works

30 with iron, a man who works with test-tubes, is more akin to a joiner, a smith, a research chemist from the other end of the earth than to a clerk or a shopkeeper in his own town. A fisherman from Ushant and a fisherman from Stornoway are both citizens of the same relentless country; and Nicollier, the farmer with whom Mrs. Miniver had made friends at the village fête, had expressed in a different tongue precisely the same feelings and opinion as Tom (Brickwall) Iggulsden.

If only, she thought, sipping her black coffee, one could

40 somehow get them together – not the statesmen and the diplomats, but Toby and Hansi, Iggulsden and Nicollier. If only all governments would spend the price of a few bombers on exchanging for the holidays, free of charge, a certain number of families from each district....

The attendant brought her bill. She paid it, burying her last thought as a dog buries a bone, to be returned to later. They had passed Boulogne now and were on the last lap of the journey to Calais. As one does when there are only a few minutes to go and it is not worth while embarking on

50 anything new, she let her gaze wander round the carriage, idly seeking the titillation of the printed word. On the window-sill she read: –

> *Ne pas se pencher en dehors.*
> *Niche hinauslehnen.*
> *E pericoloso sporgersi.*

Exactly, she thought. 'What I tell you three times is true.' But the trouble was, it still had to be said in three different languages.

2

VERSIONS OF RURAL ENGLAND

INTRODUCTION

For many of the writers featured in this book 'England' is virtually synonymous with 'rural England'. So pervasive is the presence of the countryside in accounts of Englishness that many of the passages featured in other sections of this book could equally have been placed here. Rural England is central to any account of Englishness and yet the rural England which so many writers evoked had either disappeared in the first wave of industrialisation in the nineteenth century or was being changed beyond recognition through the introduction of electricity, the impact of the wireless, increased mechanisation of agriculture, and the expansion of public transport and car ownership. In this chapter we provide a number of extracts which can be taken as attempts at defining rural England: attempts to capture its essential qualities, often in the context of their erosion or eradication by what may be glossed as modernity. Our coverage concludes with three more substantial accounts – by Stanley Baldwin, H. V. Morton and J. B. Priestley – which demonstrate the ways in which the countryside was used in accounts of Englishness which were not specifically concerned with recording a rural scene. These extracts underline the centrality of rural England to accounts of Englishness in the period, and as such may be said to represent encodings of the ideology of rural England.

Edward Thomas's and Edmund Blunden's pieces both evoke a world which is rapidly becoming more imaginary than real. This imaginary England of patchwork fields, distant spires, village greens, warm beer and inter-class solidarity has been put to service in the 1990s by John Major in his quest to unite the nation behind a Tory vision of Englishness. In the period covered by this book the rural England evoked by writers such as Blunden or Thomas was increasingly put to similarly ideological purposes. During the First World War, verse by W. H. Hudson or Edward Thomas, along with prose like Blunden's, provided an encoding of what was being fought for when you went 'over the top for King and Country'. Books such as Hugh Massingham's collection of essays on *The English Countryside* (1939) or J. B. Priestley's *Our Nation's Heritage* (1939) evoked specific features and experiences of rural England as constitutive of English identity at a time of national crisis (impending war with Nazi Germany).

Morton's account of tramp life makes an interesting contrast to Thomas's rather more idealised depiction, but both are part of a long tradition of celebrating the wanderer. This tradition receives something of a revival in the late nineteenth and early twentieth centuries – a revival which in part relies upon the notional autonomy of the tramp and his or her supposed freedom from the confines of mass society. Many readers will be familiar with Kenneth Grahame's satire upon this trend for the travelling life-style from the chapter of the *Wind in the Willows* in which Toad takes up caravanning.[1] In the context of the anxiety of the 1980s and 1990s about the traveller, the positive or at worst ambivalent response of the 1920s to the figure of the tramp may seem very remote from contemporary conceptions of Englishness.

Not all accounts of England were in the elegiac vein; Robertson-Scott's ironically titled *England's Green and Pleasant Land* offers a corrective to the preceding pieces in terms of the version of rural England disclosed, but is still an outsider's view and a middle-class one.

The three more substantial extracts which conclude our coverage of rural England serve, in part, to provide an overview of the ideological function of rural England in the period. Stanley Baldwin's 'England ...' is a carefully constructed hymn to the essential English qualities as Baldwin's middle-England voters wished to see them. Baldwin sums up what is implicit in many of the extracts in this chapter: that 'England is the country, and the country is England'. As H. V. Morton points out, the problem with such claims is that they gloss the question of 'whose England': Morton himself suggests that there is evidence – in the voracious appetite for books on England and tours through England – that a search for national identity is going on. The accessibility of 1920s England to the ordinary factory worker or suburbanite was something which many writers discussed; for Morton the English village is the well-spring of the national character, and he, like others, is concerned that day-trippers will irrevocably pollute it.

In a famous passage at the end of *English Journey*, J. B. Priestley, writing seven years after Morton, offers an assessment of the competing versions of England. He identifies three Englands, and whilst he can see the attractions of the Old England of the shires and wolds, in which the urban is present only in the containable form of market-towns and elegant cathedral cities, Priestley is only too aware of the unreality of this rural England. His second England – the increasingly decrepit and outmoded nineteenth-century-England of the northern industrial towns – is in terminal decline; but Priestley is ambivalent about the newest England, which he sees as a cheap and depressing democracy with 'Woolworths as its symbol'.

Many of the writers suffer from similar inconsistencies of perspective, and one is brought up against the fact that very few average country dwellers have left records of their life. None of the extracts in this chapter have been written by people with first-hand experience of the life of a farm labourer or even of a yeoman farmer, and that obviously informs the perspective of the pieces we have included here. Readers wishing to read first-hand accounts can begin with the material in Paul Thompson's *The Edwardians* (see selected further reading in the appendix).

Note

1   This point is also made by M. A. Crowther (Crowther 1992: 95).

18   EDWARD THOMAS
'The Village'

From *The Heart of England* (1906)

(Philip) Edward Thomas (1878–1917) was born in London of Welsh parents. Throughout his youth he struggled to support himself and his growing family by writing critical essays, book reviews and topographical and biographical prose. He was also a prolific writer of poetry, which he was encouraged to publish by the American poet Robert Frost; however, most of his poetry, written between his enlistment in the army in 1915 and his death at Arras in April 1917, was published posthumously. Thomas wrote a number of prose works about England, and was friendly with Walter de la Mare and W. H. Davies. *The Heart of England* is a celebration of a mythic English pastoralism.

75

The village stands round a triangular, flat green that has delicate sycamores here and there at one side; beneath them spotted cows, or horses, or a family of tramps; and among them the swallows waver. On two sides the houses are close together. The third, beyond the sycamores, is filled by a green hedge, and beyond it an apple orchard on a gentle hill, and in the midst of that a farmhouse and farm-buildings so happily arranged that they look like a tribe of quiet monsters that have crawled out of the sandy soil to sun

10   themselves. There the green woodpecker leaps and laughs in flight. Down each side of the green run yellow roads that cross one another at the angles, two going north, two going south, and one each to the east and west. Along these roads, for a little way, stand isolated cottages, most of them more ancient and odd than those in the heart of the village, as if they had some vagrant blood and could not stay in the neat and tranquil community about the green. Thus, one is built high above the road and is reached by a railed flight of stone steps. The roof of another slopes right to the ground on one

20   side in a long curve, mounded by stonecrop and moss, out of which an elder tree is beginning to grow; and it has a crumbling tiled porch, like an oyster shell in colour and shape. One has a blank wall facing the road, and into the mortar of it, while it was yet fresh, the workmen have stuck fragments and even complete rounds of old blue and white saucers and plates. In others the mortar is decorated by two strokes of the trowel forming a wedge such as is found on old urns. In the ruinous orchard by a fourth, among nettles and buttercups, there is always a gipsy tent and white linen

30   like blossom on the hedge. One of these houses seems to have strayed on to the green. Years ago someone pitched a tent there, and in course of time put an apple pip into the ground close by and watched it grow. The codling tree is now but a stump, standing at the doorway of the black wooden cottage named after it. Between it and the village pond go the white geese with heads in air.

    Off one of these roads the church lifts a dark tower along with four bright ash trees out of a graveyard and meadow

which are all buttercups. On three of the others there are
40 plain, square, plastered inns, 'The Chequers', 'The Black
Horse', 'The Four Elms', where tramps sit on benches
outside, and within the gamekeepers or passing carters sit
and wear a little deeper the high curved arm-rests of the
settles. But the chief inns stand opposite one another at one
corner of the green, 'The Windmill', and 'The Rose', both
of them rosy, half-timbered houses with sign-boards; the
one beneath a tall, rocky based elm which a wood pigeon
loves, the other behind a row of straight, pollarded limes;
and opposite them is a pond on the edge of the green. In
50 these inns the wayfarer drinks under the dark seventeenth-
century beams; the worn pewter rings almost like glass;
moss and ivy and lichen, and flowers in the windows, and
human beings with laughter and talk and sighs at parting,
decorate the ancient walls. The lime trees run in a line along
the whole of one side of the green, and at their feet still
creeps a stream where minnows hover and dart, and the
black and white wagtail runs. Behind the trees are half the
cottages of the village, some isolated among their bean rows
and sunflowers, some attached in fantastic unions. Most are
60 of one story, in brick, which the autumn creepers melt into,
or in timber and tiles perilously bound together by old ivy;
in one the Jacobean windows hint at the manor house of
which other memory is gone; all are tiled. Their windows
are white curtained, with geranium or fuchsia or suspended
campanula, or full of sweets, and onions, and rope, and tin
tankards, and ham, and carrot-shaped tops, dimly seen
behind leaded panes. Between the houses and the limes, the
gardens are given up to flowers and a path, or they have a
row of beehives: in one flower-bed the fragment of a
70 Norman pillar rests quietly among sweet-rocket flowers.
Instead of flower gardens, the wheel-right and the blacksmith have wagons, wheels, timber, harrows, coulters,
spades, tyres, or fragments, heaped like wreckage on the sea
floor, but with fowls and children or a robin amongst them,
and perhaps, leaning against the trees, a brave, new wagon
painted yellow and red or all blue.

On the other populous side of the green the houses are of the same family, without the limes; except that far back, among its lilac and humming maple foliage and flower, is the vicarage, a red, eighteenth century house with long, cool, open windows, and a brightness of linen and silver within or the dark glimmer of furniture, and a seldom disturbed dream of lives therein leading 'melodious days'. Of how many lives the house has voicelessly chronicled the days and nights. It is aware of birth, marriage, death; into the wall is kneaded a record more pleasing than brass. With what meanings the vesperal sunlight slips through the narrow staircase window in autumn, making the witness pause. The moon has an expression proper to the dwellers there alone, nested among the limes or heaving an ivory shoulder above the tower of the church.

From one side to the other the straight starlings fly.

Along the roads go wagons and carts of faggots, or dung, or mangolds in winter; of oak bark in spring; of hay or corn in summer; of fruit or furniture in autumn.

A red calf, with white hind legs and white socks on her forelegs, strays browsing at the edge of the road. A close flock of sheep surges out of the dust and covers the green.

We were twelve in the tap of 'The Four Elms'. Five tramps were on one side; on the other, six pure-blooded labourers who had never seen London, and a seventh. A faggot was burning in the hearth, more for the sake of its joyful sound and perfume than for its heat. The sanded floor, cool and bright, received continually the red hollowed petals that bled from a rose on the table. The pewter glimmered; the ale wedded and unwedded innumerable shades of red and gold as it wavered in the mystic heart of the tankard. The window was held fast, shut by the stems of a Gloire de Dijon rose in bloom, and through it could be seen the gloom of an ocean of ponderous, heaving clouds, with a varying cleft of light between them and the hills which darkened the woods and made the wheat fields luminous.

Now and then a labourer extended his arm, grasped the

tankard, slowly bent his arm whilst watching a gleam on the metal, and silently drank, his eyes lifted as if in prayer; then slowly put it back and saw a fresh circle being formed around it by the ale that was spilled.

120 The tramps leaned on a walnut table, as old as the house, polished so that it seemed to be coated with ice, here and there blackened with the heat transferred to it by a glass bottle standing in the sun. They looked at one another, changed their attitudes and their drinks, gesticulated, argued, swore, and sang. They became silent only when one of their number hammered a tune out on the reluctant piano. They were of several ages and types, of three nationalities, and had different manners and accents. One was a little epicurean Spanish skeleton who loved three things, his own pointed beard, a pot of cider, and the saying 130 of Sancho Panza: 'I care more for the little black of the nail of my soul than my whole body.' He was a grasshopper in the fields of religion, scandal, and politics, and wore his hat scrupulously on one side. Another was a big gentle French-man, with heavy eyelids, but a fresh boy's laugh. Early in the evening he scourged the republic; later, he laughed at the monarchy, the consulate, and the empire; and as he went to sleep touched his hat and whispered 'Vive la France!' His neighbour was fat, and repeated the Spaniard's remarks when they had been forgotten. It was to be wondered when 140 he walked, what purpose his legs were made to serve. At the inn it was to be seen that they were a necessary addition to the four legs of a chair. He wanted nothing but a seat and not often wanted that. He was, I may say, made to be a sitting rather than a sapient animal, and had been lavishly favoured by Nature with that intention. The fourth, a pale, sour anarchist, hardly ever spoke, but was apparently an honest man, whom his indignant fellows called 'parson'. The last was one that had been born a poet, but never made one. He sang when he was asked, and later when he was 150 asked not to sing; very quietly and very bitterly he cried when he had sung, indulging in a debauch of despair. Before we parted, the twelfth man sang all the sixteen verses of 'Sir

Hugh of Lincoln', in the hope of quenching their love of interminable song. 'Heaven and Hell!' said the tramp, 'ye make me feel as if I was like Sir Hugh and Lady Helen and the Jew's daughter all in one. Curse ye! bless ye!'

Half-way through the evening the tramps were asleep. The labourers were as they were at the beginning. They sat arow [sic] according to age, and nothing but age dis-
160 tinguished them. Their opinions were those of the year in which they were born; for they were of that great family which, at the prime of life or earlier, seems to begin growing backwards to quote 'grandfather' more often, and thus to give the observer a glimpse of the Dark Ages. Life to them was at once as plain and as inexplicable as the patterns on their willow cups or toby jugs. The eldest had a gift of dumbness that sometimes lasted nearly half a century, but once set going and wandering from ploughs to horses, and from horses to the king, his loyalty brought this forth:
170 'If that Edward wasn't king he ought to be.' Advancing to the subject of hay with a digression on the church, 'Which,' said the youngest, 'which came first, parson or hay?'

'What,' said the eldest in a short speech that occupied an hour of time, without interruption from the rest, who drank through his periods and sat watching him while he drank in the intervals by way of semi-colon. 'What is church for but rector to pray in? The parson prays for – for a good season, and a good season means a good hayrick like a church; well,
180 then, Robert, George, Henry, and Palmston, I say that the day after they first wanted a rick they put up a church and put rector in to pray. I,' continued he, growing confident, 'remember the Crimea. I had but four boys then, but bad times they were. But we had tea, we had tea; the wife used to grate up toast and pour boiling water on it.'

'We called that coffee,' said the youngest, a lover of truth.

As the evening darkened and pipes went out and the scent of carnations came in with the wind, their speech
190 became slower, with long intervals, as if they spoke only

after ploughing a furrow. One by one they seemed to go out like the candles overhead, were silent, but never slept. The oldest, reddest and roundest of face with white hair, looked like the sun at a mountain crest. The next seemed to be the spirit of beneficent rain, pale, vague, with moist eyes and tangled grey beard. The third was as the south wind, mild, cheerful, pink-faced, with a great rose in his button-hole. The fourth was the west wind, that lifts the hay from the level fields into the clouds at a breath, that robs the harebell
200 of its dew and stores it with rain – a mighty man with head on breast, and small hands united, and flowing hair. And the youngest was the harvest moon, glowing, with close hair and elusive features, a presence as he sat there rather than a man. So they were in the twilight, like a frieze on the white wall.

'Well, us have had fun, haven't us, George?' said the harvest moon. He received no answer as we passed out of 'The Four Elms', for all but he had left the world where words are spoken and opinions held; and the hazel lane
210 seemed to be a temple of the mysterious elements that make the harvest and the apple crop and the glory of the hops.

19 H. V. MORTON
'The fun it is to tramp from town to town ...'

From *In Search of England* (1927)

Henry Vollam Morton (1892–1979) was a journalist on the *Birmingham Gazette* from 1910 and by 1912 became assistant editor. He wrote a number of popular travelogues about the Middle East (*Through the Lands of the Bible*), Britain (the *In Search of* series) and London (*The Heart of London*). *In Search of England* was published in July 1927 and by 1947 was in its thirty-sixth edition. Morton is notably absent from the *DNB*.

I was sitting on a gate studying the map of Norfolk when there came towards me the first tramps I have seen – or rather the first obvious tramps I have seen – since Cheshire. The man was pushing a wooden box on perambulator wheels; the woman was walking a few paces behind him, carrying a small cardboard tray, and wearing the remains of

a once fashionable long-waisted tailor-made costume. She
came up to me, pulling the collar of the costume to her
throat, which made me realise that she had nothing on
10 beneath it, and asked me to buy a packet of lavender. Much
to her surprise, I bought twelve.

The man was surprised; so was the mongrel pup who had
one sharp ear cocked on the hedge and a rabbity look about
his jaw. So we all stood smiling in a group.

'Well,' I said, 'It's an awful life, isn't it? But, thank
goodness – catch – we have tobacco!'

Tramps sum you up quicker than a dog or a child. They
decide in one second whether you are dangerous or
harmless. So we got talking. . . .

20 'Steady job!' said the woman. 'You wouldn't be in no
steady job, long, Joe, would you?'

Joe narrowed his eyes and looked down the road. He was
a born tramp, a born walker, a born wanderer, half
countryman, half townsman, quite young, but one of those
people civilisation will never break in. He had served during
the war.

'Well,' he said in a tired drawl, 'well, you don't pay no
rent and you don't pay no rates, and no income tax, and you
can get all you want to eat most times, and I like the country
30 and I don't get on in towns.'

He told me that his 'people' were well-to-do village folk
somewhere who wanted him to settle down. (He spat.)

'I won't 'ave no truck with them,' he said. 'They can keep
their blinkin' money. I don't want it!'

'And you,' I said to the woman, 'how do you like it?'

She smiled. She also was a vagrant, I think; a much rarer
type in a woman. Or she may have been just slipshod and
lazy.

'I've seen better days,' she said, putting on a miserable
40 face and drawing her coat collar up.

'Go on with you!' I laughed. 'Admit you'd hate to know
where you'd sleep next week!'

She laughed. 'Perhaps I would . . . tho' it's cold sometimes and me stockings dry on me legs which gives me

82

rheumatism somethink cruel at times.'

'I wonder how long either of you would stay in a house?'

'Not long,' said the man definitely. 'Here, boy, come away there! He's a sharp dog, sir, I've been offered quids for
50   him. No, he's never caught a rabbit ...'

At this untruthful moment a stoat ran across the road, and the dog was on it like a dart. We tactfully changed the subject.

They told me far more than they realised. The fun it is to tramp from town to town as members of a lazy, irresponsible brotherhood, meeting friends in doss-houses every night, swopping news, hearing how old So-and-So did such and such a thing; putting out all the eatables on the table and holding an auction, then wandering on and on again, listless,
60   without ambition, unenvious of other men, just drifters. . . .

He whistled the dog, nodded to me; she smiled and showed teeth and they went off down the road; the man pushing the truck that held all their worldly goods; the woman a step or two behind; the mongrel questing ahead. You could not feel sorry for them. I believe they were happier than any millionaire; happier in fact, than most of us.

20 EDMUND BLUNDEN
'How much that we loved is going or gone!'

From *The Face of England* (1932)

Edmund Charles Blunden (1896–1974), poet, editor and critic, was Professor of Poetry at Oxford from 1966 to 1968. Much of his own poetry was concerned with rural experience: see *English Poems* (1922); he also wrote about his experiences in the First World War (see the poem 'Report on Experience' in *Collected Poems*, 1930). *Undertones of War* (1928) examines the impact of the conflict on man and countryside.

The fact cannot be avoided: how much that we loved is going or gone! It is not a tremendous old age that has justified me in this exclamation. I am still merely an old young man. I have known an England in which the water mill and the windmill were regular, familiar workers; already the few of them that have not been dismantled by weather or by the improver are anxiously numbered up as antiquities which ought, if we can contrive it, to be preserved. It is a great rarity to find one that is still working

10   – sometimes they suffer the indignity of being used as sheds for oil engines. The streams of my old home were kept clear and lively by a system of sluice-gates and tumbling-bays, when farmers flourished who understood the matter; those streams are now choked and stagnant. Ponds, that were felt to be valuable for just their beauty, are rubbish heaps; the owners have no eye for them. Rivers that poured a pure wave are defiled with the poisons that accompany our mechanical development; the radiant noonday pool in which you saw here a shoal of bluish bream, there a

20   hundred silvery roach, and a pike or two on the warm sandy shallow beyond, is not to be seen. Paths that were as good as roads are overwhelmed with nettles and briars; or the stiles that admitted to them are uprooted, and wire fences run in their stead; although we never needed our paths so manifestly. Meadow after meadow disappears; the rabbit scarcely has time to move out before the next row of villas is affronting the retreating woods with the confectionery of the builder's yard.

But I did not mean to be indignant – elegiac perhaps, or

30   perhaps a trifle boastful. It is something to have lived out of one epoch into another. I lived in the epoch of the horse, and went to school on a winter morning often riding on the tailboard of the long wagon loaded with apples, drawn by a team of horses – a magnificent picture, which has ceased to appear. The natty red mail-van no longer goes gliding by; the carrier's hooded wagon is forgotten; the baker no longer makes his tour from dawn till dusk behind his pony; our cricketers do not order the horsed brake for their matches in villages over the hill. And with them you can see a

40   particular effect: whereas in the old days of the brake they went out together and so returned, in the moments of the motorcycle they hurl themselves separately at their

84

destinations. The loss is not only one of a picturesque spectacle, but of a social idea.

It might be almost as difficult to put up a horse now at many wayside inns as it would have been twenty years ago to buy petrol there.

I have been one of the latest witnesses of the old kind of threshing-floor, and the skill of the thumping flail; of the
50 sickle cutting through acre after acre, of the gleaners following at their understood distance. On Sussex Downs, I once saw the oxen dragging the wooden ploughs. Almost as far away seem the processions of people to church and chapel on Sundays.

Black hoods and scarlet crossing hill and dale.

Among them, in my parish, were the boys of the little endowed school, with their tasselled caps and wide collars, conducted along by the last of the Ushers. In winter, I have been among the drove of young men and boys who went
60 out in the moonshine to slide and caper over the frozen meadow lakes – a simple pastime. 'Big Man Slide', 'Little Man Slide' – the terms are surrounded with merriment beneath a sky of terror and glory; we went forth with natural impulse, a community. I knew my village as one of great trees, and hidden beauties; the trees are mainly felled from one cause and another, there are not many surprises in the emphasised plan of roads, houses, and fences. The sweet-shops that I remember were usually indicated by nothing more than a box or two of popcorn and 'home-
70 mades' in the front window of a cottage; those were for us who had time to stop and stare; to capture attention nowadays Mrs Giles must set up a battery of posters and pictures. The inns were humble, semi-private places; they too must now bedizen themselves with proprietary labels, loud, often nearly meaningless. Thus, the windows of 'The Bull' will be found plastered with the goggling trademark of a hippopotamus or so, in dismal repetition, who has nothing to tell me, though repeated to the nine hundred and ninety-ninth time, about the cardinal points of old ale, a bite of
80 bread and cheese, and a landlord who makes one welcome.

The aeroplanes that gloriously fly over us do not make the small boys put down their bats and balls; but after all they are here and over the hill in almost less time than the writing of these words requires. I was a cricketer of the same stamp in the balloon age, and a balloon gives you some chance. I see a red balloon still, bowing and turning along above us; and I see Miss K. running out to take us to the hilltop for as long and near a sight of this magic vessel as could be had. Coming down! That ultimate pleasure of
90 approaching the vision, it is true, was not granted.

The wooden bridges which used to shake ominously under the passage of our wheels were replaced soon after I had formed my dreams upon them and the deeps below. They carried roads of no small importance. Their steepness tested the judgement of carters and the muscles of horses; life is certainly easier that way. I knew the village pound on the common, where the boys watched their cows, although it was never used in my day for the stray animal and the reward of the finder; but now the children do not know that
100 the square palings are a pound, or what, other than money, that word can mean. They have scarcely any notion, moreover, of the joys of the blacksmith's anvil and musical pyrotechnics – it was worth taking a hoop to him for repair as an excuse for loitering and admiring the red glare and the giant energies for shoeing mighty dray horses. And every day almost was the forge's day.

Even at the railway station the last age had something of its own. The stationmaster's beard and top hat have gone with it. The bell no longer rings in his ceremonious hand
110 before the trains come. The trains are not so important – they are not now what they were, the only locomotive fashioners of our lives except in our own little sphere, the messengers and agencies from and to London and the wide world. What crises, what fortunes, depended on their fiery banners on the cloud of night, their grand lowings and throbbings and hissings! They are, in a mechanical inquiry, as they then were; but their impact on one's attention and imagination is fallen away.

But my catalogue must be broken off, for in England you
120 can never be sure that the thing you miss will not meet you
round the next turn of the lane – and who, at least among
those whose days are cabined, cribbed, confined by the
demon Work, can speak of England except in such a
parochial manner as I have been doing?

21 H. V. MORTON
'We may not revive the English village of the old days ...'

From *In Search of England* (1927)

For a biographical note on Morton, see p.81.

A writer on England to-day addresses himself to a wider
and a more intelligent public than ever before, and the
reason is, I think, that never before have so many people
been searching for England. The remarkable system of
motor coach services which now penetrates every part of
the country has thrown open to ordinary people regions
which even after the coming of the railway were remote and
inaccessible. The popularity of the cheap motor-car is also
greatly responsible for this long-overdue interest in English
10 history, antiquities, and topography. More people than in
any previous generation are seeing the real country for the
first time. Many hundreds of such explorers return home
with a new enthusiasm.

The roads of England, eclipsed for a century by the
railway, have come to life again; the King's highway is once
more a place for adventures and explorations; and I would
venture to prophesy that within the next few years we shall
see a decline in the popularity of the sea-side resort,
unfortunate as this may be, and a revival of the country inn.
20 The danger of this, as every lover of England knows, is
the vulgarisation of the country-side. I have seen charabanc
parties from the large manufacturing towns, providing a
mournful text for an essay on Progress, playing cornets on
village greens and behaving with a barbaric lack of manners

which might have been outrageous had it not been unconscious, and therefore only pathetic. This, however, is
exceptional. The average townsman of no matter what class
feels a deep love for the country, and finds there the answer
to an ancient instinct.

30 Against the vulgarization of the country we must place
to the credit of this new phase in the history of popular
travel in England the fact, already mentioned, that thousands of intelligent men and women are every year discovering the country-side for themselves. The greater the
number of people with an understanding love for the
villages and the country towns of England the better seems
our chance of preserving and handing on to our children the
monuments of the past, which is clearly a sacred duty. Time
is already having its way with many a cathedral whose roots
40 are in Norman England and with many a famous strong-
hold like Durham Castle, and, in parts, with Hadrian's Wall,
which should at once be made an official 'ancient monu-
ment' and preserved from further decay by a top-dressing
of concrete. When the public really feels that these signposts
along the road which the English people have followed in
the course of their development are not dead shells of the
past but a living inspiration to the present, to the future,
and, in addition, that they possess a personal interest to
them as part of a common racial heritage, then we shall have
50 advanced a long way and – perhaps the petrol engine will
have atoned for a few of its sins!

There is another and a very interesting aspect to this
question. Since James Watt invented a new world on
Glasgow Green, the town and the country have grown
apart. They do not understand one other. Since the so-called
Industrial 'Revolution' – evolution is surely a better word
– English country life has declined, agriculture has fallen on
bad times, and the village has been drained to a great extent
of its social vitality.

60 It is difficult at first for the unaccustomed eyes of the
townsman to understand that behind the beauty of the
English country is an economic and a social cancer. An old

order is being taxed out of existence; 'our greatest industry' – as the experts call it – employs fewer men than those on the dole, and, struggling along, is facing insuperable difficulties with a blundering but historic stolidity. While our cornland is going back to grass year after year, our annual bill to the foreigner for imported foodstuffs is four hundred million pounds. Everywhere is the same story: mortgages
70 on farms; no fluid capital; the breaking up of famous estates when owners die; the impossibility of growing corn because of the expense of labour and the danger of foreign competition; the folly of keeping cattle when the Roast Beef of Old England comes so cheaply from the Argentine.

'Why should the towns be expected to understand the complex problems of the country-side? We have our own troubles. The country-side must lick its own wounds!' That is the view of the town, and I submit that it is an ignorant and a short-sighted view. The towns should understand the
80 problems of agriculture, because as the life of a country-side declines, as in England to-day, and the city life flourishes, the character and physique of a nation deteriorate. History proves to us that a nation cannot live by its towns alone: it tells us that the virile and progressive nation is that which can keep pace with the modern industrial world and at the same time support a contented and flourishing peasantry.

The 'Back to the land' cry is a perfectly sound instinct of racial survival. When a man makes money he builds himself
90 a country home. This is the history of our great families – town wave after town wave – since the earlier nobility committed suicide in the Wars of the Roses. And any man who wishes his family to survive has at some time to take it and plant it in the country. Where are the town families? Where are the Greshams of London? the Whittingtons, the Philipots?

'The Grenvilles are country squires', wrote Langton Sandford in his *The Great Governing Families of England*, 'who for five hundred years vegetated on slowly increasing
100 estates in Buckinghamshire.' For five hundred years! In half

that time the average city family has disappeared into racial anaemia.

I have introduced this note in a book which is pitched in a much lighter key because I feel that help for the woes of our agricultural districts may, quite unexpectedly, come from the cities. Political power is to-day all on the side of cities. They have a four-fifths majority in the electorate, and the countryman has no legislative tradition. His vision is bounded, as it always has been, by the line of his own 110 hedges. But granted that a healthy country-side is necessary to a nation, it is then surely the duty of every man to ponder these problems and to enter into them. If those men and women who, as my letter-bag so clearly proves, are starting out in their thousands to discover rural England will see it not merely as a pretty picture or as an old battle-field whose drama has long since departed, but as a living thing, as important to-day as it was when all men drew their bread from it, we may be a step nearer that ideal national life: on one hand the wealthy industrial cities; on the other a happy 120 country-side, ready to give its new blood to the towns, guarding the traditions of the race, ready always to open its arms to that third generation from the city in need of resurrection.

We may not revive the English village of the old days, with its industry and its arts. The wireless, the newspaper, the railway, and the motor-car have broken down that perhaps wider world of intellectual solitude in which the rustic evolved his shrewd wisdom, saw fairies in the mushroom rings, and composed those songs which he now 130 affects to have forgotten. Those days are gone. The village is now part of the country: it now realises how small the world really is! But the village is still the unit of development from which we have advanced first to the position of a great European nation and then to that of the greatest world power since Rome.

That village, so often near a Roman road, is sometimes clearly a Saxon hamlet with its great house, its church, and its cottages. There is no question of its death: it is, in fact,

a lesson in survival, and a streak of ancient wisdom warns
140 us that it is our duty to keep an eye on the old thatch
because we may have to go back there some day, if not for
the sake of our bodies, perhaps for the sake of our souls.

22 J. W. ROBERTSON-SCOTT
'A community which has almost always been hovel housed'

From *England's Green and Pleasant Land: The Truth Attempted* (1925)

Robertson-Scott (1866–1962) founded and was the first editor of the
Countryman. He worked as a journalist on the *Pall Mall Gazette,* the *Westminster Gazette* and the *Daily Chronicle.* He also served on the Ministry of
Health's advisory committee on rural housing. In this extract Robertson-Scott
offers a passionate account of the limitations of rural life in many villages in
the inter-war period.

> *If your misses had slept, squire, where they did*
> *Your misses might do the same.*
> 'The Bad Squire', *by a Canon (Kingsley)*

Dank thatch and slipped slates leak. Moisture runs down
the inside of walls. Floors are very damp where they have
always been very damp.

Two or three dumpy, blemished folk squatter [*sic*] on the
muddy road.

At one cottage door a slattern, who was not always a
slattern, takes in from the baker four ill-baked loaves that
her untidy children paw.

Within another cottage door the perky, talkative credit-
10 store man from Thurton asks the price for a skirt that poor
people pay who buy on tick. In the worst cottage a labourer
lies in his coffin, and his niece is wearily thankful and also
a little appreciative of the drama in which death has made
her a conspicuous player.

Mrs. Bloss at her back door thanking, in her kind way,
the wet postman for her monthly circular of the Polynesian
Mission, is just too late to hear the groans and the shrieks
of a woman, wraith-like for months past, giving birth and
her life to an unwanted infant in a poor cottage to which the

20 school would be returning in two hours, but for the neighbours' mercy, six children.

The parson, cycling past to take tea with the Richardsons, has in full view the five worst cottages of the hamlet we have heard about. They are in Categories IV (2) V (l) and VI (2) of the official transcript which gives particulars of all the cottages of the parish. . . .

Condition of Cottages	In our Hamlet	In rest of Parish
I. *Up to Ministry of Health's requirements*	*None*	*None*
II. *Would be so with slight alterations*	1	2
III. *Would be so by being added to*	1	2
IV. *Would be so with a large outlay*	2	2
V. *Not worth repair*	1	12
VI. *Unfit for habitation*	2	8
	7	26

These five cottages that the parson was passing have each two 'bedrooms', let us call them sleeping places. These sleeping places average 12 ft. long by 9 ft. wide by 7 ft. high.
30 If you will kindly get up from your chair and pace on the floor twelve boot-lengths by nine boot-lengths, and reach up a little on the wall beyond your height to seven feet, the facts will come home to you. The cottages are as far short of window space as they are of cubic capacity.

There slept last night in these five cottages which have two sleeping places apiece:

First Cottage: Mother, grandfather, two boys.
Second Cottage: Husband and wife, lodger, four children.

Third Cottage: Husband and wife, four girls, two boys, a
40 baby.

Fourth Cottage: Husband and wife, a young man, two
young women, two boys.

Fifth Cottage: Husband and wife, grown-up daughter, a
younger girl, two young men.

In three of the cottages there is an illegitimate. In four
cottages there are firstborn who arrived, as so many of the
firstborn in these parts do arrive, impolitely soon after the
marriage of their parents.

Consider the schoolmistress's task with the physical and
50 mental endowments, manners, sentiments, beliefs and habits of the children of these five cottages.

Consider the chances of 'social work' with their fathers
and mothers.

A recent visitor to the hamlet asked if the people were
interested in folk dancing. No, the people are not interested
in folk dancing; and there are things most of them are more
interested in than politics and the Church.

Such as, in varying degrees, what they have to eat, the
weather, gossip, how to make ends meet, the growth of
60 things, police news from the Sunday paper or local paper,
old age, the day's work, sexual relations, gardens and
allotments, tobacco, beer, betting.

The hamlet labourers ought, of course, to be better paid.
But many of them are wasteful – as the rest of us are, in
larger or smaller measure, you will agree, if you think a
little. The reason is that they have never been taught
differently by example, and rarely by precept.

With more money in hand, some labouring families
would certainly improve themselves, after their own fash-
70 ion. The lot of others would not be markedly better. Look
at the state of some of the gardens within a yard or two of
the cottage doors.

Is it more money that the hamlet needs most of all? What
it needs most of all seems to be a stiffening of moral fibre,
a development of consciousness or a stretching of minds,

better health, better hygienic notions, better ideals, spiritual regeneration.

More money would be the road to some of these things. Better chances of 'rising' in the farming life would be better
80 still. But how can the foundation of progress be laid in the depressing drowsiness of condemned cottages?

Better wages would provide the rents for better homes. But in some of these cottages, in which there are several wage-earners, there is already an income sufficient to pay the rent of a decent dwelling. There is no decent dwelling to go to, however.

And many of these people have slithered down to such a condition of fecklessness that they are incapable of putting forth the effort on their own behalf necessary to bring about
90 the building of new cottages by the local authorities.

These people have never acted on their own behalf. They have no tradition of doing so, no memory of independence. They have not the advantage of being members of churches of 'disruptions' in which minorities have taken their stand on principles, and people have held to their views though it cost them money and homes.

Not one of these people is in a trade union. These people believe, what is true, that, sooner or later, they would 'get wrong' with Farmer Richardson and the smaller masters if
100 they joined.

Better conditions of life are their due. Let us press forward, by every possible means, the urgent work of putting sanitary dwellings in the place of their hovels.

But to think that better housing alone will at once make very much better men and women of these afflicted people is folly. Something is lacking in them. It is necessary that there shall be put into these men and women that which will make them themselves require better conditions of life. How much farther on will men and women be who get into
110 a new house without being themselves renewed?

How are these people to be renewed? Can all of them be renewed? Most of the things of which they have greatest need can be brought to them only *by personal dealing, by*

patient persistence, enlightened, long-suffering personal
dealing; by, in the widest sense of the word, religious
teaching that reaches out to ALL they lack.

'True religion is a relation, accordant with season and
knowledge, which man establishes with the infinite life
surrounding him, and it is such as binds his life to that
120 infinity, and guides his conduct', wrote Tolstoy. 'A religious
man', he went on, 'will always know where the truth lies,
and where, consequently, his duty lies; and if he does not do
what he ought, he will know that he is guilty and has acted
badly, and will try not to repeat that same sin when he is
next tempted.'

It is easy to talk and toy with the problem of these poor
folk. It is not at all difficult, however, completely to
understand the problem. It can be completely understood if
the source of all the woe be held constantly in mind.

130 *There are limits to what can be done for these people,*
because there are limits to what they can be got to do for
themselves; and the reason is that they are a community
from which the spirited and hopeful men and women have
been continuously withdrawn, generation after generation –
a community which has almost always been hovel housed,
and is physically, mentally and morally impoverished. . . .

The hamlet is corroded by uncharitableness, the pettiest
feuds and jealousies, paltry snobberies, and trumpery vani-
ties. This corrosion of human nature is hidden at times by
140 little generosities. The most hopeless people are often the
most generous, the untidiest and most sly the most agreeably temperamental.

At the root of the plant there is some life.

A main trouble of the community is that it is steadily
distrustful of the unfamiliar. It always suspects the Greeks
when they bring gifts, and all strangers and 'betters' are
Greeks.

Because of its fashion of life it is difficult, almost
impossible, for it to understand, it is incredible that it
150 should fully understand life at another level.

As for those who would be the instructors, advisers or

friends of the hamlet, it is *only by long experience, only by disillusionment after disillusionment, striking sometimes at the heart, sometimes at self-will, that these would-be guides can fully realise what a gap there is between it and them.*

After a time the gap seems to narrow, for a work of grace goes on in the friend of the community as well as in the community itself. An entirely honest friend, purged of self-seeking and self-importance, comes to understand how full 160 *of weeds and darkness was his own mind, how untilled and untrained was his own heart. He recalls with shame the opportunities of improvement which he has had, from his birth up, in his happier education and environment. He remembers, in thoughts of these submerged neighbours and brethren, that, but for a good fortune, that he has done so very little to deserve or requite, there, as old Jeremy owned, there went he along with them.*

The hamlet, its friend, and the nation have to do their best without water that is past.

170   If any further stimulus were needed than the weakness of the hamlet to bring about active effort on its own behalf it is to be found in a strange and moving thing, that, out of the five miserable cottage hovels that ought to have been burnt, there came forth, of their own will, five soldiers to the War. It was a great and welcome adventure for these lads, but their sufferings were keen. Of the five there returned two only – one weakened in his head, the other to die.

Had these courageous, ignorant lads as much responsibility for the nation for which they died as the nation has 180 *resting on it for their hamlet?*

To give up hope of the hamlet were as faint-hearted as to give up hope of the nation, of civilization itself. Does anyone give up hope of the nation because it is so little developed as yet that, while its leaders declare that it cannot find the money for this or that social advance, it goes on spending 685 millions a year on drink, 548 millions on tobacco, and 750 millions on gambling, in contrast with not more than 38 millions on books?

When the nation awakens to its backwardness, its

190 obtuseness, its sinful neglects, its out-of-dateness, it will be too late, as I have tried to show, to do much for the grown-ups of the hamlet.

But a great deal can be done, and more and more every year, for the children.

With this new life we shall of a certainty begin to build Jerusalem.

23 STANLEY BALDWIN
'England is the country, and the country is England'

From *On England* (1926), a collection of Baldwin's speeches

Stanley Baldwin (1867–1947) was British Prime Minister May 1923–January 1924, November 1924–June 1929, and June 1935–May 1937 (National Government). Baldwin was the first British Prime Minister to make effective use of radio. He was very much the representative of middle England: as Thomas Jones notes in the *DNB*, '"My worst enemy", it was Baldwin's pride to maintain, "could never say that I do not understand the people of England, especially middle-class England".'

ON ENGLAND AND THE WEST

ENGLAND

AT THE ANNUAL DINNER OF THE ROYAL SOCIETY

OF ST. GEORGE, AT THE HOTEL CECIL

6th May, 1924

Though I do not think that in the life of a busy man there could be placed into his hands a more difficult toast than this, yet the first thought that comes into my mind as a public man is a feeling of satisfaction and profound thankfulness that I may use the word 'England' without some fellow at the back of the room shouting out 'Britain'. I have often thought how many of the most beautiful passages in the English language would be ruined by that substitution which is so popular to-day. I read in your Dinner-book,

10 'When God wants a hard thing done, He tells it', not to His Britons, but 'to His Englishmen'. And in the same way, to come to a very modern piece of poetry, how different it would be with the altered ending, 'For in spite of all

temptations to belong to other nations, he remains a Briton.' We have to-night to celebrate our country and our Patron Saint. It always seems to me no mere chance that besides being the Patron Saint of England, St. George was the Patron Saint of those gallant sailors around the shores of the Adriatic, and that in his honour there exists one of the 20 most beautiful chapels in Venice to-day. The Patron Saint of sailors is surely the most suitable Patron Saint for men of the English stock; and I think to-night amongst ourselves we might for a minute or two look at those characteristics, contradictory often, peculiar as we believe, in that great stock of which we are all members.

The Englishman is all right as long as he is content to be what God made him, an Englishman, but gets into trouble when he tries to be something else. There are chroniclers, or were chroniclers, who said it was the aping of the French 30 manners by our English ancestors that made us the prey of William the Norman, and led to our defeat at Hastings. Let that be a warning to us not to ape any foreign country. Let us be content to trust ourselves and to be ourselves.

Now, I always think that one of the most curious contradictions about the English stock is this: that while the criticism that is often made of us is not without an element of truth, and that is that as a nation we are less open to the intellectual sense than the Latin races, yet though that may be a fact, there is no nation on earth that has had the same 40 knack of producing geniuses. It is almost a characteristic of the English race; there is hardly any line in which the nation has not produced geniuses, and in a nation which many people might think restrained, unable to express itself, in this same nation you have a literature second to none that has ever existed in the world, and certainly in poetry supreme.

Then, for a more personal characteristic, we grumble, and we always have grumbled, but we never worry. Now, there is a very great truth in that, because there are foreign 50 nations who worry but do not grumble. Grumbling is more superficial, leaves less of a mark on the character, and just as

98

the English schoolboy, for his eternal salvation, is impervious to the receipt of learning, and by that means preserves his mental faculties further into middle age and old age than he otherwise would (and I may add that I attribute the possession of such faculties as I have to the fact that I did not overstrain them in youth), just as the Englishman has a mental reserve owing to that gift given him at his birth by St. George, so, by the absence of worry he keeps his nervous
60 system sound and sane, with the result that in times of emergency the nervous system stands when the nervous system of other peoples breaks.

The Englishman is made for a time of crisis, and for a time of emergency. He is serene in difficulties, but may seem to be indifferent when times are easy. He may not look ahead, he may not heed warnings, he may not prepare, but when he once starts he is persistent to the death, and he is ruthless in action. It is these gifts that have made the Englishman what he is, and that have enabled the English-
70 man to make England and Empire what it is.

It is in staying power that he is supreme, and fortunately, being, as I have said, to some extent impervious to intellectual impressions as a nation, he is equally impervious to criticism – a most useful thing for an English statesman. That may be the reason why English statesmen sometimes last longer than those who are not English. I admit that in past generations we carried that virtue to an excess, and by a rebound the sins of the fathers are being visited on the children. For instance, there was a time when this particular
80 epithet was more in vogue in political society, and the Englishman invariably spoke of the 'damned' foreigner. Those days are gone, but the legacy has come to us in this, that by the swing of the pendulum we have in this country what does not exist in any other, a certain section of our people who regard every country as being in the right except their own. It largely arises, I think, among a section of the population who hold beliefs which they cannot persuade their fellow-countrymen to adopt.

There is yet one other point. I think the English people

90 are at heart and in practice the kindest people in the world.
    With some faults on which I have touched, there is in
    England a profound sympathy for the under-dog. There is
    a brotherly and a neighbourly feeling which we see to a
    remarkable extent through all classes. There is a way of
    facing misfortunes with a cheerful face. It was shown to a
    marvellous degree in the war, and in spite of all that he said
    in criticism of his own people, Ruskin said one thing of
    immortal truth. He said: 'The English laugh is the purest
    and truest in the metal that can be minted. And indeed only
100 Heaven can know what the country owes to it.' There is a
    profound truth in that. As long as a people can laugh, they
    are preserved from the grosser vices of life, political and
    moral. And as long as they can laugh, they can face all the
    ills that fortune may bring upon them.

    Then, in no nation more than the English is there a
    diversified individuality. We are a people of individuals, and
    a people of character. You may take the writings of one of
    the greatest and one of the most English of writers, Charles
    Dickens, and you will find that practically all his characters
110 are English. They are all different, and each of us that has
    gone through this world with his eyes open and his heart
    open, has met every one of Dickens's characters in some
    position or another in life. Let us see to it that we never
    allow our individuality as Englishmen to be steam-rollered.
    The preservation of the individuality of the Englishman is
    essential to the preservation of the type of the race, and if
    our differences are smoothed out and we lose that great gift,
    we shall lose at the same time our power. Uniformity of
    type is a bad thing. I regret very much myself the uni-
120 formity of speech. Time was, two centuries ago, when you
    could have told by his speech from what part of England
    every member of Parliament came. He spoke the speech of
    his fathers, and I regret that the dialects have gone, and I
    regret that by a process which for want of a better name we
    have agreed among ourselves to call education, we are
    drifting away from the language of the people and losing
    some of the best English words and phrases which have

lasted in the country through centuries, to make us all talk one uniform and inexpressive language. Now, I have very
130 little more that I want to say to you to-night, but on an occasion like this I suppose there is no one who does not ask himself in his heart and is a little shy of expressing it, what it is that England stands for to him, and to her. And there comes into my mind a wonder as to what England may stand for in the minds of generations to come if our country goes on during the next generation as she has done in the last two, in seeing her fields converted into towns. To me, England is the country, and the country is England. And when I ask myself what I mean by England, when I think
140 of England when I am abroad, England comes to me through my various senses – through the ear, through the eye, and through certain imperishable scents. I will tell you what they are, and there may be those among you who feel as I do.

The sounds of England, the tinkle of the hammer on the anvil in the country smithy, the corncrake on a dewy morning, the sound of the scythe against the whetstone, and the sight of a plough team coming over the brow of a hill, the sight that has been seen in England since England was
150 a land, and may be seen in England long after the Empire has perished and every works in England has ceased to function, for centuries the one eternal sight of England. The wild anemones in the woods in April, the last load at night of hay being drawn down a lane as the twilight comes on, when you can scarcely distinguish the figures of the horses as they take it home to the farm, and above all, most subtle, most penetrating and most moving, the smell of wood smoke coming up in an autumn evening, or the smell of the scutch fires: that wood smoke that our ancestors, tens of
160 thousands of years ago, must have caught on the air when they were coming home with the result of the day's forage, when they were still nomads, and when they were still roaming the forests and the plains of the continent of Europe. These things strike down into the very depths of our nature, and touch chords that go back to the beginning

101

of time and the human race, but they are chords that with every year of our life sound a deeper note in our innermost being. These are the things that make England, and I grieve for it that they are not the childish inheritance of the
170 majority of the people to-day in our country. They ought to be the inheritance of every child born into this country, but nothing can be more touching than to see how the working man and woman after generations in the towns will have their tiny bit of garden if they can, will go to gardens if they can, to look at something they have never seen as children, but which their ancestors knew and loved. The love of these things is innate and inherent in our people. It makes for that love of home, one of the strongest features of our race, and it is that that makes our race seek its new home in the
180 Dominions over seas, where they have room to see things like this that they can no more see at home. It is that power of making homes, almost peculiar to our people, and it is one of the sources of their greatness. They go overseas, and they take with them what they learned at home: love of justice, love of truth, and the broad humanity that are so characteristic of English people. It may well be that these traits on which we pride ourselves, which we hope to show and try to show in our own lives, may survive – survive among our people so long as they are a people – and I hope
190 and believe this, that just as to-day more than fifteen centuries since the last of those great Roman legionaries left England, we still speak of the Roman strength, and the Roman work, and the Roman character, so perhaps in the ten thousandth century, long after the Empires of this world as we know them have fallen and others have risen and fallen, and risen and fallen again, the men who are then on this earth may yet speak of those characteristics which we prize as the characteristics of the English, and that long after, maybe, the name of the country has passed away,
200 wherever men are honourable and upright and persevering, lovers of home, of their brethren, of justice and of humanity, the men in the world of that day may say, 'We still have among us the gifts of that great English race.'

24 J. B. PRIESTLEY
'The Three Englands'

From *English Journey* (1934)

For a biographical note on Priestley, see p.26.

Southampton to Newcastle, Newcastle to Norwich:
memories rose like milk coming to the boil. I had seen
England. I had seen a lot of Englands. How many? At once,
three disengaged themselves from the shifting mass. There
was, first, Old England, the country of the cathedrals and
minsters and manor houses and inns, of Parson and Squire;
guide-book and quaint highways and byways England:

> Visit ancient York with its 1,300-year-old Minster;
> and Durham where lies the Venerable Bede. Wander
10   through the historic streets of Norwich, once the
> second city of England. Look down from the battle-
> ments of Conway Castle. Visit Lichfield Cathedral,
> renowned for its three beautiful spires, and put
> yourself back in the Middle Ages at Warwick. Every
> county of Great Britain speaks to you of your
> ancestors ...

as our railway companies tell the readers of American
magazines, most of whose ancestors never saw a county of
Great Britain. But we all know this England, which at its
20 best cannot be improved upon in this world. That is, as a
country to lounge about in; for a tourist who can afford to
pay a fairly stiff price for a poorish dinner, an inconvenient
bedroom and lukewarm water in a small brass jug. It has
few luxuries, but nevertheless it is a luxury country. It has
long ceased to earn its own living. I am for scrupulously
preserving the most enchanting bits of it, such as the
cathedrals and the colleges and the Cotswolds, and for
letting the rest take its chance. There are people who believe
that in some mysterious way we can all return to this Old
30 England; though nothing is said about killing off nine-
tenths of our present population, which would have to be

103

the first step. The same people might consider competing in a race at Brooklands with a horse and trap. The chances are about the same. And the right course of conduct, I reflected, was not, unless you happen to be a professional custodian, to go and brood and dream over these almost heart-breaking pieces of natural or architectural loveliness, doing it all at the expense of a lot of poor devils toiling in the muck, but to have an occasional peep at them, thus to steel
40 your determination that sooner or later the rest of English life, even where the muck is now, shall have as good a quality as those things.

Then, I decided, there is the nineteenth-century England, the industrial England of coal, iron, steel, cotton, wool, railways; of thousands of rows of little houses all alike, sham Gothic churches, square-faced chapels, Town Halls, Mechanics' Institutes, mills, foundries, warehouses, refined watering-places, Pier Pavilions, Family and Commercial Hotels, Literary and Philosophical Societies, back-to-back
50 houses, detached villas with monkey-trees, Grill Rooms, railway stations, slag-heaps and 'tips', dock roads, Refreshment Rooms, doss-houses, Unionist or Liberal Clubs, cindery waste ground, mill chimneys, slums, fried-fish shops, public-houses with red blinds, bethels in corrugated iron, good-class drapers and confectioners shops, a cynically devastated countryside, sooty dismal little towns, and still sootier grim fortress-like cities. This England makes up the larger part of the Midlands and the North and exists everywhere; but it is not being added to and has no new life
60 poured into it. To the more fortunate people it was not a bad England at all, very solid and comfortable. A great deal of very good literature has come out of it, though most of that literature never accepted it but looked either backward or forward. It provided a good parade ground for tough, enterprising men, who could build their factories in the knowledge that the world was waiting for their products, and who also knew that once they had accumulated a tidy fortune they could slip out of this mucky England of their making into the older, charming one, where their children,

70 well schooled, groomed and finished, were almost indis-
tinguishable, in their various uniforms, pink hunting coats
to white ties and shiny pumps, from the old inhabitants, the
land-owning aristocrats. But at first you had to be tough. I
reminded myself how more than once I had thought that
the Victorians liked to weep over their novels and plays, not
because they were more sensitive and softer than we are but
because they were much tougher and further removed from
emotion, so that they needed good strong doses of pathos
to move them at all. The less fortunate classes were very
80 unlucky indeed in that England. They had some sort of
security, which is more than many of them have now, but it
was a security of monstrously long hours of work, miserable wages, and surroundings in which they lived like black-
beetles at the back of a disused kitchen stove. Many of their
descendants are still living in those surroundings, but few
people now have the impudence to tell them to be resigned
and even thankful there, to toil in humble diligence before
their Maker and for His chosen children, the debenture-
holders. Whether they were better off in this England than
90 in the one before, the pre-industrial one, is a question that
I admitted I could not answer. They all rushed into the
towns and the mills as soon they could, as we know, which
suggests that the dear old quaint England they were
escaping from could not have been very satisfying. You do
not hurry out of Arcadia to work in a factory twelve hours
a day for about eighteen-pence. Moreover, why did the
population increase so rapidly after the Industrial Revolution? What was it about Merrie England that kept the
numbers down?
100   One thing, I told myself, I was certain of and it was this,
that whether the people were better or worse off in this
nineteenth-century England, it had done more harm than
good to the real enduring England. It had found a green and
pleasant land and had left a wilderness of dirty bricks. It had
blackened fields, poisoned rivers, ravaged the earth, and
sown filth and ugliness with a lavish hand. You cannot make
omelettes without breaking eggs, and you cannot become

rich by selling the world your coal and iron and cotton goods and chemicals without some dirt and disorder. So
110 much is admitted. But there are far too many eggshells and too few omelettes about this nineteenth-century England. What you see looks like a debauchery of cynical greed. As I thought of some of the places I had seen, Wolverhampton and St. Helens and Bolton and Gateshead and Jarrow and Shotton, I remembered a book I had just read, in which we are told to return as soon as possible to the sturdy Victorian individualism. But for my part I felt like calling back a few of these sturdy individualists simply to rub their noses in the nasty mess they had made. Who gave them leave to turn
120 this island into their ashpit? They may or may not have left us their money, but they have certainly left us their muck. If every penny of that money had been spent on England herself, the balance would still be miles on the wrong side. It is as if the country had devoted a hundred years of its life to keeping gigantic sooty pigs. And the people who were choked by the reek of the sties did not get the bacon. The more I thought about it, the more this period of England's industrial supremacy began to look like a gigantic dirty trick. At one end of this commercial greatness were a lot of
130 half-starved, bleary-eyed children crawling about among machinery and at the other end were the traders getting natives boozed up with bad gin. Cynical greed – *Damn you, I'm all right*: you can see as much written in black letters across half England. Had I not just spent days moving glumly in the shadow of their downstrokes?

The third England, I concluded, was the new post-war England, belonging far more to the age itself than to this particular island. America, I supposed, was its real birth place. This is the England of arterial and by-pass roads, of
140 filling stations and factories that look like exhibition buildings, of giant cinemas and dance-halls and cafes, bungalows with tiny garages, cocktail bars, Woolworths, motorcoaches, wireless, hiking, factory girls looking like actresses, grey hound racing and dirt tracks, swimming pools, and every thing given away for cigarette coupons. If the fog had

106

lifted I knew that I should have seen this England all round
me at that northern entrance to London, where the smooth
wide road passes between miles of semi-detached bungalows, all with their little garages, their wireless sets, their
150 periodicals about film stars, their swimming costumes and
tennis rackets and dancing shoes. The fog did not lift for an
instant, however; we crawled, stopped, crawled again; and I
had ample time to consider carefully this newest England,
from my richly confused memory of it. Care is necessary
too, for you can easily approve or disapprove of it too
hastily. It is, of course, essentially democratic. After a social
revolution there would, with any luck, be more and not less
of it. You need money in this England, but you do not need
much money. It is a large-scale, mass-production job, with
160 cut prices. You could almost accept Woolworths as its
symbol. Its cheapness is both its strength and its weakness.
It is its strength because being cheap it is accessible; it nearly
achieves the famous equality of opportunity. In this England, for the first time in history, Jack and Jill are nearly as
good as their master and mistress; they may have always
been as good in their own way, but now they are nearly as
good in the *same way*. Jack, like his master, is rapidly
transported to some place of rather mechanical amusement.
Jill beautifies herself exactly as her mistress does. It is an
170 England, at last, without privilege. Years and years ago the
democratic and enterprising Blackpool, by declaring that
you were all as good as one another so long as you had the
necessary six pence, began all this. Modern England is
rapidly Blackpooling itself. Notice how the very modern
things, like the films and wireless and sixpenny stores, are
absolutely democratic, making no distinction whatever
between their patrons: if you are in a position to accept
what they give – and very few people are not in that position
– then you get neither more nor less than what anybody else
180 gets, just as in the popular restaurants there are no special
helpings for favoured patrons but mathematical portions
for everybody. There is almost every luxury in this world
except the luxury of power or the luxury of privacy. (With

the result that these are the only luxuries that modern autocrats insist upon claiming for themselves. They are far more austere than most of the old tyrants ever were, but they are all greedy for power and sticklers for privacy.) The young people of this new England do not play chorus in an opera in which their social superiors are the principals; they
190 do not live vicariously, enjoy life at second-hand, by telling one another what a wonderful time the young earl is having or how beautiful Lady Mary looked in her court dress; they get on with their own lives. If they must have heroes and heroines, they choose them themselves, from the ranks of film stars and sportsmen and the like. This may not seem important, but nevertheless it is quite new in English life, where formerly, as we may see from memoirs and old novels, people lived in an elaborate network of relations up and down the social scale, despising or pitying their
200 inferiors, admiring or hating their superiors. You see this still in the country and small towns, but not in this new England, which is as near to a classless society as we have got yet.

Unfortunately, it is a bit too cheap. That is, it is also cheap in the other sense of the term. Too much of it is simply a trumpery imitation of something not very good even in the original. There is about it a rather depressing monotony. Too much of this life is being stamped on from outside, probably by astute financial gentlemen, backed by
210 the Press and their publicity services. You feel that too many of the people in this new England are doing not what they like but what they have been told they would like. (Here is the American influence at work.) When I was a boy in Yorkshire the men there who used to meet and sing part-songs in the upper rooms of taverns (they called themselves Glee Unions) were not being humbugged by any elaborate publicity scheme on the part of either music publishers or brewers, were not falling in with any general movement or fashion; they were singing glees over their beer because they
220 liked to sing glees over their beer; it was their own idea of the way to spend an evening and they did not care tuppence

whether it was anybody else's idea or not; they drank and yarned and roared away, happy in the spontaneous expression of themselves. I do not feel that any of the activities in this new England have that spontaneity. Even that push towards the open which we have now decided to call 'hiking' has something regimented about it. Most of the work, as we have already seen, is rapidly becoming standardised in this new England, and its leisure is being handed
230 over to standardisation too. It is a cleaner, tidier, healthier, saner world than that of nineteenth century industrialism. The difference between the two Englands is well expressed by the difference between a typical nineteenth-century factory, a huge dark brick box, and a modern factory, all glass and white tiles and chromium plate. If you remember the old factories at closing time, go and see the work people coming out of one of these new factories. The change is startling. Nevertheless, I cannot rid myself of a suspicion that the old brick boxes had more solid lumps of character
240 inside them than the new places have.

... I cannot help feeling that this new England is lacking in character, in zest, gusto, flavour, bite, drive, originality, and that this is a serious weakness. Monotonous but easy work and a liberal supply of cheap luxuries might between them create a set of people entirely without ambition or any real desire to think and act for themselves, the perfect subjects for an iron autocracy. There is a danger of this occurring in the latest England.

3

WAR AND NATIONAL
IDENTITY

INTRODUCTION

Wars are obvious occasions when ideas about national identity become particularly visible. In time of war Governments and war leaders will call upon a sense of nationhood in order to both enlist support for the war effort and to foster a sense of unity. Between 1900 and 1950 Britain was involved in two major wars: wars which had short- and long-term economic consequences as well as far-reaching social ramifications in terms of both the welfare of its citizens and the structure of its society. Moreover, the global political and economic position of Britain changed radically during this period – by 1950 the idea and reality of Empire which had sustained belief in Britain's world supremacy had been seriously attacked.

The idea of Englishness which existed in 1900 and which was called upon between 1914 and 1918 was not the same sense of Englishness for which men were exhorted to fight in 1939, although it inherited certain aspects from the Edwardian and Georgian eras. Throughout the 1920s and 1930s Englishness was constantly debated, re-worked and re-formulated: the 1940s' idea of 'a people's war' to combat Nazi Germany was a very different (and notably more inclusive) concept than that of the 'hero's war' of 1914. The extracts in this chapter have been chosen to suggest some of the ways in which war, and the sense of a national identity necessary to wage it, changed between 1900 and 1950.

Rupert Brooke's 'The Soldier' and Ernest Raymond's *Tell England* offer a certain version of Englishness prevalent before 1918: a version which, with its insistence on the public school codes of honour and loyalty, worked to legitimate the forms of heroism and self-sacrifice represented in the idea of 'dying for King and Country'. Raymond's heroes, Rupert Ray and Edgar Doe, come to believe that dying for your country is the ultimate religious self-sacrifice, akin to Christ's death at Calvary. Raymond represents this view without irony, and the novel's popularity (it was later made into a film) in the 1920s suggests that, despite a growing climate of anti-heroism and a disavowal of Victorian sentiment, many continued to need or desire the particular pleasures offered by such a text. In this context it is worth remembering that Rupert Brooke's elegiac poetry, celebrating heroism and Englishness, remained esteemed and popular long after the more savage poetry of Owen, Sassoon and other accounts of the historical realities of the First World War had rendered its values deeply problematic.

It is precisely the codes of patriotism and public school honour which Virginia Woolf attacks in *Three Guineas*. As she asserts so trenchantly, women's relation to the idea of 'our country' is deeply ambiguous, and, like many feminists and pacifists of the inter-war years, she repudiates the rituals and symbols which perpetuate militarism and aggressive nationalism. Whilst recognising the particularly masculine construction of militarism, Woolf does not exclude women from perpetuating the codes which sustain war in their relationships with men as brothers, sons and husbands. Siegfried Sassoon's poem 'Memorial Tablet' evokes one of the most potent symbols of patriotism and uses this as the basis for a scathing attack not only on the values of heroism but on the class structure which underpinned British society in 1914. Sassoon's reference to 'Squire' ironically undermines the notion of a benevolent social order to be found in the idealised pastoralism of a rustic England. In contrast Edward Thomas's poem 'As the Team's Head-Brass' conjures up and attempts to capture a version of this rural England which the poem's speaker believes is fast disappearing. Thomas links the loss of this older rural England to the losses sustained by the war, and does so in a way which eschews the high rhetoric of patriotism but nevertheless invites the reader to identify wholeheartedly with the particular England he evokes.

The kind of report filed by the Mass Observation panellist in 1940, on conscripts' attitude to politics and by implication to the war they are engaged in, could not have been written in the First World War. For one thing it demonstrates an egalitarianism and a willingness to hear the views of 'ordinary' people which would have been inconceivable to many in 1914. The vote had been extended to all males over 21 in 1918 and to all women over 21 in 1928; throughout the 1920s and 1930s the idea of citizenship for all social groups had been fostered by successive governments and social agencies, despite the obvious dispossession of poverty and unemployment experienced by many. In this context you might consider Baldwin's speech, 'On England' (see the extract in chapter 2, Versions of Rural England), in which he envisions a more socially-inclusive version of Englishness than Raymond's public-school, upper-class version.

As a result of extended civil and political rights, the political attitudes of working-class conscripts were significant for any government planning post-war reconstruction. Equally, the note of cynicism and boredom amongst conscripts in Second World War, recorded by the Mass Observation panellist, contrasts strongly with the intense, patriotic fervour of some First World War accounts. This is not to suggest that conscripts in the First World War were neither cynical nor unenthusiastic, but that such expressions were perhaps not seen worthy of recording or retaining.

Churchill's Second World War speeches draw on a sense of a war to be fought not only by the armed forces but also by civilians; a war which requires stoical endurance and a refusal to be beaten, rather than the fervent self-sacrifices of patriotic heroism. Nonetheless, it is interesting to note the ways in which Churchill deploys a repertoire of traditional iconography associated with the idea of Englishness – the little man who stands up to the big bully, the idea of 'our island home' and the quasi-religious equation of England with the will of God and a manifest destiny. Finally, note Churchill's address to King George VI in which he sums up the role of the monarchy not only as a symbol of England in time of war but also as a reminder of England's constitutional history and social unity. This echoes Phillip Gibbs's essay on the occasion of the 1935 Jubilee, and you could consider the function of the monarchy as a rallying-point for ideas of Englishness in times of national crisis.

Labour MP Herbert Morrison's speech uses the same rhetoric and ideals, and should remind us that discourses of Englishness were never the prerogative of conservatism and the Right. Throughout the 1930s and during the Second World War many writers, politicians and commentators attempted to capture a version of England which included the 'ordinary' man and woman. Morrison's speech, like Churchill's, is targeted not just at the potential soldiers but also at those, working long hours in factories, whose job it was to produce munitions.

Churchill in his victory speeches addresses 'ordinary' Londoners. However, the Mass Observation diarist's account of the VE celebrations captures a sense of ambivalence amongst the 'ordinary people' targeted by such speeches – on the one hand there is elation that the war in Europe is over and a desire to celebrate; on the other there is a recognition of what has been lost, a refusal to be duped by bombastically nationalistic gestures (for example, Churchill singing the chorus of 'Rule Britannia'), and an anxiety about the future.

London's survival of the Blitz became an icon for Englishness: in 1940 Humphrey Jennings directed the Ministry of Information film, *London (Britain) Can Take It*, in which the title itself makes explicit the metonymic function of 'London' and in which German bombing is depicted as being unable to kill 'the unconquerable spirit and courage of the people of London'.[1] The extract from the *Documentary Newsletter* on wartime film propaganda makes explicit the images, ideals and icons which together constitute 'British life and character'. Any wartime propaganda tends to simplify issues: values are positive or negative; complexity or ambiguity is suppressed in order to construct certain versions of history. This is evident in the extracts from J. B. Priestley's wartime radio broadcast in which he urges his listeners to look forward to a post-war society founded upon community and creation – an England which he found little evidence of in his earlier *English Journey*.

The myths created in wartime, however potent, do not emerge from a cultural vacuum, and many of the ideas emphasised in this Newsletter had their origins in earlier conceptualisations of Englishness. Moreover, the Ministry of Information was only too well aware in 1940 that the aims of post-war reconstruction, conventionally glossed as a refusal to return to the 'bad old days' of the inter-war years, had to be promoted if public morale was to be strengthened for the impending Blitz. Thus Priestley promotes a post-war dream of community as one of the ideals that make the war worth fighting. Whilst the Government's deployment of a vast propaganda machine aimed at sustaining civilian morale is more evident in 1940 than in 1914, it is worth stressing that propaganda played an important role in 1914. George Orwell noted in 1943 that writers of whatever political persuasion or history had been sucked into 'the various Ministries or the BBC' (Orwell 1945/1968: 335), but in 1914 writers as different as Arnold Bennett and Ford Madox Ford worked for the Ministry of Information (see Wright 1978).

Jan Struther's Mrs. Miniver wrote her final contributions for the *Times* column during the autumn of 1939. Mrs. Miniver's 'letter' to her sister-in-law, 'From Needing Danger', sounds precisely the kind of note the Ministry of Information, if it had commissioned Mrs. Miniver, would have wished for. England is imaged as a national family who, having made mistakes, has been brought to its senses and given another chance to get things right. This image of England as a united family 'muddling through' was a far cry from the bombast of Victorian imperialism; it suggests what Alison Light has called 'a patriotism of private life' in which to be English was to value the pleasures of 'privacy and domesticity' (Light 1991: 154). MGM made *Mrs. Miniver* into a highly successful film in 1942, and in doing so offered a specific version of the British civilian in time of war to both British and American audiences. It is worth considering how, in the space of thirty years, popular representations of wartime heroism have replaced the public-schoolboy officer with the middle-class housewife. Jan Struther's Mrs. Miniver captured 'our country' for the 'daughters of educated men' in ways Virginia Woolf could not have foreseen or wished.

Note

1 Commentary of the film *London (Britain) Can Take It*, 1940 from *Documentary Newsletter*, November 1940, pp.6–7, reprinted in Open University *A309 Documents 1918–1970* (Milton Keynes, Open University Press).

25 VIRGINIA WOOLF
'Her sex and class has very little to thank England for ...'

From *Three Guineas* (1938)

Virginia Woolf (1882–1941) was educated at home in London where she lived until the death of her father, Leslie Stephen, in 1904. Thereafter she moved to Bloomsbury, and with her brothers and sister, Vanessa, formed the nucleus of the Bloomsbury group so influential in literature and the arts in the 1920s and 1930s. She was an innovative novelist (*Mrs Dalloway, To The Lighthouse, The Waves*), a literary critic and a journalist. Her polemical essays, *A Room of One's Own* (1929) and *Three Guineas* (1938) are classics of the feminist movement. In this extract from *Three Guineas*, written in response to the death of her nephew in the Spanish Civil War, Woolf argues that national identity and patriotism cannot have the same meaning for middle-class women ('the daughters of educated men') as they do for men.

114

... Let us then draw rapidly in outline the kind of society which the daughters of educated men might found and join outside your society but in co-operation with its ends. In the first place, this new society, you will be relieved to learn, would have no honorary treasurer, for it would need no funds. It would have no office, no committee, no secretary; it would call no meetings; it would hold no conferences. If name it must have, it could be called the Outsiders Society. That is not a resonant name, but it has the advantage that it squares with facts – the facts of history, of law, of biog-raphy; even, it may be, with the still hidden facts of our still unknown psychology. It would consist of educated men's daughters working in their own class – how indeed can they work in any other? – and by their own methods for liberty, equality and peace. Their first duty, to which they would bind themselves not by oath, for oaths and ceremonies have no part in a society which must be anonymous and elastic before everything, would be not to fight with arms. This is easy for them to observe, for in fact, as the papers inform us, 'the Army Council have no intention of opening recruiting for any women's corps'. The country ensures it. Next they would refuse in the event of war to make munitions or nurse the wounded. Since in the last war both these activities were mainly discharged by the daughters of working men, the pressure upon them here too would be slight, though probably disagreeable. On the other hand the next duty to which they would pledge themselves is one of considerable difficulty, and calls not only for courage and initiative, but for the special knowledge of the educated man's daughter. It is, briefly, not to incite their brothers to fight, or to dissuade them, but to maintain an attitude of complete indifference. But the attitude expressed by the word 'indifference' is so complex and of such importance that it needs even here further definition. Indifference in the first place must be given a firm footing upon fact. As it is a fact that she cannot understand what instinct compels him, what glory, what interest, what manly satisfaction fighting provides for him – 'without war there would be no outlet

for the manly qualities which fighting develops' – as
40 fighting thus is a sex characteristic which she cannot share,
the counterpart some claim of the maternal instinct which
he cannot share, so is it an instinct which she cannot judge.
The outsider therefore must leave him free to deal with this
instinct by himself, because liberty of opinion must be
respected, especially when it is based upon an instinct which
is as foreign to her as centuries of tradition and education
can make it. This is a fundamental and instinctive distinction upon which indifference may be based. But the
outsider will make it her duty not merely to base her
50 indifference upon instinct, but upon reason. When he says,
as history proves that he has said, and may say again, 'I am
fighting to protect our country' and thus seeks to rouse her
patriotic emotion, she will ask herself, 'What does "our
country" mean to me an outsider?' To decide this she will
analyse the meaning of patriotism in her own case. She will
inform herself of the position of her sex and her class in the
past. She will inform herself of the amount of land, wealth
and property in the possession of her own sex and class in
the present – how much of 'England' in fact belongs to her.
60 From the same sources she will inform herself of the legal
protection which the law has given her in the past and now
gives her. And if he adds that he is fighting to protect her
body, she will reflect upon the degree of physical protection
that she now enjoys when the words 'Air Raid Precaution'
are written on blank walls. And if he says that he is fighting
to protect England from foreign rule, she will reflect that for
her there are no 'foreigners', since by law she becomes a
foreigner if she marries a foreigner. And she will do her best
to make this a fact, not by forced fraternity, but by human
70 sympathy. All these facts will convince her reason (to put it
in a nutshell) that her sex and class has very little to thank
England for in the past; not much to thank England for in
the present; while the security of her person in the future is
highly dubious. But probably she will have imbibed, even
from the governess, some romantic notion that Englishmen,
those fathers and grandfathers whom she sees marching in

116

the picture of history, are 'superior' to the men of other countries. This she will consider it her duty to check by comparing French historians with English; German with
80 French; the testimony of the ruled – the Indians or the Irish, say – with the claims made by their rulers. Still some 'patriotic' emotion, some ingrained belief in the intellectual superiority of her own country over other countries may remain. Then she will compare English painting with French painting; English music with German music; English literature with Greek literature, for translations abound. When all these comparisons have been faithfully made by the use of reason, the outsider will find herself in possession of very good reasons for her indifference. She
90 will find that she has no good reason to ask her brother to fight on her behalf to protect 'our' country. '"Our country,"' she will say, 'throughout the greater part of its history has treated me as a slave; it has denied me education or any share in its possessions. "Our" country still ceases to be mine if I marry a foreigner. "Our" country denies me the means of protecting myself, forces me to pay others a very large sum annually to protect me, and is so little able, even so, to protect me that Air Raid precautions are written on the wall. Therefore if you insist upon fighting to protect me, or
100 "our" country, let it be understood soberly and rationally between us, that you are fighting to gratify a sex instinct which I cannot share; to procure benefits which I have not shared and probably will not share; but not to gratify my instincts, or to protect either myself or my country. For,' the outsider will say, 'in fact, as a woman, I have no country. As a woman I want no country. As a woman my country is the whole world.' And if, when reason has said its say, still some obstinate emotion remains, some love of England dropped into a child's ears by the cawing of rooks in an elm
110 tree, by the splash of waves on a beach, or by English voices murmuring nursery rhymes, this drop of pure, if irrational, emotion she will make serve her to give to England first what she desires of peace and freedom for the whole world.
Such then will be the nature of her 'indifference' and

from this indifference certain actions must follow. She will bind herself to take no share in patriotic demonstrations; to assent to no form of national self-praise; to make no part of any claque or audience that encourages war; to absent herself from military displays, tournaments, tattoos, prize-
120 givings and all such ceremonies as encourage the desire to impose 'our' civilization or 'our' dominion upon other people. The psychology of private life, moreover, warrants the belief that this use of indifference by the daughters of educated men would help materially to prevent war. For psychology would seem to show that it is far harder for human beings to take action when other people are indifferent and allow them complete freedom of action, than when their actions are made the centre of excited emotion. The small boy struts and trumpets outside the window;
130 implore him to stop; he goes on; say nothing; he stops. That the daughters of educated men then should give their brothers neither the white feather of cowardice nor the red feather of courage, but no feather at all; that they should shut the bright eyes that rain influence, or let those eyes look elsewhere when war is discussed – that is the duty to which outsiders will train themselves in peace before the threat of death inevitably makes reason powerless.

26 ERNEST RAYMOND
'I see a death in No Man's Land to-morrow as a wonderful thing'

From *Tell England: A Study in a Generation* (1922)

Ernest Raymond (1888–1974) was ordained, but on the outbreak of the First World War he resigned orders and joined up. He fought in Gallipoli, Egypt and Russia, and was demobilised in 1919. *Tell England* was the first of many novels. Today he is perhaps best remembered for his 1936 crime novel *We, the Accused*.

Tell England tells the story of two boys, Rupert Ray and Edgar Doe, growing up in the years before the First World War, their relationship to each other and to their public school and their war experience at Gallipoli, where Doe sacrifices his life at the end of the doomed campaign, and where both boys come to believe that to die for their country is the purest form of religious self-sacrifice. The boys' beliefs are represented as deeply rooted in and sustained by the values of the public school, the bourgeois family and the Church of England. The film of *Tell England* made eight years later in 1930 presented a more ambivalent version of the public school code and wartime heroism in line with changing attitudes to the First World War and to ideals of patriotism. This extract is from the novel's ending in which Rupert, the story's narrator, contemplates the next day's offensive, when, as we know from the novel's opening, he will be killed. Monty is the padre who has been with both boys on the sea journey (which is represented as also a spiritual journey) to Gallipoli; Pennybet is another boy from the same public school.

'Only by turning your sufferings into the seeds of God-like things will you make their memory beautiful.'

As I copied just now those last words of Monty's sermon I laid down my pencil on the dug-out floor with a little start. As in a flashlight I saw their truth. They created in my mind the picture of that Aegean evening, when Monty turned the moment of Doe's death, which so nearly brought me discouragement and debasement, into an ennobling memory. And I foresaw him going about healing the sores
10   of this war with the same priestly hand.

Yes, there are reasons why such wistful visions should haunt me now. Everything this evening has gone to produce a certain exaltation in me. First, there has been the bombardment, with its thought of going over the top to-morrow. Then comes my mother's glowing letter, which somehow has held me enthralled, so that I find sentences from it reiterating themselves in my mind, just as they did in the old schooldays. And lastly, there has been the joyous sense of having completed my book, on which for three
20   years I have laboured lovingly in tent, and billet, and trench.

I meant to close it on the last echo of Monty's sermon. But the fascination was on me, and I felt I wanted to go on writing. I had so lost myself in the old scenes of school-room, playing-fields, starlit decks, and Grecian battle-grounds, which I had been describing, that I actually ceased to hear the bombardment. And the atmosphere of the well-loved places and well-loved friends remained all about me. It was the atmosphere that old portraits and fading old

119

30   letters throw around those who turn them over. So I took
up again my pencil and my paper.

I thought I would add a paragraph or two, in case I go
down in the morning. If I come through all right, I shall
wipe these paragraphs out. Meanwhile, in these final hours
of wonder and waiting, it is a happiness to write on.

I fear that, as I write, I may appear to dogmatize, for I am
still only twenty-two. But I must speak while I can.

What silly things one thinks in an evening of suspense
and twilight like this! One minute I feel I want to be alive
40   this time to-morrow, in order that my book, which has
become everything to me, may have a happy ending.
Pennybet fell at Neuve Chapelle, Doe at Cape Helles, and
one ought to be left alive to save the face of the tale. Still, if
these paragraphs stand and I fall, it will at least be a *true*
ending – true to things as they were for the generation in
which we were born.

And the glorious bombardment asserts itself through my
thoughts, and with a thrill I conceive of it – for we would-be
authors are persons obsessed by one idea – as an effort of
50   the people of Britain to make it possible for me to come
through unhurt and save my story. I feel I want to thank
them.

Another minute I try to recapture that moment of ideal
patriotism which I touched on the deck of the *Rangoon*. I
see a death in No Man's Land to-morrow as a wonderful
thing. There you stand exactly between two nations. All
Britain with her might is behind your back, reaching down
to her frontier, which is the trench whence you have just
leapt. All Germany with her might is before your face.
60   Perhaps it is not ill to die standing like that in front of your
nation.

I cannot bear to think of my mother's pain, if to-morrow
claims me. But I leave her this book into which I seem to
have poured my life. It is part of myself. No, it *is* myself –
and I shall only return her what is her own.

Oh, but if I go down, I want to ask you not to think it
anything but a happy ending. It will be happy, because

victory came to the nation, and that is more important than
the life of any individual. Listen to that bombardment
70 outside, which is increasing, if possible, as the darkness
gathers – well, it is one of the last before the extraordinary
Sabbath-silence, which will be the Allies' Peace.

And, if these pages can be regarded as my spiritual
history, they will have a happy ending, too. This is why.

In the Mediterranean on a summer day, I learned that I
was to pursue beauty like the Holy Grail. And I see it now
in everything. I know that, just as there is far more beauty
in nature than ugliness, so there is more goodness in
humanity than evil. There is more happiness in life than
80 pain. Yes, there is. As Monty used to say, we are given now
and then moments of surpassing joy which outweigh
decades of grief. I think I knew such a moment when I won
the swimming cup for Bramhall. And I remember my
mother whispering one night; 'If all the rest of my life,
Rupert, were to be sorrow, the last nineteen years of you
have made it so well worth living.' Happiness wins hands
down. Take any hundred of us out here, and for ten who are
miserable you will find ninety who are lively and laughing.
Life is good – else why should we cling to it as we do? – oh,
90 yes we surely do, especially when the chances are all against
us. Life is good, and youth is good. I have had twenty
glorious years.

I may be whimsical to-night, but I feel that the old
Colonel was right when he saw nothing unlovely in Penny's
death; and that Monty was right when he said that Doe had
done a perfect thing at the last, and so grasped the Grail.
And I have the strange idea that very likely I, too, shall find
beauty in the morning.

27 RUPERT BROOKE
'The Soldier'

From *1914 and Other Poems* (1915)

Rupert Brooke (1887–1915) was educated at Rugby where his father was a master, won a scholarship to King's College, Cambridge and travelled in Germany, the USA, Canada and the Pacific, before enlisting in the army in 1914. He died of blood poisoning in 1915 on his way to the Dardanelles. His 'War Sonnets' precisely caught the early war mood of exalted heroism, and for a while he was considered the national poet of war. 'The Old Vicarage, Grantchester' (see chapter 5, Domestic and Urban Englands) offers a far more light-hearted, even ironic, view of England and Englishness than 'The Soldier'.

The Soldier

If I should die, think only this of me:
That there's some corner of a foreign field
That is for ever England. There shall be
In that rich earth a richer dust concealed;
A dust whom England bore, shaped, made aware,
Gave, once, her flowers to love, her ways to roam,
A body of England's, breathing English air,
Washed by the rivers, blest by suns of home.

And think, this heart, all evil shed away,
10   A pulse in the eternal mind, no less
Gives somewhere back the thoughts by England given;
Her sights and sounds; dreams happy as her day;
And laughter, learnt of friends; and gentleness,
In hearts at peace, under an English heaven.

28 SIEGFRIED SASSOON
'Memorial Tablet' (1919)

From *Georgian Poetry*, ed. J. Reeves (1962)

Siegfried Sassoon (1886–1967) was educated at Marlborough and Cambridge. He fought in the trenches of the First World War, was invalided out with shellshock and was awarded an MC which he later repudiated. His war poetry attacked the kind of patriotism invoked in *Tell England* and by the poetry of Rupert Brooke. Sassoon survived the war, continued to write poetry and also established a reputation for himself as a prose writer with his semi-autobiographical work, *Memoirs of a Fox-Hunting Man*. 'Memorial Tablet', like much of his war poetry, satirises with contempt the valorisation of war as heroic and honourable by society's leaders and by civilian society generally.

Memorial Tablet
(Great War)

Squire nagged and bullied till I went to fight,
(Under Lord Derby's scheme), I died in hell –
(They called it Passchendaele). My wound was slight,
And I was hobbling back; and then a shell
Burst slick upon the duck-boards; so I fell
Into the bottomless mud and lost the light.

At sermon-time, while Squire is in his pew,
He gives my gilded name a thoughtful stare;
For, though low down upon the list, I'm there;
10   *'In proud and glorious memory'* ... that's my due.
Two bleeding years I fought in France, for Squire:
I suffered anguish that he's never guessed,
Once I came home on leave; and then went west ...
What greater glory could a man desire?

29 EDWARD THOMAS
'As the Team's Head-Brass' (c. 1915)

From *The Collected Poems of Edward Thomas*

For a biographical note on Thomas, see p.75.

Thomas's poetry evokes a rural England which is on the verge of decay and collapse: a moment of transition between one world and another when it becomes imperative to affirm an enduring and stable vision of England.

As the Team's Head Brass

As the team's head-brass flashed out on the turn
The lovers disappeared into the wood,
I sat among the boughs of the fallen elm
That strewed the angle of the fallow, and
Watched the plough narrowing a yellow square
Of charlock. Every time the horses turned
Instead of treading me down, the ploughman leaned
Upon the handles to say or ask a word,
About the weather, next about the war,
10 Scraping the share he faced towards the wood,

And screwed along the furrow till the brass flashed
Once more.

The blizzard felled the elm whose crest
I sat in, by a woodpecker's round hole,
The ploughman said. 'When will they take it away?'
'When the war's over.' So the talk began –
One minute and an interval of ten,
A minute more and the same interval.
'Have you been out?' 'No.' 'And don't want to, perhaps?'
20 'If I could only come back again, I should.
I could spare an arm. I shouldn't want to lose
A leg. If I should lose my head, why, so,
I should want nothing more.... Have many gone
From here?' 'Yes.' 'Many lost?' 'Yes, a good few.

Only two teams work on the farm this year.
One of my mates is dead. The second day
In France they killed him. It was back in March,
The very night of the blizzard, too. Now if
He had stayed here we should have moved the tree.'
30 'And I should not have sat here. Everything
Would have been different. For it would have been
Another world.' 'Ay, and a better, though
If we could see all all might seem good.' Then
The lovers came out of the wood again,
The horses started and for the last time
I watched the clods crumble and topple over
After the ploughshare and the stumbling team.

30 J. B. PRIESTLEY
Talk from 21 July 1940

From *All England Listened: The Wartime Broadcasts of J. B. Priestley*

For a biographical note on Priestley, see p.26.

Now, there are two ways of looking at this war. The first
way, which, on the whole, we are officially encouraged to

adopt, is to see this war as a terrible interruption. As soon as we can decently do it, we must return to what is called peace, so let's make all the munitions we can, and be ready to do some hard fighting, and then we can have done with Hitler and his Nazis and go back to where we started from, the day before war was declared. Now this, to my mind, is all wrong. It's wrong because it simply isn't true. A year
10 ago, though we hadn't actually declared war, there wasn't real peace, or the year before, or the year before that. If you go back to the sort of world that produces Hitlers and Mussolinis, then no sooner have you got rid of one lot of Hitlers and Mussolinis than another lot will pop up somewhere, and there'll be more wars.

This brings us to the second, and more truthful, way of looking at this war. That is, to regard this war as one chapter in a tremendous history, the history of a changing world, the breakdown of one vast system and the building
20 up of another and better one. In this view of things Hitler and Mussolini have been thrown up by this breakdown of a world system. It's as if an earthquake cracked the walls and floors of a house and strange nuisances of things, Nazists and Fascists, came running out of the woodwork. We have to get rid of these intolerable nuisances but not so that we can go *back* to anything. There's nothing that really worked that we can go back to. But so that we can go forward, without all the shouting and stamping and bullying and murder, and really plan and build up a nobler
30 world in which ordinary, decent folk can not only find justice and security but also beauty and delight. And this isn't a 'pipe dream' because many of our difficulties have arrived not because man's capacity is feebler than it used to be, but just because it's actually so much greater. The modern man, thanks to his inventiveness, has suddenly been given a hundred arms and seven-league boots. But we can't go forward and build up this new world order, and this is our real war aim, unless we begin to think differently, and my own personal view, for what it's worth, is that we
40 must stop thinking in terms of property and power and

begin thinking in terms of community and creation.

Now, I'll explain just what I mean. First, take the change from power to creation. Now, power – whether on a large or small scale – really boils down to the ignoble pleasure of bossing and ordering other people about because you have the whip-hand of them. All these Nazi and Fascist leaders are power worshippers, they're almost drunk on it. I suspect it's simply a bad substitute for the joy of creation, which everybody understands, whether you're creating a
50 vast educational system or a magnificent work of art, or bringing into existence a vegetable garden or a thundering good dinner. People are never so innocently happy as when they're creating something. So, we want a world that offers people not the dubious pleasures of power, but the maximum opportunities for creation. And even already, in the middle of this war, I can see that world shaping itself.

And now we'll take the change from property to community. Property is that old-fashioned way of thinking of a country as a thing, and a collection of things on that
60 thing, all owned by certain people and constituting property; instead of thinking of a country as the home of a living society, and considering the welfare of that society, the community itself, as the first test. And I'll give you an instance of how this change should be working. Near where I live is a house with a large garden, that's not being used at all because the owner of it has gone to America. Now, according to the property view, this is all right, and we, who haven't gone to America, must fight to protect this absentee owner's property. But on the community view, this is all
70 wrong. There are hundreds of working men not far from here who urgently need ground for allotments so that they can produce a bit more food. Also, we may soon need more houses for billeting. Therefore, I say, that house and garden ought to be used whether the owner, who's gone to America, likes it or not. That's merely one instance, and you can easily find dozens of others.

Now, the war, because it demands a huge collective effort, is compelling us to change not only our ordinary,

social and economic habits, but also our habits of thought.
80 We're actually changing over from the property view to the
sense of community, which simply means that we realize
we're all in the same boat. But, and this is the point, that
boat can serve not only as our defence against Nazi
aggression, but as an ark in which we can all finally land in
a better world. And when I say We, I don't mean only the
British and their allied peoples, but all people everywhere,
including all the Germans who haven't sold themselves
body and soul to the evil Nazi idea. I tell you, there is
stirring in us now, a desire which could soon become a
90 controlled but passionate determination to remodel and
recreate this life of ours, to make it the glorious beginning
of a new world order, so that we might soon be so fully and
happily engrossed in our great task that if Hitler and his
gang suddenly disappeared we'd hardly notice that they'd
gone. We're even now the hope of free men everywhere but
soon we could be the hope and lovely dawn of the whole
wide world.

31 MASS OBSERVATION NATIONAL PANEL MEMBER
'Conscripts' attitudes to war politics' (April 1940)

From *Speak for Yourself: A Mass Observation Anthology 1937–49*, eds A.
Calder and D. Sheridan (1984)

Mass Observation (M-O) began as the brain-child of Tom Harrisson, an
anthropologist, Charles Madge, poet and journalist, and Humphrey Jennings,
painter, film-maker and writer. Humphrey Jennings directed a number of
wartime films, including *London Can Take It*, *Listen to Britain* and *Diary for
Timothy*. M-O's aim was to observe and record the day-to-day life and
thoughts of 'ordinary' people. To this end M-O recruited a panel of volunteer
'observers' whose task it was to write about themselves. Throughout the war
about 300 of these volunteer 'observers' submitted regular diaries.

General report on conscripts' attitudes to war politics

First of all I must say that I have to generalise a great deal in this report and that these generalisations should not be taken as applying to every conscript. They merely give the broad impression I have received from the contacts I have made in the few months I have been in the RAF. These impressions may not be typical. I imagine, for instance, that on the whole a more intelligent type gets into the RAF than in the Army or even the Navy. I have compared notes, however, with a friend in the Navy who is also a Mass-Observer and his impressions
10   have been much the same as mine.

The first impression then is that, as shown by M-O's survey of those about to be called up, there is no enthusiasm for war as such and not a great deal of enthusiasm for this particular war. Also without exception, the conscripts, and also many volunteers, want the war to end so that they can get back to civilian life. They are not deeply in love with life in the RAF, tho' of course they like certain aspects of it but on the whole they bear it because they know that it is preferable to life in the Army, who are generally acknowl-
20   edged to have the worst of everything. A number of conscripts have confessed to me that they would have been 'COs' if they had 'had the guts' but on closer questioning they nearly always revealed that they had no conscientious objection to war (tho' of course they thought it rather silly and pointless), but merely an objection to being in H.M. Forces at all.

There is not a great deal of hatred expressed against the Germans. Hitler of course is generally referred to as a bastard. In the last few days since the invasion of Scandina-
30   via, I have heard more condemnation than in all the rest of the time. Neither is there in the RAF that tendency so common in civilians to underestimate the enemy. It is realised that we have a hard nut to crack. Indeed to listen to some RAF men talk you would imagine we had practically no chance of winning at all. I believe that a good deal of this pessimism is affected.

Conscripts I have met have not often been what the Communists call 'politically conscious' and they seldom talk politics. There are exceptions to this tho'. I have met
40 Communists, Socialists, an ex-Fascist and so forth. But mostly conscripts do not talk incessantly politics. When they do, however, they seem to display a good deal of political intelligence and many can argue quite coherently.

The foremost characteristic of their outlook is a cynicism about everything. They like democracy but they know damn well that all we are fighting for is British capital. Patriotism, the Flag and the Empire are a lot of tripe – only they don't say tripe. Mr Chamberlain's ears must be red at some of the nouns and adjectives I have heard applied to
50 him. Churchill is far and away the most liked member of this government. Indeed his was the only talk I have heard a barrack room listen to on the wireless.

Conscientious objectors cause a good deal of heart-burning and I have heard many heated arguments about them. Many dismiss them all as unnatural and meet to be shot but the more thinking usually concede that it requires a good deal of guts to be a CO and that we have taken the easy way out by following the crowd. Complaints usually made over the fact that many COs are merely swinging the
60 lead. There is probably some justification for this complaint but I have heard the more uncompromising assert that 95 per cent of COs were not genuine. Generally speaking, broad streak of tolerance runs thro' opinions of most of the conscripts I have met.

32 WINSTON S. CHURCHILL
'Victory – victory at all costs ...'

From *Into Battle: War Speeches by Right Hon. Winston S. Churchill,* compiled by Randolph S. Churchill (1941)

Winston S. Churchill was born in 1874 and died in 1965. The following is an extract from Churchill's speech to the House of Commons, 13 May 1940, on his taking office as Prime Minister. Neville Chamberlain had resigned, accused of mishandling diplomatic negotiations and the war effort, and Churchill, long in the political wilderness, rose to the occasion, forming and heading a wartime Coalition government, one of whose aims was to raise the flagging morale of the British people in the face of continued German war successes.

'I have nothing to offer but blood, toil, tears and sweat.'

We have before us an ordeal of the most grievous kind. We have before us many, many long months of struggle and of suffering. You ask, what is our policy? I will say: it is to wage war, by sea, land and air, with all our might and with all the strength that God can give us: to wage war against a monstrous tyranny never surpassed in the dark, lamentable catalogue of human crime. That is our policy. You ask, what is our aim? I can answer in one word: Victory – victory at all costs, victory in spite of all terror, victory, however long and hard the road may be; for without victory, there is no survival. Let that be realised; no survival for the British Empire; no survival for all that the British Empire has stood for, no survival for the urge and impulse of the ages, that mankind will move forward towards its goal. But I take up my task with buoyancy and hope. I feel sure that our cause will not be suffered to fail among men. At this time I feel entitled to claim the aid of all, and I say, 'Come, then, let us go forward together with our united strength.'

33 WINSTON S. CHURCHILL
'We shall go on to the end ...'

From *Into Battle: War Speeches by Right Hon. Winston S. Churchill,* compiled by Randolph S. Churchill (1941)

For a biographical note on Churchill, see p. 129.

This extract is from a speech delivered to the House of Commons by Churchill on the occasion of the Dunkirk evacuation, 4 June 1940.

Turning once again, and this time more generally, to the question of invasion, I would observe that there has never been a period in all these long centuries of which we boast when an absolute guarantee against invasion, still less against serious raids, could have been given to our people. In the days of Napoleon the same wind which would have

carried his transports across the Channel might have driven away the blockading fleet. There was always the chance, and it is that chance which has excited and befooled the
10   imaginations of many Continental tyrants. Many are the tales that are told. We are assured that novel methods will be adopted, and when we see the originality of malice, the ingenuity of aggression, which our enemy displays, we may certainly prepare ourselves for every kind of novel stratagem and every kind of brutal and treacherous manoeuvre. I think that no idea is so outlandish that it should not be considered and viewed with a searching, but at the same time, I hope, with a steady eye. We must never forget the solid assurances of sea-power and those which belong to air
20   power if it can be locally exercised.

I have, myself, full confidence that if all do their duty, if nothing is neglected, and if the best arrangements are made, as they are being made, we shall prove ourselves once again able to defend our island home, to ride out the storm of war, and to outlive the menace of tyranny, if necessary for years, if necessary alone. At any rate, that is what we are going to try to do. That is the resolve of His Majesty's Government – every man of them. That is the will of Parliament and the nation. The British Empire and the French Republic, linked
30   together in their cause and in their need, will defend to the death their native soil, aiding each other like good comrades to the utmost of their strength. Even though large tracts of Europe and many old and famous States have fallen or may fall into the grip of the Gestapo and all the odious apparatus of Nazi rule, we shall not flag or fail. We shall go on to the end, we shall fight in France, we shall fight on the seas and oceans, we shall fight with growing confidence and growing strength in the air, we shall defend our island, whatever the cost may be, we shall fight on the beaches, we shall fight on
40   the landing grounds, we shall fight in the fields and in the streets, we shall fight in the hills; we shall never surrender, and even if, which I do not for a moment believe, this island or a large part of it were subjugated and starving, then our Empire beyond the seas, armed and guarded by the British

Fleet, would carry on the struggle, until, in God's good time, the new world, with all its power and might, steps forth to the rescue and the liberation of the old.

34 HERBERT MORRISON
'Let us take stock of ourselves'

From *Looking Ahead: Wartime Speeches by the Right Hon. Herbert Morrison* (1943)

This extract is from a speech broadcast by Herbert Morrison (1888–1965), Labour member of the Wartime Coalition Government on 22 May 1940 – the day the new Government took office.

Today we are at grips with a more deadly menace than has threatened the people of this island since Philip's Great Armada set out to storm our coasts, and bring us under his yoke. Indeed, the present threat looms nearer. To-day there is not 'time enough to finish the game and beat the enemy too'. There is time for nothing but an intense, concentrated effort of muscle, and mind and will. It must begin *now*.

Let us take stock of ourselves. We have our backs to the wall, surely enough. You know that, all of you, men and
10 women. You know what is at stake – you know what fate awaits us if those ruthless desperadoes succeed in making us the next victims of their Juggernaut ride to world-mastery and the enslavement of all mankind. If they could they would yoke us in bondage to their war machine, setting us to turn out bombs to drop on our friends elsewhere, as other people are being slave-driven to make arms for use against us.

You read and hear, day by day, how our magnificent young men are striving to buy with their flesh and blood the
20 time that we need to build up our strength. At this hour of all hours we at home cannot take things easy. For, whether we have deserved it or not, the men of our fighting forces are struggling to give us time to make up leeway – to their undying honour.

What are we going to do with it – with this crucial time

that we yet possess? The question answers itself. We, men and women alike, are going to work our fingers to the bone for our sons and for their future. We are going to do whatever lies in our power to match, and to be worthy of, 30 the sacrifices that are being made for us. We are going to cut down our leisure, going to cut down our comfort, blot out of our thought every private and sectional aim. We *must*! We are going to guard our health and strength, for these are assets in the fight; but we shall be careless of all else, thinking only of arms for the men – arms for victory, arms for liberty.

After all, these young fighting men are our sons. We bred them. There must be something of their spirit in us.

I ask you to remember this one thing. The enemy's first 40 blow against us at home is being struck now. As always, that first blow is his attempt to sow fear and confusion in our minds. We – all of us – will defeat that attempt; and with it we shall have beaten the enemy's first offensive – even though not a single serious attack has yet been made upon this country. The enemy is trying that trick upon the wrong people. Each of you, individually, can help to win this first moral phase in the battle for these islands.

Remember that the underlying thought the enemy is trying to convey to you is the thought that nothing counts 50 but material methods and material might. That is what he would like you to believe. At the moment his material position may seem superior to ours; if we accept his standard, we have opened the door for the first success of his attempt to weaken our confidence, our strength of mind and our will to work. But we do not accept his standard. We know that even in this terrible conflict of mechanical armed power, it is the moral factor that counts in the last resort. Napoleon said – and who should know better? – that in war the moral is to the material as ten to one. Because we fight 60 for the highest things, against the powers of darkness, our will to hold on and hold out is stronger than any will that rears itself to strike us down.

The British are a brave people and a kind people; even

now, under the shadow of the threat to our own security, countless little dramas of personal comradeship among ourselves and gracious welcome to the unhappy allied refugees among us, are being enacted in many parts of the country. Courage and kindness know no defeat.

70 Not for nothing have these islands been for centuries the home and the haven of freedom. Whatever our past mistakes have been, there are, deep within us, stronger and richer than we ourselves may realise, resources of mind and spirit that cannot be matched by the feverish, propaganda-fed, self-deluded spirit of our enemies.

Let us count on that. Let us refresh ourselves with the realisation of our own strength. And let us express that strength now – tonight, tomorrow, every moment until victory is won. Work is the call. Work at WAR SPEED. Good night – and go to it.

35 WINSTON S. CHURCHILL
VE speeches

From *Victory: War Speeches by Right Hon. Winston S. Churchill*, compiled by Charles Eade (1945)

For a biographical note on Churchill, see p.129.

During the VE celebrations following the announcement of Germany's surrender, Churchill made two short speeches to the crowds from the balcony of the Ministry of Health in Whitehall. These are the speeches referred to in the Mass Observation diarist's account (see extract 37).

May 8th, 1945

God bless you all. This is your victory! It is the victory of the cause of freedom in every land. In all our long history we have never seen a greater day than this. Everyone, man or woman, has done their best. Everyone has tried. Neither the long years, nor the dangers, nor the fierce attacks of the enemy, have in any way weakened the independent resolve of the British nation. God bless you all.

May 9th, 1945
My dear friends, I hope you have had two happy days.
Happy days are what we have worked for, but happy days
10 are not easily worked for. By discipline, by moral, by
industry, by good laws, by fair institutions – by those ways
we have won through to happy days for millions and
millions of people.

You have been attacked by a monstrous enemy – but you
never flinched or wavered.

Your soldiers were everywhere in the field, your airmen
in the skies – and never let us forget our grand Navy. They
dared and they did all those feats of adventure and audacity
which have ever enabled brave men to wrest victory from
20 obstinate and bestial circumstances. And you people at
home have taken all you had to take – which was enough,
when all is said and done. You never let the men at the front
down. No one ever asked for peace because London was
suffering.

London, like a great rhinoceros, a great hippopotamus,
saying: 'Let them do their worst. London can take it.'
London could take anything.

36 WINSTON S. CHURCHILL
Address to the King

From *Victory: War Speeches by Right Hon. Winston S. Churchill*, compiled by
Charles Eade (1945)

For a biographical note on Churchill, see p.129.

A week after the victory celebrations Churchill made the following speech to
the House of Commons, celebrating the role of the monarch as a symbol of
national unity.

May 15th, 1945
I beg to move,
that an humble Address be presented to His Majesty as
followeth:
Most Gracious Sovereign,
We, Your Majesty's most dutiful and loyal subjects, the

Commons of the United Kingdom of Great Britain and
Northern Ireland in Parliament assembled, beg leave to
convey to Your Majesty our heartfelt congratulations on the
victorious conclusion of the war in Europe, and to assure
10   Your Majesty of our resolute support in the continuing war
against Japan.

We rejoice with Your Majesty in the deliverance brought
both to the Nation and to the enslaved peoples of Europe
by the success of Your Majesty's Forces fighting in comradeship with those of Your Majesty's Allies.

We would acknowledge the powerful help given without
hesitation and without stint to the common cause by the
peoples of Your Empire and Commonwealth of Nations
overseas.

20   We would wish to express the deep feeling which exists
throughout the whole country that Your Majesty and Your
gracious Consort have from the beginning contributed in a
wonderful manner to the courage and constancy of the
people by your inspiring example, by the extreme personal
exertions you have made year after year, by your willingness to share all their trials, and your constant sympathy
with them in the losses which they have endured.

It is our earnest prayer that, under God's grace, the
glorious victory won in Europe may be followed by a
30   speedy and successful conclusion of the struggle against
Japan, and that Your Majesty's reign, so many years of
which have been darkened by war and the threats of war,
may long continue in a world at peace.

It is fitting, and in accordance with the precedents,
which I have carefully consulted, that on emerging
victorious from a great peril and calamity, like the German
war, we should express our sentiments of gratitude and
loyalty to the Sovereign. The King is the Commander of
all our Armed Forces, and is the symbol of the whole war
40   effort of the British Nation in the innumerable forms in
which it has been manifested by all his subjects, in their
various posts and stations, according to their strength and
opportunity. The King is also, since the Statute of

Westminster, in a very special sense the constitutional link which joins us to the self-governing Dominions. He embodies a multiple Kingship unique in the world of to-day and, so far as I know, in the history of the past.

Of this multiple Kingship, we in these Islands, the Mother country, are but a single member, namely the
50 United Kingdom of Great Britain and Northern Ireland; but it is a Kingship to which all the other Governments of the Empire feel an equal allegiance and an equal right. Governments so proud and independent that they would not brook the slightest sign of interference from this House, vie with each other, and with us, in the respect for the ancient and glorious institution of the British Monarchy. It is the golden circle of the Crown which alone embraces the loyalties of so many States and races all over the world. It is the symbol which gathers together and expresses those
60 deep emotions and stirrings of the human heart which make men travel far to fight and die together, and cheerfully abandon material possessions and enjoyments for the sake of abstract ideas.

Woeful would it be in this modern age, were such forces to be used in a wrongful cause of greedy aggression, in a lust for conquest, or in a vain conceit of earthly grandeur. Glorious is it when all the mysterious powers of the British Commonwealth and Empire come together by a spontaneous impulse to face unmeasured and immeasurable dan-
70 gers, when they fight for honour and win the fight. That is glorious indeed. It is at such moments that the House expresses its respect and its loyalty by formal and reasoned Resolution, not only for the institution of the Monarchy but for the person of the Sovereign who occupies the Throne. We are fortunate indeed that an office of such extraordinary significance should be filled by one who combines with an intense love of our country and of all his people a thorough comprehension of our Parliamentary and democratic Constitution. Well may it be said, well was it
80 said, that the prerogatives of the Crown have become the privileges of the people.

Sincere affection, quite apart from constitutional respect, is given to King George VI from all parts of his Empire and Commonwealth. He is well beloved because of his courage, of his simple way of living, and of his tireless attention to duty.

I will give just one instance of many, but one which has been brought much before my eyes in my daily work. In all, 92,000 decorations have been awarded to those who have
90 done brave or arduous service in this war. Of this great number of 92,000, over 37,000 have been personally presented to the recipients by the hands of His Majesty the King.

The continuous discharge of every function helpful to the peace and happiness of the country and to the prosecution of the war by the King and by the Royal Family has been long remarked and admired by people in all parts of the country engaged in all kinds of functions, and most especially those in the areas which have been shattered by
100 the bombing of the enemy. His Majesty's visits to the battlefronts have involved his Royal person in that element of danger which cannot be divorced from travel by air, but we must also remember him as a sailor King who fought as a young officer in the greatest of all naval battles, the battle of Jutland. It would be altogether unfitting if I mentioned these personal aspects of His Majesty's work without referring also to his gracious Consort the Queen, who has been everywhere with him to scenes of suffering and disaster, to hospitals, to places shattered the day before by
110 some devastating explosion, to see the bereaved, the sufferers and the wounded, and I am sure that many an aching heart has found some solace in her gracious smile.

I do not think that any Prime Minister has ever received so much personal kindness and encouragement from his Sovereign as I have. Every week I have my audience, the greater part of which occurs most agreeably at luncheon, and I have seen the King at close quarters in every phase of our formidable experiences. I remember well how in the first months of this administration the King would come in

120 from practising with his rifle and his tommy-gun in the garden at Buckingham Palace, and if it had come to a last stand in London, a matter which had to be considered at one time, I have no doubt that His Majesty would have come very near departing from his usual constitutional rectitude by disregarding the advice of his Ministers.

It is in no perfunctory sense that we sing the National Anthem. We have a King and Queen well fitted to sit at the summit of all that the British nation stands for, and has largely achieved in these tremendous times.

130 I have only one more observation to make. If it be true, as has been said, that every country gets the form of government it deserves, we may certainly flatter ourselves. The wisdom of our ancestors has led us to an envied and enviable situation. We have the strongest Parliament in the world. We have the oldest, the most famous, the most honoured, the most secure and the most serviceable monarchy in the world. King and Parliament both rest safely and solidly upon the will of the people expressed by free and fair election on the basis of universal suffrage. Thus this system

140 has long worked harmoniously both in peace and war, and I think that this is indeed a fitting occasion when we should give our wholehearted thanks to the Sovereign in the Resolution which has appeared upon the Paper and which I now, Mr. Speaker, have the honour to move.

37 MASS OBSERVATION ATS CLERK
Diary account of VE Day

From the Mass Observation diary of a 23-year-old clerk in the ATS, in *Wartime Women*, ed. D. Sheridan (1990)

For a note on Mass Observation, see p.127.

May 9th

VE 1, and a dull, close day. In spite of drizzling rain, we set out in the early evening for London, and the 'lights'. By the time we reached Victoria, the rain had stopped, the pavements were dry and it was a lovely evening. We made for Buckingham Palace where a large crowd was milling. As the sun set, the crowd grew larger and larger, singing, cheering and whistling at intervals. Loudspeakers relayed popular music, and everyone stood patiently, occasionally chanting, 'We want the King.' A group of young people behind us sang 'Come out, come out, wherever you are.' It grew darker, and a lamp lighter leisurely lit gas lamps in front of the Palace; a wan searchlight climbed into the warm air, and beyond Green Park a flag was floodlit.

In the room behind the red-draped balcony of the Palace, lights came on, showing through the blitz-shuttered windows. A roar went up from the crowd. Then, against the dark sky the Palace sprang into light, like an immense wedding cake. The crowd burst into life, swaying and roaring, and on the crest of the cheers, the Royal Family came on to the balcony – the King in naval uniform, the Queen in white, with a tiara gleaming in her dark hair, Princess Elizabeth in grey, and Princess Margaret in blue – an attractive group. They stayed for a few minutes, smiling and waving, with the people happy and noisy below. As they left the balcony, the crowd dispersed, swarming in all directions.

I left my parents at Victoria, and made for Westminster alone. Victoria St. and Parliament Sq. were practically empty, but Westminster Bridge was packed with people admiring the lights on the river. As I stood there, a roar went up behind me. I turned around, and started back towards Whitehall; I was soon swept along by a hurrying crowd, and east up at the corner of Whitehall and Bridge St. As I expected, Churchill was on the floodlit balcony of the Ministry of Health, puffing at a huge cigar, and saluting the cheers through a cloud of smoke. After a few moments, he indicated that he was going to speak, and the crowd tried to hush itself. After a few attempts, he made himself heard over a microphone; it was a short, disconnected, but impressive speech, about London and the Londoners, and even I felt moved. Personally, I have no great admiration for the *man* Churchill, but as a war leader he has been unsurpassed, and his command of the language is wonderful. He recited the verse of 'Rule Britannia', then lifted his hand, and with a tuneless voice roared out the first notes of the chorus: 'R ... Rule ...' and the crowd took up the refrain. It was impossible not to be moved.

Amid the cheers, he left the balcony, and the lights went out. Excitedly, the crowd broke up and tried to get away. It
50 was impossible to move for fully 10 minutes; trying to get away in all directions at once, the mob was bogged down. Finally, I broke through into the comparatively clear space around the Cenotaph, and proceeded up Whitehall. Trafalgar Sq. was surrounded by floodlit buildings, with searchlights playing on Nelson's column. Long queues were formed at the entrances of tube stations, the only means of transport available. I decided to walk, and proceeded by way of Pall Mall, ablaze with burning torches and coloured lights. Movie cameras, with people festooned
60 all over the trolleys, moved through the gay streets.

Along Piccadilly and Knightsbridge, the crowds had thinned slightly. Instead of Mafeking throngs, there were merry groups tramping steadily towards Hammersmith and heaven only knows what points west. Searchlights wagged all over the sky, and an exuberant pilot zoomed up and down, throwing out coloured flares with gay abandon. London is having a wonderful time.

38 MINISTRY OF INFORMATION
Programme for film propaganda

From *Documentary Newsletter* (1940)

With the establishment of the Coalition government in May 1940, the evacuation of Dunkirk, and the start of the Battle of Britain, a sustained campaign by the Labour Party, the Ministry of Information and Home Intelligence aimed to construct the idea and ideal of a 'People's War' from which would emerge a peace based on social democracy and social reconstruction.

1 This memorandum assumes the importance of films as a medium of propaganda. It follows the principles outlined in

Lord Macmillan's memorandum to the War Cabinet with such changes as are made necessary by adapting abstract ideas to the concrete, dramatic and popular medium of the films. An appendix sets out the same conclusions in practical form.

2 The Themes of our propaganda (Minister's memorandum 4) are:

10   I. What Britain is fighting for.

     II. How Britain fights.

     III. The need for sacrifices if the fight is to be won.

3 I. *What Britain is fighting for.* This can be treated in

(a) Feature films.

(b) Documentaries.

(c) Cartoons.

4 (a) The main objects of feature films can be:

(i) *British life and character*, showing our independence, toughness of fibre, sympathy with the under-dog, etc.

20 *Goodbye Mr. Chips* is an obvious example of this kind. But British characteristics are perhaps more acceptable (especially in the USA) when less obviously stressed e.g., in *The Lady Vanishes*. In this category we may also consider films of heroic actions, histories of national heroes (Captain Scott).

(ii) *British ideas and institutions.* Ideals such as freedom, and institutions such as parliamentary government can be made the main subject of a drama or treated historically. It might be possible to do a great film on the history of British

30 Liberty and its repercussions in the world (Holland in the 17th century, France in the 18th century). The value of our institutions could also be brought home to us by showing what it would be like to have them taken away, e.g., a film about a part of the British Isles (e.g. Isle of Man) that the Germans had cut off, showing the effect of the Gestapo on everyday life, breaking up the family, taking away liberties hitherto unnoticed. The 'knock on the door and tap on the shoulder' motif could come in here as well as the next section.

40 (iii) *German ideals and institutions in recent history.* This

might include an historical film of the growth of Pan-German ideas from Bismarck onwards. There should be a number of themes for films in the activities of the Gestapo stressing, as more easily credible, the sinister rather than the sadistic aspect, but the Germans should also be shown as making absurd errors of judgement. There should be room for several refugee films, some of which might end in England for contrast; e.g., heavy step, knock on the door, automatic wave of fear, enter an English policeman. . . .

50   6 (c) *Animated Cartoons.* These are a very flexible medium of propaganda and have the advantage that ideas can be inserted under cover of absurdity. They can present (as in Mickey Mouse) a system of ethics in which independence and individuality are always successful, bullies are made fools of, the weak can cheek the strong with impunity, etc. With a slight twist they can be made topical without being recognizable as propaganda. There are several artists in England who can do them really well.

7 II. *How Britain fights.* This also can be treated in
60   (a) Feature films.
(b) Documentaries.
(c) News Reels.

8 (a) *Feature Films* of the present war are already being made by private companies (Note: *The Lion Has Wings* may be reckoned as three documentaries strung together to attain feature length. This is its principal defect). A film on *Contraband* is well under way; another on *Convoys* has been begun, a third on *Minesweepers* is in preparation. In all these the documentary element is made part of a dramatic
70   story. Similar treatment should be given to the Army, the Indian war effort, and to one or more of the Dominions. An important feature film could deal with the good relations of French and English troops in France. . . .

9 (b) *Documentaries.* A long series should be undertaken to show this country, France and the neutrals the extent of our war effort. There should be, in the first place, full and carefully worked out films of each of the fighting services; then shorter films of all the immediately subsidiary services,

i.e., merchant navy, munitions, shipbuilding, coastal com-
80 mand, fishermen, etc. Most of these subjects are susceptible
of detailed treatment from different angles, e.g., one-reel
films on the Bren Gun, the training of an anti-aircraft
gunner, etc. The change from peace to war time conditions
should be shown in a whole series drawn from every
department of State, e.g. the Ministry of Transport provides
the following subjects:

Railways – the change over, night work, troop movements, evacuees, etc.

Roads – lorries at night, bridges ready to be replaced in
90 case of damage, etc.

Ports – control and diversion (a model of the port
control room could be built)

Canals – their gradual return to use.

Other Departments (e.g. Agriculture, Education, Health,
Home Security, etc.) will provide subjects in the same ratio
so that ultimately there should be a complete survey of the
Government's war effort....

10 (c) *News Reels*. The selection and proper presentation
of news reel material is one of the most vital factors in
100 propaganda. At present the five news reel companies in
France have to pool their results and submit to censorship,
but no effort is made to direct their initial policy of
selection. This system is wasteful for the news reel companies (they have three cameramen on the same spot) and
results in trouble with the censorship. It is therefore highly
desirable that they should be asked to agree to a plan by
which the selection and arrangement of all news reel
material was in the hands of a single office controlled by the
Film Division. In this way it would be possible to treat the
110 news in a manner both more coherent and more in keeping
with our common aims. The news reel material so produced
would then be handed to the five companies to comment on
and distribute. Failing this it is absolutely necessary to
persuade the five companies to create a single, fortnightly
cine-magazine of selected British news for distribution to
France and neutrals.

11 *The need for sacrifice if the fight is to be won.* This cannot be made the subject of separate treatment but must be emphasized in certain of the foregoing: e.g. in I(a)(i) British
120 character must be shown as capable of great sacrifices; in I(a)(ii) British institutions must be shown as having been won and retained by sacrifices; in I(a)(iii) the refugee films should show our sacrifices as trifling compared to the hardships suffered by a defeated people. The sections II(a) and (b), *How Britain fights*, must stress the sacrifices made by merchant-men, fishermen (as minesweepers) and, in documentaries, by railwaymen and all classes of workers. These sacrifices can be shown not as something which the Government is afraid to ask, and the public expected to resent, but as something to be
130 accepted with courage and pride.

12 Apart from this general scheme of film propaganda, the Government will often wish to use the film as an immediate means of communication with the people, e.g., to prevent gossip, to induce greater caution in pedestrians, to explain the shortage of food, etc. These urgent needs are best served by short dramatic films on the model of the American *Crime Does Not Pay* series. They can be quickly made and have a wide appeal. Cartoon films, which are a useful medium of communication, cannot generally be used for
140 this purpose as they take too long to make.

13 Before passing to the practical examination of this programme in the appendix, certain general principles of film propaganda remain to be stated.

14 The same treatment is not equally valid at home, on the Continent, in the USA and in the Dominions. For example, pictures of English liberty and honour welcomed at home are interpreted on the Continent as evidence of slackness and stupidity. Shots of our soldiers laughing or playing football must be cut out of all newsreels and documentaries
150 sent to France. So sharp is the division that it will be necessary to make documentary films specially for France and neutral countries. For many neutrals specially prepared cine-magazines will be necessary. Feature films will often have to be cut, or given alternative endings to bring them

into consonance with local feelings.

15 The film being a popular medium must be good entertainment if it is to be good propaganda. A film which
induces boredom antagonizes the audience to the cause
which it advocates. For this reason, an amusing American
160 film with a few hits at the Nazi regime is probably better
propaganda than any number of documentaries showing
the making of bullets, etc.

16 This leads to the further consideration that film propaganda will be most effective when it is least recognizable as
such. Only in a few rare prestige films, reassurance films
and documentaries should the Government's participation
be announced. The influence brought to bear by the
Ministry on the producers of feature films, and encouragement given to foreign distributors must be kept secret. This
170 is particularly true of any films which it is hoped to
distribute in America and other neutral countries, which
should in some instances actually be made in America and
distributed as American films.

17 This programme deals only with production. It will be
remembered, however, that an almost equally important
part of the Film Division's duty is the effective distribution
throughout the world of all films showing British life and
the war effort. The problems of distribution differ in each
country and it is only possible to state one general principle:
180 that theatrical distribution through ordinary commercial
channels is incomparably more effective, although more
difficult to achieve, than distribution through diplomatic or
other private agencies.

39 JAN STRUTHER
'From Needing Danger'

From *Mrs. Miniver* (1939)

For a note on Struther and *Mrs. Miniver*, see p.71.

The thing is, we're all so buoyed up just now with the
crusading spirit, and so burningly convinced of the infamy

146

of the Government we're fighting against (this time, thank goodness, one doesn't say 'the nation we're fighting against') – that we're a little inclined to forget about our own past idiocies. The fact that we are now crusaders needn't blind us to the fact that for a very long time we have been, as Badger would say, echidnas. I can think of a hundred ways already in which the war has 'brought us to

10 our senses'. But it oughtn't to *need* a war to make a nation paint its kerbstones white, carry rear-lamps on its bicycles, and give all its slum children a holiday in the country. And it oughtn't to need a war to make us talk to each other in buses, and invent our own amusements in the evenings, and live simply, and eat sparingly, and recover the use of our legs, and get up early enough to see the sun rise. However, it *has* needed one: which is about the severest criticism our civilization could have.

I wonder whether it's too much to hope that afterwards,

20 when all the horrors are over, we shall be able to conjure up again the feelings of these first few weeks, and somehow rebuild our peace-time world so as to preserve everything of war which is worth preserving? What we need is a kind of non-material war museum, where, instead of gaping at an obsolete uniform in a glass case, we can press a magic button and see a vision of ourselves as we were while this revealing mood was freshly upon us. I know that this sounds silly and that there are no such magic buttons. The nearest approach to them, I think, are the poems and articles – and even the

30 letters and chance phrases – which are struck out of people like sparks at such moments as this. So write all the letters you can, Susan, please (to me, if you feel like it, but at any rate to somebody), and keep all the ones you get, and put down somewhere, too, everything you see or hear which will help later on to recapture the spirit of this tragic, marvellous, and eye-opening time: so that, having recaptured it, we can use it for better ends. We may not, of course, ever get the chance: but if we do, and once more fail to act upon it, I feel pretty sure we shan't be given another one.

40 As usual in all moments of stress, I've been falling back

on Donne. It's a pity preachers never seem to take their texts from anything but the Bible: otherwise they could base a perfectly terrific sermon for the present day on verse 16 of his *Litany* – the one which begins 'From needing danger...' Do look it up – I know there's a copy in the library at Quern, in the little bookshelf just on the left of the fireplace.

Yours ever, with much love,

CAROLINE.

4

CULTURE AND ENGLISHNESS

INTRODUCTION

Our use of the term 'culture' in this context reflects the older sense of the term which refers to 'the "spirit" which informed the "whole way of life" of a distinct people' (Williams 1981: 10). We wanted to give access to some of the key debates and to accounts of central forms of English culture but, as with any selection, we have had to exclude much material. The suggested further reading for this chapter (see the Appendix) makes several suggestions for work on topics such as music, radio, cinema and popular fiction. We have deliberately avoided engaging with the period's canonical fiction as this raises debates which are outside the scope of this book. However, in assessing the forms of culture at work during our period it is important to identify the ways in which antagonism towards the perceived obscurities and elitism of much modernist textual and artistic practice acted as a goad to other forms of culture.

As has been well documented, the period's literary history is filled with factions, and presents an often confusing picture. What should be stressed is the way in which literary and artistic experiments became associated with a 'foreign' liking for theory and also (post Wilde's trial) even a frisson of sexual 'deviancy'. In a period when Britain faced a series of external and internal crises – two wars, mass unemployment, a series of (at times potentially revolutionary) labour disputes, etc. (see the Chronology) – deviation from perceived norms was unacceptable, and the hostility of many critics to new forms of art or literature was informed by both a conservative *and* a xenophobic hostility to the new. Whilst it would be inaccurate to claim that there had ever been a close link between avant garde art or literature and the popular taste of a period it is fair to say that from the late nineteenth century there was an increasing divergence between those forms of culture found acceptable by the majority of people and those forms which a small minority enjoyed.

Ironically this occurs at a time when literary culture was fast becoming a currency to employment for many and also being promoted as a handy tool in the rebuilding of a sense of national unity. There was a growth in the demand for university-educated teachers and a parallel growth in the educational opportunities available to middle-class women and working- and lower-middle-class men.[1] English became the leading non-technical subject in the Mechanics' Institutes and a core component of the university extension lectures given in the provinces under the auspices of Oxford and Cambridge. English was established 'as the only academic discipline which embodied not only the high culture of "polite society" but also the "national character", the discipline... [was] promoted as uniquely suited to the mission of national cultivation' (Doyle, 1989: 12). English was promoted as a 'poor man's classics'; it was presented by groups like the English Association as the means of offering an equivalent (but 'necessarily' restricted) range of sensibilities to those who would not have experienced a classical education and as a consequence – so the 'logic' went – might have aspirations and values at odds with those of the dominant social group. Thus the promotion of English Studies enabled both an evasion of and a reaction to the increasing divergence between popular and 'polite' culture which is a feature of this period.

In this chapter we provide extracts from a range of material which allow the reader to examine some dominant positions within these debates. Our first section, 'Functions for English', contains extracts from the 1921 report on the *Teaching of English in England* – usually referred to as the Newbolt Report since it was written under the chairmanship of Sir Henry Newbolt. For modern readers debates over the place of English in the school curriculum are only too familiar, and with the Newbolt Report we have one of the first interventions by central government into the teaching of literature. The report sees English rather as recent Tory ministers see Shakespeare – as a passport to what it calls 'the right kind of national pride': since so much of English literature is actually working against the status quo (government gets short shrift from Dickens, for example) this argument seems as specious then as it does today.

The Newbolt Report seeks to promote literature as the opium of the masses. Provided it was the 'right' literature – i.e. not 'misguidedly written according to the dictates of foreign theory' – then it was, according to the Newbolt Committee, the ideal source of values for the lower orders. Chunks of Milton and lashings of Shakespeare were, according to the Newbolt Report, just the thing to head off any disaffection amongst the working classes.

The Report also turns to the Middle Ages (as William Morris did in *News from Nowhere* (1891) for politically rather different ends) to find a model of the united nation whose literature reflects the interests of all its people. Like other commentators on the state of the nation, the Report identifies the Industrial Revolution as a prime cause of the lamentable state of the nation, in this case seeing it as a cause of a disassociation of populist and highbrow sensibility. The Report lays at the feet of the professors of English the mission of heading out into the smokey cities to 'wean the ignorant millions' from their horrid penny-dreadfuls, dance-halls and other forms of 'misguided' entertainment.

It is important not to overemphasise the impact of the Newbolt Report. Whilst the Newbolt Committee were calling for academic missionaries, the professors and their fellow academic missionaries were in the main too busy writing belle-lettrist reviews or conducting pseudo-psychological tests about the reading process to worry too much about the needs of the working classes. Meanwhile the mass of people got on with having a good time.

The new literature and art of the early twentieth century, today so revered, were likely to excite contempt or perhaps only apathy amongst the majority of people in the period. In our second section, 'Reactions to modernism', we offer four pieces which strike some of the key notes in the period's responses to the new movements in art and literature. James Bone's account of 'The Tendencies of Modern Art' makes the point that the English Spirit of Compromise means that all that will come of modernism in English hands is 'something with which we can live harmoni-ously'. The unintelligibility ascribed to much modern writing is captured in Pont's wonderful satire of the kind of prose to be found in the short stories of Katherine Mansfield or the novels of Virginia Woolf. Even Oxford undergraduates, such as Winifred Holtby, had little time for modern poetry or art as our extract from her letter makes clear. The final piece in this section, by the critic Frank Swinnerton, is a bitchy attack on Bloomsbury and its writers – whom Swinnerton dismisses as 'ill mannered and pretentious dilettanti'. What is of particular interest here is that Swinnerton accuses Bloomsbury of doing exactly what the Newbolt Committee would like the professors to do: 'to boss and impress people into reading' what it thinks is good literature.

Our third section looks at sport, and begins with Vita Sackville-West's argument that in sporting life 'certain fundamental traits of the English character become floodlit' and that '[t]he English man is seen at his best the moment that another man starts throwing a ball at him'. The remaining piece in this section, Neville Cardus's nostalgic account of school cricket, resonates with that mournfulness we have already met in many of the elegiac pieces in our chapter on rural England. For Cardus, the innocent summers of school cricket are both 'forever England' and forever lost in the tawdry world of 'professionalism' which leads cricketers to debase themselves with Morris-Cowley motor cars, suede shoes and the other trappings of success.

Our final section, 'Popular culture and everyday life', is concerned with those forms of culture which involved many more people than the literary and artistic trends addressed in our second section. We begin with an extract from J. B. Priestley's *English Journey* on the monotony of Sunday evenings. This extract has also been included because Priestley cogently points up the problems with expecting a literary culture to develop amongst the majority of people, and as such serves as a corrective to the missionary zeal of the Newbolt Report. Our second extract in this section, Priestley's account of Blackpool, offers a cogent – if not altogether positive – reading of the resort which even today is Britain's number one holiday destination. Priestley's piece adopts the 'pre-war: good, post-war: bad' notion which we have already seen from many of the other commentators featured in this book.

Whilst the Newbolt Report laid the blame for cultural dislocation at the door of the industrial revolution, the vulgarisation of Blackpool culture is laid at the feet of American culture and read as a sign of the 'Blackpooling' of England. It should be noted that this line of argument recurs again and again in the latter part of our period and becomes the central thesis in Richard Hoggart's influential book *The Uses of Literacy* (1958).

This section concludes with two longer pieces which complement each other as accounts of the reading habits of the majority. In both George Orwell's 1939 essay on 'Boys' Weeklies' and Pearl Jephcott's 1943 study of *Girls Growing Up* there is anxiety about the material which many people are reading, coupled with an appalled fascination at the content of some of the comics and magazines intended for children and young adults. Many of the attitudes that inform Orwell's and Jephcott's pieces are still influential today: the comic book and the 'pulp' romance remain among the most marginalised and yet the most popular forms of print culture; and, whilst there is a history of academic interest in the genre from cultural studies, comics are unlikely to feature on reading lists for literature courses, despite the fact that *Gem* or *Magnet* provided far more influential encodings (in terms of their ability to engage with the beliefs of a large number of people) of English values in the 1930s than, say, the poems of W. H. Auden or the novels of Graham Greene.

Note

1   See Baldick 1983, pp.62 and 67. See also Doyle 1989, pp.24–25.

FUNCTIONS FOR ENGLISH

40 NEWBOLT COMMITTEE
'The bulk of our people ... are unconsciously living starved existences'

From *The Teaching of English in England* (1921)

Sir Henry Newbolt (1862–1938) was a poet, barrister and novelist, member of the English Association (from 1913), Chair of the Government Commission (1919) which produced *The Teaching of English in England*, and author of numerous articles and patriotic ballads (see, for example, *Admiral's All and Other Verses* (1897), which includes 'Drake's Drum'). During the First World War he was controller of wireless and cables. He was knighted in 1915.

We believe that such an education based upon the English language and literature would have important social, as well as personal, results; it would have a unifying tendency. Two causes, both accidental and conventional rather than national, at present distinguish and divide one class from another in England. The first of these is a marked difference in their modes of speech. If the teaching of the language were properly and universally provided for, the difference between educated and uneducated speech, which at present

10   causes so much prejudice and difficulty of intercourse on both sides, would gradually disappear. Good speech and great literature would not be regarded as too fine for use by the majority, nor, on the other hand, would natural gifts for self-expression be rendered ineffective by embarrassing faults of diction or composition. The second cause of division amongst us is the undue narrowness of the ground on which we meet for the true purposes of social life. The associations of sport and games are widely shared by all classes in England, but with mental pleasures and mental
20   exercises the case is very different. The old education was not similar for all, but diverse. It went far to make of us not one nation, but two, neither of which shared the associations or tastes of the other. An education fundamentally English would, we believe, at any rate bridge, if not close, this chasm of separation. The English people might learn as a whole to regard their own language, first with respect, and then with a genuine feeling of pride and affection. More than any mere symbol it is actually a part of England: to maltreat it or deliberately to debase it would be seen to be
30   an outrage; to become sensible of its significance and splendour would be to step upon a higher level. In France, we are told, this pride in the national language is strong and universal; the French artisan will often use his right to object that an expression 'is not French'. Such a feeling for our own native language would be a bond of union between classes, and would beget the right kind of national pride. Even more certainly should pride and joy in the national literature serve as such a bond. This feeling, if fostered in all our schools without exception, would disclose itself far
40   more often and furnish common meeting ground for great numbers of men and women who might otherwise never come into touch with one another. We know from the evidence of those who are familiar with schools of every type that the love of fine style and the appreciation of what is great in human thought and feeling is already no monopoly of a single class in England, that it is a natural and not an exceptional gift, and that though easily discouraged

by unfavourable circumstances it can also, by sympathetic treatment, be easily drawn out and developed. Within the
50 school itself all scholars, though specialising perhaps on different lines, will be able to find a common interest in the literature class and the debating or dramatic society. And this common interest will be likely to persist when other less vital things have been abandoned. The purely technical or aesthetic appeal of any art will, perhaps, always be limited to a smaller number but, as experience of life, literature will influence all who are capable of finding recreation in something beyond mere sensation. These it will unite by a common interest in life at its best, and by the
60 perpetual reminder that through all social differences human nature and its strongest affections are fundamentally the same.

41 NEWBOLT COMMITTEE
'Middle-class trivialities'

From *The Teaching of English in England* (1921)

We were told that the working classes, especially those belonging to organised labour movements, were antagonistic to, and contemptuous of, literature, that they regarded it 'merely as an ornament, a polite accomplishment, a subject to be despised by really virile men'. Literature, in fact, seems to be classed by a large number of thinking working men with antimacassars, fish knives and other unintelligible and futile trivialities of 'middle-class culture', and, as a subject of instruction, is suspect as an attempt
10 'to side-track the working class movement'. We regard the prevalence of such opinions as a serious matter, not merely because it means the alienation of an important section of the population from the 'confort' and 'mirthe' of literature, but chiefly because it points to a morbid condition of the body politic which if not taken in hand may be followed by lamentable consequences. For if literature be, as we

155

believe, an embodiment of the best thoughts of the best minds, the most direct and lasting communication of experience by man to men, a fellowship which 'binds
20 together by passion and knowledge the vast empire of human society, as it is spread over the whole earth, and over all time', then the nation of which a considerable portion rejects this means of grace, and despises this great spiritual influence, must assuredly be heading to disaster....

At the same time we are unable to subscribe to the dictum that literature, as generally interpreted, is a part of 'middle-class culture'. We sincerely wish it were. We find, on the contrary, an indifference among middle-class persons
30 to the claims of literature, even more disheartening than the open hostility which we are told exists among certain circles of working-class opinion. Here, quite as much as there, is to be found a striking contrast with mediaeval conditions. No doubt there were Hotspurs in those times, who would

> ... rather be a kitten and cry mew
> Than one of these same metre ballad-mongers;

but the almost interminable 'cycles of romance', together with the honour paid to minstrel and troubadour, are a sufficient indication of how men whiled away the long hours
40 of winter in mead-hall and castle. Moreover, this section of medieval literature was intimately concerned with the ideals and occupations of the public for which it was composed, that is to say its theme was chivalry and its chief subject-matter fighting. Does poetry play anything like the same part in the domestic economy of the average well-to-do household to-day? The question answers itself. Children at the Secondary or Public School learn to pay a certain lip-service to literature, but it is safe to say that more than 90 per cent of middle-class people have ceased to read poetry in adult life.
50 Why is this? We can find no more satisfactory answer than that already given in dealing with the attitude of the working man, namely, that poetry is not recognised as having any vital connection with a workaday world.

It is natural for man to delight in poetry; the history of medieval society, to say nothing of all primitive societies, proves this. Further, we claim that no personality can be complete, see life steadily and see it whole, without that unifying influence, that purifying of the emotions, which art and literature can alone bestow. It follows from what we
60 have said above that the bulk of our people, of whatever class, are unconsciously living starved existences, that one of the richest fields of our spiritual being is left uncultivated – not indeed barren, for the weeds of literature have never been so prolific as in our day. It is easy to blame Education for this, but Education cannot proceed far in advance of the general outlook of its age. The true cause lies deeper, is rooted among the very foundations of our civilisation. Yet we believe that it belongs to a transitory phase of human development and will, therefore, in course of time cease to
70 operate.

No one who regards the literature of the middle ages can fail to notice two obvious facts about it, namely, (i) its close association with the traditions and history (as then understood) of the society which rejoiced in it, and (ii) its constant preoccupation with the vocation – whether in fighting, 'in dyking or in delving or travailing in prayer' – of the particular public which it addressed. The same is true of Greek literature. Both sprang from the life of the people and gave to that life its spiritual sanction, together with a
80 sense of stability, by linking it up with the immemorial past. If, on the other hand, we inquire why, for example, the United States of America, with all its intellectual vigour and its tremendous achievements in other directions, has not been able as yet to produce a literature which can in any sense be called national,[1] we find the explanation in the fact that its origins are too recent and the occupations of its people too 'modern' to have taken upon them that colouring of the imagination which must lie upon the poet's palette before he can make them the objects of his art. To
90 adopt the language of Wordsworth, the traditions and activities of the great society of the Republic of the West are

157

not yet sufficiently 'familiarised to men ... to put on, as it were, a form of flesh and blood', and therefore the poet cannot 'lend his divine spirit to aid the transfiguration' or 'welcome the Being thus produced, as a dear and genuine inmate of the household of man'. In our own country the contrast is less glaring, though scarcely less real. We have a traditional culture, which comes down to us from the time of the Renaissance, and our literature, which is rich, draws
100 its life-blood therefrom. But the enormous changes in the social life and industrial occupations of the vast majority of our people, changes begun in the sixteenth century and greatly accentuated by the so-called Industrial Revolution, have created a gulf between the world of poetry and that world of everyday life from which we receive our 'habitual impressions'. Here, we believe, lies the root cause of the indifference and hostility towards literature which is the disturbing feature of the situation, as we have explored it. Here too lies our hope; since the time cannot be far distant
110 when the poet, who 'follows wheresoever he can find an atmosphere of sensation in which to move his wings', will invade this vast new territory, and so once more bring sanctification and joy into the sphere of common life. It is not in man to hasten this consummation. The wind bloweth where it listeth. All we can do here is to draw attention to the existing divorce, and to suggest measures that may lead to reunion.

The interim, we feel, belongs chiefly to the professors of English literature. The rise of modern Universities
120 has accredited an ambassador of poetry to every important capital of industrialism in the country, and upon his shoulders rests a responsibility greater we think than is as yet generally recognised. The Professor of Literature in a University should be – and sometimes is, as we gladly recognise – a missionary in a more real and active sense than any of his colleagues. He has obligations not merely to the students who come to him to read for a degree, but still more towards the teeming population outside the University walls, most of whom have not so much as 'heard

130 whether there be any Holy Ghost'. The fulfilment of these
obligations means propaganda work, organisation and the
building up of a staff of assistant missionaries. But first, and
above all, it means a right attitude of mind, a conviction that
literature and life are in fact inseparable, that literature is not
just a subject for academic study, but one of the chief
temples of the human spirit, in which all should worship.
We say 'all', for there is a tendency to suppose that literature
is the preserve of the 'cultured', a tendency from which
Matthew Arnold, the apostle of culture, was himself not
140 entirely free. 'The great men of culture', he wrote, 'are those
who have had a passion for diffusing, for making prevail, for
carrying from one end of society to the other, the best
knowledge, the best ideas of their time; who have laboured
to divest knowledge of all that was harsh, uncouth, difficult,
abstract, professional, exclusive; to humanise it, to make it
efficient outside the clique of the cultivated and learned, yet
still remaining the *best* knowledge and thought of the time,
and a true source, therefore, of sweetness and light.' A noble
ideal, yet one that is incomplete without Henry Sidgwick's
150 comment upon it: 'If any culture really has what Mr. Arnold
in his finest mood calls its noblest element, the passion for
propagating itself, for making itself prevail, then let it learn
to call nothing common or unclean. It can only propagate
itself by shedding the light of its sympathy liberally; by
learning to love common people and common things, to feel
common interests. Make people feel that their own poor life
is ever so little beautiful and poetical; then they will begin
to turn and seek after the treasures of beauty and poetry
outside and above it. Culture, like all spiritual gifts, can only
160 be propagated by enthusiasm; and by enthusiasm that
has got rid of asperity, that has become sympathetic; that
has got rid of Pharisaism, and become humble.' The
ambassadors of poetry must be humble, they must learn to
call nothing common or unclean – not even the local dialect,
the clatter of the factory, or the smoky pall of our industrial
centres.

1 Whitman, who seems to us a representative American, is apparently repudiated in America.

REACTIONS TO MODERNISM

42 JAMES BONE
'We make two pretty things grow where one idea grew before'

From 'The Tendencies of Modern Art' (1913)

James Bone (1872–1962) wrote a number of travel guides to cities in Scotland and England (e.g. *The Perambulator in Edinburgh* (1901)). From 1912 until 1945 he was London Editor of the *Manchester Guardian*. The *DNB* describes him as 'an artist with a painter's vision and a poetic pen'.

England, at least, need have little fear of Post-Impressionism or any other form of imported art. England only imports what can be dealt with by her national temperament, that she speedily transforms into a home product on which the original exporter cannot find his trade marks. How different is the wayward, dainty impressionism of Steer, Clausen, McTaggart (who got Impressionism by wireless, for he never saw a Monet till he was over sixty), of the Glasgow School, of Brabazon, Holmes and Houston,
10 from the impressionism that seized and possessed Monet, Renoir and Pissarro, to whom their art was a new religion! The prevailing instinct of English art is the desire for beauty, and we pay the penalty in the national cult of prettiness, which is as far into her territory as most of us can enter. Our boast might be that we make two pretty things grow where one idea grew before. However the mandarins may rage against them, even our pioneers are never ahead of beauty. But the French can forget her in their search for truths, and it is they who must take their consolation from Whitman's
20 lines:

> ... The Great Masters
> Do not seek beauty, they are sought;
> For ever touching them, or close upon them,
>   follows beauty,

Longing, fain, lovesick

No characteristic of the Englishman is more clearly
expressed in his art than his love of an harmonious life
within the walls of that much-vaunted castle of his, which
is inviolate, because the authorities know perfectly well that
30   nothing dangerous is concealed within. (Who ever heard of
a really dangerous English anarchist?) We have an incurable
gift (called 'Spirit of Compromise') for taking an ideal,
domesticating it, and making it something with which we
can live harmoniously. Life must be pleasant and seemly.

43 PONT
'Short story in the new manner'

From *The British Character: Studied and Revealed by Pont* (1938)

'Pont' (Gavin Graham Laidler) (1908–1940). Despite boyhood wishes to be a
cartoonist Laidler trained as an architect, but following an illness which
forced him to give up office work he worked as a cartoonist. In 1932 he
submitted cartoons to *Punch* which led to an exclusive contract. *The British
Character* was originally introduced by E. M. Delafield.

... the old carpet sweeper... three pieces... all in bits...
what on earth did we ever buy that for... if i shut my eyes
i can see kingscrossstation... i wonder why that is...
somebody told me once... i must think... no time to
think... through the trapdoor i can see janet with the
feather duster but if i shut my eyes i can see kingscrossstation... hullo janet *there* you are... hullo mum
there *you* are... now then janet i've spokentoyouaboutthat-
before... let us throw all these things out of the skylight...
10   but not that or these and certainly not that i bought it the
year freddie felldownstairs mrs henry tuddy... mrs henry
tuddy... oh yes i remember now the women with the
arms... if i shut my eyes now i can see mrs tuddys arms...
what exceptionally fine arms mrs tuddy had... the boxes
might come in useful janet... i said the boxes might come
in yes in... idiot the girl is... i wonder what she did to have
suchveryfinearms... no janet i said these things in this

trunk look like something orother palms... palms...
PALMS... why mum they look more to me like your old
20 fur coat... that is exactly what they are janet... dear mrs
tuddy... i have been wondering all day...

44 WINIFRED HOLTBY
'Mistaking the grotesque for the beautiful'

From *Letters to a Friend* (1937)
Winifred Holtby (1898–1935), feminist, journalist and novelist; her works
include *Anderby Wold* (1923) and *South Riding* (1936). From 1926 she was a
director of the feminist periodical *Time and Tide*.

9, Bevington Road,
Oxford, Feb. 20th, 1921.

DEAREST ROSALIND,
    First of all, to thank you for your letter of January 25th,
1921. I love writing the weekly epistle, so you are not in my
debt, but rather I in yours, for the fair things one sees and
hears become fairer when one gives them to a friend, and all
'brave, gay, amusing things' lose their splendour on a lonely
road. Don't you like the phrase I put in inverted commas?
I met it in a review of one of the modern, dismal,
psychological stories. The reviewer asked the author if the
world was barren now of all gay things that once adorned
10 it – and he laughed at the solemn 'newly brutal and direct'
touch, as, indeed, it needs to be laughed at. I think modern
art, in England anyway, has fallen under the pernicious
influence of Augustus John. The Slade School calls every
charming picture 'pretty-pretty' and flies to the other
extreme, in mistaking the grotesque for the beautiful. The
poets are just as bad; for those who have energy and
freshness fear to become Sunday-magazinish and write their
Wheels[1] and *Rolls* and other atrocities under the impression
that they are out-Henleying Henley, and discovering a new
20 pathless world of *vers libre*, free from the trammels of such
minor accessories of poetry such as rhyme or metre or even
musical language.

1 An Oxford publication edited by Edith Sitwell.

45 FRANK SWINNERTON
'Ill mannered and pretentious dilettanti'

From *The Georgian Literary Scene* (1935)

Frank Swinnerton (1884–1982), novelist and among the last of the 'men of letters'. He was President of the Royal Literary Fund (1962–1966). Swinnerton began as a clerk in a publisher's office and eventually became a reader for Chatto & Windus. These rather ordinary beginnings, coupled with his lack of any consistent education, may in part inform his anti-Bloomsbury attitudes.[1]

Before saying another word about books, I must explain to those who know no better that Central London is mapped for some forgotten reason into different quarters. Thus, Soho, which lies between Shaftesbury Avenue on the south and some not quite clearly defined point to the north of Oxford Street, is the home of a part of London's foreign population and is a centre for French and Italian restaurants; Belgravia is the old highly fashionable district west of the Green Park, Mayfair the extraordinarily aristocratic

10 section north of Piccadilly and east of Hyde Park, and so on. And Bloomsbury, which I have made the title of this chapter, lies to the north of New Oxford Street, between Tottenham Court Road upon the one side and Gray's Inn Road upon the other. It is the great quarter for squares and private hotels, straight plain Georgian houses (but Georgian in its eighteenth-century sense), publishers, a few prostitutes, and, residentially, a kind of bourgeois or aesthetic-bourgeois selectness. In it lie the British Museum and the great Foundling Hospital of Thomas Coram; and it is the

20 spiritual home of exiles from Cambridge University. It is an actual home for some of them.

Other members of this fraternity, the so-called Intelligentsia, live upon the farther side of Tottenham Court Road, and these are the artists and rebels; more still live in Chelsea, down by the River Thames, where artists, poets, and mere frequenters of studios have given rise to more self-expository novels than any other class of people living at the present day. Such younger aesthetes are not the real thing; they see themselves as characters in a 'modn' tale by Murger

30 or a satirical novel by Aldous Huxley, and are of no
account. The seat of intellectual *ton* lies in Bloomsbury.
There, in the shadow of learning's home from home,
Bloomsbury (as the embodiment of an assumption) feels
strongly its intellectual superiority to the rest of British
mankind. It represents culture. It is full of what Desmond
MacCarthy (to whom Bloomsbury is a shrine and even its
parents sacrosanct) calls 'alert, original men and women':
and what I call ill-mannered and pretentious dilettanti.

I must make two things clear. First that I write harshly
40 of Bloomsbury from sheer malice. I have suffered no ill
from Bloomsbury: whenever I have had any relation with
its chief figures that relation has been mutually kind. My
dislike of it (which I avow, although in writing of its leaders
I shall try as usual to explain their incontestable excellences)
is due entirely to what seems to me to be a conflict between
its performance and its presumption. The second thing to be
made clear is that – in consequence of my inability to share
it – I believe the love of Bloomsbury on Mr MacCarthy's
part to be an aberration. I by no means include Mr
50 MacCarthy among my dilettanti. He is a critic with whom
I seldom agree (that can't be helped); but he is an intelligent
man, an excellent and informative talker (given, perhaps, to
monologue, but ever courteous to interrupters), and he
reads poetry very well indeed. He has been, it is clear, the
best of all speakers employed by the British Broadcasting
Corporation to instruct the public about literature; and he
does not live in Bloomsbury. He is only dazzled by its
glory.

Whether that glory is genuine or not, I cannot say; it is
60 not a modest glory, and for me modesty is the only true
glory. It has no love for others; and for me a love of others,
which was good enough for Shakespeare, is essential to the
production of great literature. I call it pretentious, because
it seems to me to claim aristocracy. Criticism it regards as
lèse-majesté, and meets it, or anticipates it, with personal
insult – but that, perhaps, is a consequence of not being
quite sure of its own superiority to criticism? I think it bad

manners. Can I illustrate what seems to me the spirit of
Bloomsbury towards criticism by means of a true story of
70 two children, both of literary parents, who had had a slight
breeze? The little boy, tenderly resentful, said: '*Your* father
doesn't write books about *you*'; and the little girl answered:
'No; and I haven't got knock-knees, either'. Horrid little
girl; very alert, conceited, ill-mannered, retaliatory, and
'priceless'; quite obviously born, I think, to dwell, and
write, in a Bloomsbury of the next generation.

I presume that there is another side to the picture; and
that Bloomsbury really does imagine itself as suffering from
the assaults of Philistia. I do not know why it should do so.
80 If the complaint is that ordinary people are too stupid to
read the books of Bloomsbury, that seems to me a paradox,
and Mahomet, you remember, went to the mountain. If
nobody read my books, I should be sorry; but I should
think it was because they were not interesting. Bloomsbury,
as to its own books, takes a different view. It wants to boss
and impress people into reading what it has written,
whether they like it or not; that is, it wants to be read from
snobbery – a snobbery of culture; – and by writing above
the heads of Tom, Dick, and Harry, to lead Tom, Dick, and
90 Harry to higher things. In the same way, very stupid
Englishmen shout in English at Foreigners, and then say
'They're fools; they don't understand English.' It is a kind
of insularity – insulatedness – of mind, and arises from lack
of familiar contact with other modes of thought and feeling
than its own.

The odd thing about that is that Bloomsbury is
politically Left, and only intellectually Royalist – royalist,
you understand, to itself. It has a powerful wish to
dominate the Labour Party, but it will not do this in the
100 end because it wants to form an aristocratic caucus, a kind
of group dictatorship of brains, after, I suppose, the
Russian model, in ignorance of the fact that the English
as a nation (apart from the unemployed) are practically a
petty bourgeoisie. Further, it alienates the very people it
would impress by its determined patronage of the arts (and

artists) and a tremendous parade of refinement. Ostenta-
tious refinement, indeed, is a part of its assertion of
superiority; and I have so long believed all ostentation to
be vulgar that I am sure Bloomsbury, at heart, is vulgar.
110 It loves the eighteenth century – the wits, you know – and
is fashionably coarse in its conversation. That you would
expect, if you had read Hazlitt's book of talks with
Northcote; for Northcote said (I have telescoped two
passages):

> As the common people sought for refinement as a
> *treat*, people in high life were fond of grossness as a
> relief to their overstrained affectation of gentility...
> Fashion is gentility running away from vulgarity, and
> afraid of being overtaken by it. It is a sign the two
> 120   things are not very far asunder.

It dresses distinctively and – in the female part of it – does
its hair as Mrs Gaskell used to do hers a hundred years ago,
wearing long earrings and in some way managing always to
look sickly. When it laughs, it grimaces desperately; for its
laughter is painfully self-conscious. It speaks with great
affectation, introducing all the vowels into so simple a word
as 'no'. It is conversationally insincere, what one would call
'strained'; but although its tones are the tones of wit I
constantly hear far wittier talk at my Club, where men think
130 less of showing off than of contributing to the general
gaiety. It was very sensitive and sarcastic ('ahrony'); is full
of jealous contempts; is spiteful and resents being ignored,
although it goes in a good deal for the wilful ignoring of
others. And it has the impudence to accuse all who do not
support its pretensions to superiority of being fatuous
(having knock-knees) or of selling the pass to the enemy.
The enemy is Democracy.

1 This tension is further contextualised by H. G. Wells in *The Wife of Sir
Issac Harman* when Lady Harman, 'who wants inside information about
suburbia, is advised to read Gissing, Pugh and Swinnerton' (Trotter 1993:
129).

SPORT AND NATIONAL IDENTITY

46 VITA SACKVILLE-WEST
'The English man is seen at his best the moment that another man starts throwing a ball at him'

From *The Character of England* (1947)

Vita Sackville-West (1892–1962) was a poet, novelist (see her *The Edwardians* (1930)) and author of numerous journalistic pieces. A close friend of Virginia Woolf, her home, Knole House, Kent, and her lifestyle inform Woolf's *Orlando*. See Nigel Nicolson's *Portrait of a Marriage* (Weidenfeld & Nicolson, 1973) for details of his mother's unconventional marriage (recently made into a BBC series).

Sport – it is not only that the young gentleman from Eton and the son of the village blacksmith meet on equal terms on the village cricket ground and in the hunting-field, the one on his father's hunter, the other on a tubby pony, each to be judged entirely on his own merits of pluck and performance: but that in this very dominant aspect of English life certain fundamental traits of the English character become floodlit. It is a great bond, to have such standards in common: a sort of cement, welding at least one section of
10 our queer ramshackle nation together. Let us admit that; but at the same time let us examine with impartiality, for better or worse, with approbation or condemnation, or with a mixture of both (which is the more civilised estimate to adopt), the effect of the sport-obsession on its votaries.

An obsession it is, with two facets: games and sport... the love of games with its attendant character-building qualities of fair play, team-spirit, generosity in victory, cheerfulness in defeat, respect for the better man, and all the rest of the platitudes is in fact responsible for many of the
20 less offensive traits in our national make-up. The English man is seen at his best the moment that another man starts throwing a ball at him. He is then seen to be neither spiteful, nor vindictive, nor mean, nor querulous, nor desirous of taking an unfair advantage; he is seen to be law-abiding, and to respect the regulations which he himself generally has

made; he takes it for granted that his adversary will respect them likewise; he would be profoundly shocked by any attempt to cheat; his scorn would be as much aroused by any exultation displayed by the victor as by any ill-temper 30 displayed by the loser. He really loves the thing for its own sake, and the resultant purity of motive is remarkable enough to be recorded. In this field we need look for no division; there is no hypocrisy, no evasion of awkward facts. It is all quite simple. One catches, kicks, or hits the ball, or else one misses it; and the same holds good for the other chap. It is all taken in good part.

But when we come to sport the discussion immediately becomes far more complicated and the arc-lights thrown against the great facade of the English character produce 40 shadows which we cannot ignore. This is no longer a flat surface that we contemplate. It has its planes of light, but it has also the deep arcades offering shelter to something worse than nocturnal depravity: the intellectual dishonesty of false thinking, which has given us a half-deserved, half-undeserved reputation for actual perfidy among the clearer sighted nations of Europe. Perfidious Albion! a phrase consecrated to world politics – since of our island life our neighbours know little – but a phrase which unconsciously reflects something deeply based in the strange composition 50 of our misty nature. It might be true to say, not that we think wrongly, but that we do not think at all, or at any rate stop thinking the moment thought threatens to become unpleasant or to interfere with what we want to do – a proposition extremely hard for the more lucid and uncompromising mind to entertain.

Yet our capacity for self-delusion is genuine; it is neither a pose nor, consciously, a convenience. It explains many of the remarkable contradictions of the English, for we are surely the most contradictory race on earth.

47 NEVILLE CARDUS
'Cricket at Shastbury'

From *Good Days* (1931)

Sir John Frederick Neville Cardus (1889–1975), writer and critic. After a colourful childhood in Manchester he began a lifelong involvement with cricket in 1912 with his appointment as assistant cricket coach at Shrewsbury School. He wrote on cricket and music for the *Guardian* and *Sunday Times*. In 1964 he received a CBE and in 1967 he was knighted.

In a day or two the cricket field at Shastbury will be empty and the boys gone home for holidays. I used to watch them go, happy as only boys can be when they have weeks and weeks of fun and freedom before them. But I did not like the end of the summer term at Shastbury: it meant that for me cricket on green grass was over and done with for the year; it meant that I had to go back to a noisy, dusty city. Sometimes I would stay on at Shastbury a day or two, and at evening-time I would walk over the playing-fields in the
10 sunset. I shall never forget the peacefulness of those solitary hours, with the little chapel huddled in the trees. The crows came home one by one, flapping their way overhead. It was good to sit under the great oak and watch the light leave the sky and hear the hum of the town in the distance.

I see those years at Shastbury now as years full of the thoughtless happiness of youth. When we get older our pleasures no doubt gain subtlety and fineness, but the habit of criticism sets in; the middle-aged temperament places every precious moment against a moving background of
20 time – and no longer is it possible to live a life of pure sensation, every pulse of it deliciously to be felt for its own sake, with no bitter-sweet sense creeping in of the onward movement of life and of the bloom that makes the hour blessed, maybe, but fugitive.

When you have lived in a lovely place until, at the time, you were part of it, and could feel every day the fragrance of it going into the texture of your being, it is hard afterwards not to get a sort of resentment that the place still

goes on and exists complete as ever, though you yourself
30 have left it and have not seen it for years. Many a day in
recent summers I have sat on a crowded county cricket
ground and sent my thoughts far away to the school over
the river. And I have seen in fancy the field white with boys
playing cricket, hundreds of them, the bat cracking noisily
– and I not there. Old William is not there any longer, either.
Yet, in his day, he seemed as permanent at Shastbury as the
ancient oak tree near the wooden pavilion. Year after year
he came at the springtime and I with him. My first summer
at Shastbury happened when I was young enough to retain
40 the boy's hero-worship for great cricketers of the past. I had
seen William play for his county in my schooldays, and now
I was at Shastbury on a fresh May evening eager to meet him
in the flesh and the next day to begin bowling with him in
the nets. I remember walking up the hill in the narrow High
Street (it is changed nowadays, a noisy habitation of motor-
cars). And I remember going into the small house where
William was, as he called it, 'lodging'. I introduced myself,
and he shook hands with me while still lying on a sofa, his
shirt-sleeves rolled up. I wanted him to know that I knew
50 all about the splendour of his first-class cricket, and I spoke
of a day at Brighton when he had bowled Ranjitsinhji and
Fry with consecutive balls. He did not remember it, not
until I had prompted his memory. Then it all came back to
him, and he reflected for a while and said, 'But it were a long
time ago.'

When I knew William he did not often talk of his great
days at the game; he even seemed to regret that he had given
his life entirely to cricket. Once I was writing a letter in the
sitting room we shared, and he watched me carefully. I
60 dashed off my note home in a few seconds. William, when
he had to write a letter, gave up a whole evening to it, and
took off his coat. He gazed at me as I wrote rapidly. 'By
Gow,' said he (avoiding what he would have called blas-
phemy, for he was religious in a simple old-world way), 'By
Gow, if I'd'a' been able to write like that I'd'a' never wasted
my life at a game.'

Then he spoke of the blessings of education, and asserted that his own son, thank the Lord, was doing well in the 'Co-op.', and might some day become a head cashier. Bless
70 you, old William, wherever you may be to-day; it never occurred to you that playing for England at Lord's and Melbourne was achievement proud enough. No; he believed, at the end of his life, in 'education'. One evening, after net practice, we walked into the park of the township and listened to the band. William was moved by the 'Brightly dawns' of Sullivan. He listened intently, and at the closing cadence he said; 'By Gow, that were beautiful. I'd give all my cricket to play music like that. It was William, as I have written before, who laid his head on his hands one
80 evening at the end of a long afternoon of bowling, and asked, 'What have we done to-day? We've bowled and bowled and bowled – and for what good? We've prodooced nowt.'

He was one of the old school of professional cricketers; I cannot see him in a Morris-Cowley, as any day I can see many contemporary Test match players. And I cannot see him in suede shoes, or any sort of shoes. William wore enormous boots which had some sort of metal protection built into the edge of the heel. You could hear him coming
90 up the street miles away. 'I pays a lot for my boots,' he was fond of telling me, 'but they lasts!' I am glad that he loved Shastbury and knew it was a beautiful place. Often he sat with me under the big tree, at the day's end. He would smoke his pipe and talk about the time of the year and of weather lore. 'The swallers are high to-night; it'll be fine tomorrow.' Or 'Red at night's a sailor's delight, Red at morning's a sailor's warning.' And something about the oak and the ash and a summer of 'wet and splash'. He was very fond of that one because the rhymes brought it within his
100 view of poetry. We would sit there on the darkening field until the last red bar in the west had gone. Then we walked home to our room, and William would have his supper, a glass of beer, a chunk of bread, and an onion. As the lamplight fell on his fine old face I used to think of all the

sunshine that had burned on it in his lifetime, here and at the other end of the earth.

I wonder who has taken William's place at the school up the hill, across the ferry. Perhaps a cricketer of the age that succeeded William; perhaps somebody who does not sit on 110 the seat under the big tree at evenings, but goes about the countryside in a car. As I say, I cannot think of William in a Morris-Cowley. He was fond of telling me how he and Bill Lockwood and Tom Richardson often came back on a late train after a cricket tour and walked at midnight three or four miles to their villages. But next morning they were at practice on the county ground at half-past ten, and no doubt ready if not anxious to tackle W. G. Grace on a good wicket. Does the 'cotton' tree drop white blossoms yet at Shastbury? Is the little grey master of mathematics still 120 there, with his passion for the game keen as ever? He lived for cricket every summer, kept a huge set of ledgers in which he entered all his runs. He loved to come to the school nets on quiet Monday afternoons and ask William and me to bowl him into form. He was always depressed when he was out of form. He had a peculiar way with him while he was batting in a match. After he had made ten he gave the umpire a batting-glove; after he made fifteen he gave the umpire his other batting-glove. When his score was twenty he took off one pad and gave it to the umpire. When 130 he made thirty he took off the other pad and gave that to the umpire, too. He wore sleeves to his shirt that were divided at the elbows by buttons, so that the lower half could be detached. When his score was forty he would take off one sleeve like a glove; when he had reached fifty he would take off the other. William acted as umpire once in a match while the little master of mathematics batted. Without comment he received the various articles of wear as they were handed to him. But at last William found a chance to say to me quietly: 'I should like to see him someday when he's got a 140 hundred!'

Good-days, indeed, long drawn out in the heat, with all Shropshire stretching away in the distance, while we bowled and bowled, William and I, sometimes until we were fit to drop. Often I walked hopelessly over to him as the field was changing positions, and said, 'What a wicket, William; there's not a spot on it anywhere; we'll never get them out.' And this is how he would reply: 'Don't worrit; somebody'll make a mistake. And all's one; it'll come half-past six long afore t'day is over.'

POPULAR CULTURE AND EVERYDAY LIFE

48 J. B. PRIESTLEY
'Sunday Evenings'

From *English Journey* (1934)

For a note on Priestley and on *English Journey*, see p.26.

Although it was such a poor night, there were lots of people, mostly young men, hanging about the streets. What were they doing there? Some of them, no doubt, were waiting for girls, or hoping that in some miraculous fashion they would quite casually make the acquaintance of a pretty and amiable young woman. But most of them, I think, were not baffled amorists: they were there simply to pass the time. They had to do something with their Sunday evening. They might have attended at one of the many and various
10   places of worship; but obviously they did not like places of worship. They might have stopped at home or visited a friend's house; but then it was probably neither comfortable nor convenient for them to stay at home or for their friends to stay at home. If you have a lot of people, of very different ages and tastes, all crowded into one small house, in which, willy-nilly, they all have to eat and sleep and wash and dress, spending a whole evening at home, for some of the residents anyhow, may be a most disagreeable and unprofitable business. Thus, if you like reading quietly in a corner, you
20   are unlucky if the rest of the family, including your sister's young man and your brother's girl, have a passion for very

noisy gramophone records or the wireless at full strength. Moreover, even if it is not too rowdy for your taste, you get sick of the miserable little hole. Far too many opinions about staying quietly at home happen to be expressed by comfortable professional men writing in warm, well-lighted, book lined apartments thirty feet long by fifteen broad. And again, even if they have quite pleasant homes, the fact remains that most young people like to go out at the
30 week end: it is not some temporary aberration of the tribe: such is their nature. They want to go out, to get on with their individual lives, which have a secret urgency of their own at such periods, to join their friends, to stare at and talk and giggle and flirt with and generally begin operations upon the other sex. Many, too, have stirring in them a desire for colour, rhythmical movement and sound, drama; in short, for some form of artistic expression and appreciation. Such is their nature, fortunately for the history of the race. If the facts of our social life do not conform to this nature,
40 then it is useless preaching sermons or writing grumbling letters to the paper about modern youth: the only thing to do is to alter the structure of our social life. Bluntly, the position is this: the good old-fashioned English Sunday – the Sabbath, as it is called by a great many people who do not seem to realise, first, that they are not Jews, and secondly, that anyhow they are a day out in their calculations – is still being imposed upon large numbers of people, especially younger people, who no longer want the good old-fashioned English Sunday.

49 J. B. PRIESTLEY
'Blackpool'

From *English Journey* (1934)

For a note on Priestley and on *English Journey,* see p.26.

[A]s I went I thought about Blackpool. There is a good deal to be said about it and for it. To begin with, it is entitled to some respect because it has amply and triumphantly

succeeded in doing what it set out to do. Nature presented
it with very bracing air and a quantity of flat firm sand; and
nothing else. There is no less charmingly situated resort
anywhere. Its citizens must have realised at once that charm
and exclusiveness were not for them and their town. They
must have decided immediately to make a move in the
10 opposite direction. They would turn it into a pleasure resort
for the crowd, and especially the Lancashire crowd from the
cotton mills. Blackpool should give them what they wanted,
and make no bones about it. Blackpool did. Compared with
this huge mad place, with its miles and miles of promenades,
its three piers, its gigantic dance-halls, its variety shows, its
switch-backs and helter-skelters, its array of wine bars and
oyster saloons and cheap restaurants and tea houses and
shops piled high and glittering with trash; its army of
pierrots, bandsmen, clowns, fortune-tellers, auctioneers,
20 dancing partners, animal trainers, itinerant singers, hawk-
ers; its seventy special trains a day, its hundreds and
hundreds of thousands of trippers; places like Brighton and
Margate and Yarmouth are merely playing at being popular
seaside resorts. Blackpool has them all licked. It has recently
built a bathing pool that does not hold mere hundreds of
people but thousands, the population of a small town. It has
decided that it ought to extend its season into October,
while the beds are still aired and the frying-pans hot, and so
now every autumn it has the whole front, miles of it,
30 illuminated with coloured lights, not a few thousand
coloured lights but hundreds of thousands of them. That is
Blackpool. It is a complete and essential product of industrial democracy. If you do not like industrial democracy,
you will not like Blackpool. I know people who would have
to go into a nursing home after three hours of it. (In the
season, of course.) I am not one of those people. I have
never actually been in Blackpool at the crazy height of its
season, during the various Lancashire 'wakes' weeks; but I
knew it before the war and I have seen something of it since.
40 It is not, in my opinion, as good as it used to be. There are
various reasons for this. One of them is that like all

originators it has suffered from the mere passing of time, during which time others have been able to follow its example. Thus, for years before the war, public dancing on a big and rather luxurious scale was part of Blackpool's programme, and the great ballrooms in the Tower and the Winter Gardens, where spinners and weavers by the thousand could dance on perfect floors to the music of good orchestras, were famous throughout the North. Now,
50 public dancing of this kind is to be found everywhere. Even the Potteries have got an enormous new dance-hall, in which on occasion notable dance bands from London scream and croon. The rest of the world, we can say, is catching up with Blackpool, our first great entertainment caterer to the sixpenny crowd. There is, however, another and better reason why I think it is not as good as it was. From the few glimpses I have had of the place since the war, I gather the impression that it lacks something of its old genuine gaiety. Its amusements are becoming too mecha-
60 nised and Americanised. Talkies have replaced the old roaring variety turns. Gangs of carefully drilled young men and women (with nasal accents), employed by the music publishers to 'plug' their 'Hot Broadway Hits', have largely replaced the pierrots and nigger minstrels. The entertainers are more calculating, their shows more standardised, and the audiences more passive. It has developed a pitiful sophistication – machine-made and not really English – that is much worse than the old hearty vulgarity. But then in the meantime there have been changes in the class for which it
70 caters. One section of it has gone ahead and does not want the new Blackpool and would probably have rejected the old: it does not care for mass entertainment and prefers to spend its leisure in quieter places, cycling and walking and playing games in the sun. There are plenty of young working class people of that quality now in the North. The rest of them, the less intelligent and enterprising, are, I feel, fit patrons of the new Blackpool, which knows what to do with the passive and the listless, but would not have been quite up to the energetic old Blackpool, crowded with vital

80 beings who burst out of their factories for the annual spree
as if the boilers had exploded and blown them out. In those
days, I remember, they used to descend upon the town as if
it were about to be besieged, for they were loaded with
eatables, whole boiled hams and sides of bacon and round
tin trunks filled with cake. More often than not, they paid
for their lodgings on arrival, for then they knew that every
penny left could be spent; and they returned home with a
stick or two of pink or yellow Blackpool rock, a plush-
framed photograph of the Tower and the Wheel, the other
90 half of their excursion ticket, and nothing else. And for the
next week or month at home, they had to live on 'tick' or
'tally'. But they had enjoyed, rapturously enjoyed, their
Blackpool, and had never once insulted its breezy majesty
by singing about their 'blues'. In those days you did not
sing the woes of distant Negroes, probably reduced to such
misery by too much gin or cocaine. You sang about dear old
Charlie Brown and his pals, and the girls, those with the
curly curls. These songs were nonsense too, but they were
our own silly innocent nonsense and not another country's
100 jaded weary nonsense; they had a fresh lilting quality, and
expressed high spirits not low spirits. The Blackpool that
sang about Charlie Brown and the girls with their curly
curls was the Mecca of a vulgar but alert and virile
democracy. I am not so sure about the new Blackpool of the
weary negroid ditties. It would not be difficult, I feel, to
impose an autocracy upon young people who sound as tired
as that. Fortunately, there are other young people who do
not come this way at all, but go climbing on to the moors,
into the sun, and they may have their own ideas about
politics just as they apparently have about holidays.

50 GEORGE ORWELL
'Boys' Weeklies'

From *Collected Letters, Essays and Journalism* (1939)

George Orwell (1903–1950) was born in India, educated at Eton, and served in the Indian Imperial Police in Burma. He was wounded in the Spanish Civil War, fighting on the side of the Republicans, and during the 1930s worked to establish himself as a documentary writer, reporting on the poor and dispossessed. Although the Spanish Civil War left Orwell disillusioned with Communism, he continued to count himself a socialist. In this extract from an essay on 'Boys' Weeklies' Orwell argues against the conservatism of boys' comics and calls for a popular culture which raises the political issues associated with socialism and the left.

Naturally the politics of the *Gem* and *Magnet* are Conservative, but in a completely pre-1914 style, with no Fascist tinge. In reality their basic political assumptions are two: nothing ever changes, and foreigners are funny. In the *Gem* of 1939 Frenchmen are still Froggies and Italians are still Dagoes. Mossoo, the French master at Greyfriars, is the usual comic-paper Frog, with pointed beard, pegtop trousers, etc. Inky, the Indian boy, though a rajah, and therefore possessing snob-appeal, is also the comic babu of the Punch
10 tradition. ('The rowfulness is not the proper caper, my esteemed Bob,' said Inky. 'Let dogs delight in the barkfulness and bitefulness, but the soft answer is the cracked pitcher that goes longest to a bird in the bush, as the English proverb remarks.') Fisher T. Fish is the old-style stage Yankee ('Waal, I guess,' etc.) dating from a period of Anglo-American jealousy. Wun Lung, the Chinese boy (he has rather faded out of late, no doubt because some of the *Magnet*'s readers are Straits Chinese), is the nineteenth-century pantomime Chinaman, with saucer-shaped hat,
20 pigtail and pidgin-English. The assumption all along is not only that foreigners are comics who are put there for us to laugh at, but that they can be classified in much the same way as insects. That is why in all boys' papers, not only the *Gem* and *Magnet*, a Chinese is invariably portrayed with a pigtail. It is the thing you recognize him by, like the Frenchman's beard or the Italian's barrel-organ. In papers of this kind it occasionally happens that when the setting of a story is in a foreign country some attempt is made to describe the natives as individual human beings, but as a rule
30 it is assumed that foreigners of any one race are all alike and

will conform more or less exactly to the following patterns:

FRENCHMAN: Excitable. Wears beard, gesticulates wildly.
SPANIARD, MEXICAN etc.: Sinister, treacherous.
ARAB, AFGHAN etc.: Sinister, treacherous.
CHINESE: Sinister, treacherous. Wears pigtail.
ITALIAN: Excitable. Grinds barrel-organ or carries stiletto.
SWEDE, DANE etc.: Kind-hearted, stupid.
NEGRO: Comic, very faithful.

The working classes only enter into the *Gem* and *Magnet* as
40   comics or semi-villains (race-course touts etc.). As for class-
friction, trade unionism, strikes, slumps, unemployment,
Fascism and civil war – not a mention. Somewhere or other
in the thirty years' issue of the two papers you might
perhaps find the word 'Socialism', but you would have to
look a long time for it. If the Russian Revolution is
anywhere referred to, it will be indirectly, in the word
'Bolshy' (meaning a person of violent disagreeable habits).
Hitler and the Nazis are just beginning to make their
appearance.... The war crisis of September 1938 made just
50   enough impression to produce a story in which Mr Vernon-
Smith, the Bounder's millionaire father, cashed in on the
general panic by buying up country houses in order to sell
them to 'crisis scuttlers'. But that is probably as near to
noticing the European situation as the *Gem* and *Magnet*
will come, until the war actually starts. That does not mean
that these papers are unpatriotic – quite the contrary!
Throughout the Great War the *Gem* and *Magnet* were
perhaps the most consistently and cheerfully patriotic
papers in England. Almost every week the boys caught a
60   spy or pushed a conchy into the army, and during the
rationing period 'EAT LESS BREAD' was printed in large
type on every page. But their patriotism has nothing
whatever to do with power politics or 'ideological' warfare.
It is more akin to family loyalty, and actually it gives one a
valuable clue to the attitude of ordinary people, especially
the huge untouchable block of the middle class and the
better-off working class. These people are patriotic to the

middle of their bones, but they do not feel that what happens in foreign countries is any of their business. When
70 England is in danger they rally to its defence as a matter of course, but in between times they are not interested. After all, England is always in the right and England always wins, so why worry? It is an attitude that has been shaken during the past twenty years, but not so deeply as is sometimes supposed. Failure to understand it is one of the reasons why left-wing political parties are seldom able to produce an acceptable foreign policy.

. . . But now turn from the *Gem* and *Magnet* to the more up-to-date papers which have appeared since the Great
80 War. The truly significant thing is that they have more points of resemblance to the *Gem* and *Magnet* than points of difference. But it is better to consider the differences first. There are eight of these newer papers, the *Modern Boy, Triumph, Champion, Wizard, Rover, Skipper, Hotspur* and *Adventure*. All of these have appeared since the Great War, but except for the *Modern Boy* none of them is less than five years old. Two papers which ought also to be mentioned briefly here, though they are not strictly in the same class as the rest, are the *Detective Weekly* and the
90 *Thriller*, both owned by the Amalgamated Press. *The Detective Weekly* has taken over Sexton Blake. Both of these papers admit a certain amount of sex interest into their stories, and though certainly read by boys, they are not aimed at them exclusively. All the others are boys' papers pure and simple, and they are sufficiently alike to be considered together. There does not seem to be any notable difference between Thomson's publications and those of the Amalgamated Press. As soon as one looks at these papers one sees their technical superiority to the *Gem*
100 and *Magnet*. To begin with, they have the great advantage of not being written entirely by one person. Instead of one long complete story, a number of the *Wizard* or *Hotspur* consists of half a dozen or more serials, none of which goes on for ever. Consequently there is far more variety and far less padding, and none of the tiresome stylization and

facctiousness of the *Gem* and *Magnet*.

... Examination of a large number of these papers shows
that putting aside school stories, the favourite subjects are
Wild West, Frozen North, Foreign Legion, crime (always
110 from the detective's angle), the Great War (Air Force or
Secret Service, not the infantry), the Tarzan motif in
varying forms, professional football, tropical exploration,
historical romance (Robin Hood, Cavaliers and Round-
heads, etc.) and scientific invention. The Wild West still
leads, at any rate as a setting, though the Red Indian seems
to be fading out. The one theme that is really new is the
scientific one. Death-rays, Martians, invisible men, robots,
helicopters and interplanetary rockets figure largely; here
and there are even far-off rumours of psychotherapy and
120 ductless glands. Whereas the *Gem* and *Magnet* derive from
Dickens and Kipling, the *Wizard, Champion, Modern Boy*,
etc. owe a great deal to H. G. Wells, who, rather than Jules
Verne, is the father of 'Scientifiction'. Naturally, it is the,
magical, Martian aspect of science that is most exploited,
but one or two papers include serious articles on scientific
subjects, besides quantities of informative snippets. (Examples: 'A Kauri tree in Queensland, Australia, is over 12,000
years old'; 'Nearly 50,000 thunderstorms occur every day';
'Helium gas costs £?? per 1,000 cubic feet'; 'There are over
130 500 varieties of spiders in Great Britain'; 'London firemen
use 14,000,000 gallons of water annually', etc. etc.) There
is a marked advance in intellectual curiosity and, on the
whole, in the demand made on the reader's attention. In
practice the *Gem* and *Magnet* and the post-war papers are
read by much the same public, but the mental age aimed
at seems to have risen by a year or two years – an
improvement probably corresponding to the improvement
in elementary education since 1909.

The other thing that has emerged in the post-war papers,
140 though not to anything like the extent one would expect, is
bully-worship and the cult of violence. If one compares the
Gem and *Magnet* with a genuinely modern paper, the thing
that immediately strikes one is the absence of the leader-

principle. There is no central dominating character; instead there, are fifteen or twenty characters, all more or less on an equality, with whom readers of different types can identify. In the more modern papers this is not usually the case. Instead of identifying with a schoolboy of more or less his own age, the reader of the Skipper, Hotspur, etc. is led to
150 identify with a G-man, with a Foreign Legionary, with some variant of Tarzan, with an air ace, a master spy, an explorer, a pugilist – at any rate with some single all-powerful character who dominates everyone about him and whose usual method of solving any problem is a sock on the jaw. This character is intended as a superman, and as physical strength is the form of power that boys can best understand, he is usually a sort of human gorilla; in the Tarzan type of story he is sometimes actually a giant, eight or ten feet high.... Of course no one in his senses would
160 want to turn the so-called penny dreadful into a realistic novel or a Socialist tract. An adventure story must of its nature be more or less remote from real life. But, as I have tried to make clear, the unreality of the *Wizard* and the *Gem* is not so artless as it looks. These papers exist because of a specialized demand, because boys at certain ages find it necessary to read about Martians, death-rays, grizzly bears and gangsters. They get what they are looking for, but they get it wrapped up in the illusions which their future employers think suitable for them. To what extent people
170 draw their ideas from fiction is disputable. Personally I believe that most people are influenced far more than they would care to admit by novels, serial stories, films and so forth, and that from this point of view the worst books are often the most important, because they are usually the ones that are read earliest in life. It is probable that many people who could consider themselves extremely sophisticated and 'advanced' are actually carrying through life an imaginative background which they acquired in childhood from (for instance) Sapper and Ian Hay. If that is so, the boys'
180 twopenny weeklies are of the deepest importance. Here is the stuff that is read somewhere between the ages of twelve

and eighteen by a very large proportion, perhaps an actual majority, of English boys, including many who will never read anything else except newspapers; and along with it they are absorbing a set of beliefs which would be regarded as hopelessly out of date in the Central Office of the Conservative Party. All the better because it is done indirectly, there is being pumped into them the conviction that the major problems of our time do not exist, that there
190 is nothing wrong with laissez-faire capitalism, that foreigners are unimportant comics and that the British Empire is a sort of charity-concern which will last for ever. Considering who owns these papers, it is difficult to believe that this is unintentional. Of the twelve papers I have been discussing (i.e. twelve including the *Thriller* and *Detective Weekly*) seven are the property of the Amalgamated Press, which is one of the biggest press-combines in the world and controls more than a hundred different papers. The *Gem* and *Magnet*, therefore, are closely linked up with the *Daily*
200 *Telegraph* and the *Financial Times*. This in itself would be enough to rouse certain suspicions, even if it were not obvious that the stories in the boys' weeklies are politically vetted. So it appears that if you feel the need of a fantasy-life in which you travel to Mars and fight lions bare-handed (and what boy doesn't?) you can only have it by delivering yourself over, mentally, to people like Lord Camrose. For there is no competition. Throughout the whole of this run of papers the differences are negligible, and on this level no others exist. This raises the question, why is there no such
210 thing as a left-wing boys' paper? ...

Now, suppose that at this moment somebody started a left-wing paper deliberately aimed at boys of twelve or fourteen.... Inevitably such a paper would either consist of dreary uplift or it would be under Communist influence and given over to adulation of Soviet Russia; in either case no normal boy would ever look at it. Highbrow literature apart, the whole of the existing left-wing press, in so far as it is at all vigorously 'left', is one long tract. The one Socialist paper in England which could live a week on its

220 merits as a paper is the *Daily Herald*, and how much
Socialism is there in the *Daily Herald*? At this moment,
therefore, a paper with a 'left' slant and at the same time
likely to have an appeal to ordinary boys in their teens is
something almost beyond hoping for.... But it does not
follow that it is impossible. There is no clear reason why
every adventure story should necessarily be mixed up with
snobbishness and gutter patriotism. For, after all, the stories
in the *Hotspur* and the *Modern Boy* are not Conservative
tracts; they are merely adventure stories with a conservative
230 bias. It is fairly easy to imagine the process being reversed.
It is possible, for instance, to imagine a paper as thrilling and
lively as the *Hotspur*, but with subject-matter and 'ideology'
a little more up to date. It is even possible (though this raises
other difficulties) to imagine a women's paper at the same
literary level as the *Oracle*, dealing in approximately the
same kind of story, but taking rather more account of the
realities of working-class life. Such things have been done
before, though not in England. In the last years of the
Spanish monarchy there was a large output in Spain of left-
240 wing novelettes, some of them evidently of Anarchist
origin. Unfortunately at the time when they were appearing
I did not see their social significance, and I lost the
collection of them that I had, but no doubt copies would
still be procurable. In get-up and style of story they were
very similar to the English fourpenny novelette, except that
their inspiration was 'left'. If, for instance, a story described
police pursuing Anarchists through the mountains, it would
be from the point of view of the Anarchists and not of the
police. An example nearer to hand is the Soviet film
250 Chapayev, which has been shown a number of times in
London. Technically, by the standards of the time when it
was made, Chapayev is a first-rate film, but mentally, in
spite of the unfamiliar Russian background, it is not so very
remote from Hollywood. The one thing that lifts it out of
the ordinary is the remarkable performance by the actor
who takes the part of the White officer (the fat one) – a
performance which looks very like an inspired piece of

184

gagging. Otherwise the atmosphere is familiar. All the usual paraphernalia is there – heroic fight against odds, escape at
260 the last moment, shots of galloping horses, love interest, comic relief. The film is in fact a fairly ordinary one, except that its tendency is 'left'. In a Hollywood film of the Russian Civil War the Whites would probably be angels and the Reds demons. In the Russian version the Reds are angels and the Whites demons. That also is a lie, but, taking the long view, it is a less pernicious lie than the other. . . . Here several difficult problems present themselves. Their general nature is obvious enough, and I do not want to discuss them. I am merely pointing to the fact that, in England,
270 popular imaginative literature is a field that left-wing thought has never begun to enter. All fiction from the novels in the mushroom libraries downwards is censored in the interests of the ruling class. And boys' fiction above all, the blood-and-thunder stuff which nearly every boy devours at some time or other, is sodden in the worst illusions of 1910. The fact is only unimportant if one believes that what is read in childhood leaves no impression behind. Lord Camrose and his colleagues evidently believe nothing of the kind, and, after all, Lord Camrose ought to know.

51 PEARL JEPHCOTT
'Girls Growing Up'

From *Girls Growing Up* (1943)

Pearl Jephcott was a youth worker and educationalist.

Girls' Crystal is published every week, and has been so for more than five years. Originally priced at twopence it costs threepence now. For this sum you are given five stories, and even pictures of boys and girls doing entrancing things like tobogganing and riding. The same young people, all beautifully unencumbered by work, school or parents, appear week after week, and readers can be certain every Friday of meeting the Merrymakers, Fay, Sally, John and Don, and

Noel Raymond, the young, suave and handsome detective.
10 *Crystal* incorporates *The Schoolgirl* but it does not contain
more than one tale about schoolgirls and the characters in
general are older and altogether grander than the girl who
attends any ordinary senior school. The issue for 1st March
1941 (No. 280), contains a full three pennyworth. *The
Fourth Formers at St Chads School*, the *Followers of the
Phantom Rebel*, expose the evil doings of their form
mistress, Miss Petson, a lady who is not only unjustly
critical of their work, but also a crook. *The Cruising
Merrymakers* is a rather older group of girls and boys,
20 members of a club which Sally, aged fifteen, has founded on
board ship. These youngsters also expose a crook, a grey-
beard of thirty-five, recover a stolen diamond, and claim the
reward – which they spend on a 'grand spread'. An
impecunious (girl) racehorse owner and rider, her ancient
but faithful groom, Old Barney, and a dashing young
detective, play their expected parts in outwitting a rather
mild villain in *Danger at the Haunted Cross Roads*, a story
with stage properties of ruins, a secret 'cellar-like room with
a narrow skylight' and Lady Rosalind's will hidden in a
30 riding whip. *The Skating Imposter* deals with mysterious
strangers, masked men, more ruins, a female rival, and a
hidden letter. Carol, the heroine of this story, has a brother
who is wrongfully accused of stealing. He poses as a famous
skater and visits the hotel where Carol has been a skating
instructress, but his 'daring imposture' is about to be
discovered unless Carol can think of a plan of escape which
she will no doubt do in the next number. The last tale goes
into foreign parts, with Jean Varden as companion to
Jasmin, daughter of the Emir of Marakand. Jean meets Brian
40 Carfax who is eager to capture the White Sheik [*sic*], an
outlaw of the desert (but also Jean's own father). Can Jean
possibly put things right? To find out this you have to 'be
sure to read next Friday's splendid instalment'.

On the whole *Crystal* is a mild little magazine. It deals
with an oddly old-fashioned world of rusty bolts, hidden
rooms and secret passages. Its stories are not love-stories,

although a rather dashing young man – in the early twenties
– appears in most of them. A *Crystal* reader can see herself
as any one of its unjustly oppressed heroines, for whom
50 right always triumphs. In other words these are tales which
compensate for the difficulty of growing up. And what
child bound all day by an elementary school classroom or
the walls of a factory does not long to be cruising, skating,
riding or giving a garden party at an Emir's palace?

Here are some of the contents of a typical 'erotic blood',
Silver Star of 19th July 1941 (No. 197), which would be
principally intended for rather older readers. The main
serial is called *Love's Sinner* (author unnamed). It has been
a very popular story, and girls have been following it
60 carefully, week by week. The headpiece to this tale shows an
open Bible where one verse is set out in large print. 'Now
Sarah Abram's wife bare him no children: and she had an
hand maiden an Egyptian whose name was Hagar.' The
synopsis says, 'So that her husband, Andrew, might have a
son to inherit his farm, Esther Craig, herself childless,
brought Hagar Sandlands, a friendless girl, to live at the
farm. Hagar fell in love with Andrew.... After a night when
Esther had shut Andrew from her room, Hagar confessed
that she was to have Andrew's child.... To save gossip,
70 Esther took the child to bring up as her own. But Ruby
Stebbing, the landgirl, found out about Hagar. Determined
to win Andrew for herself, she put poison in some milk that
was to be drunk by Esther...'

This week's issue wrings your heart for Hagar. 'Little
clinging thing that she was ... so humble with her love, so
devoted in her affection, how could he forget her? Yet he
loved Esther. Was it possible for a man to love two women
at the same time?' Ruby, the milk poisoner, is different. 'She
would never get her man. Clenching her fists, tears of fury
80 in her eyes, Ruby ran upstairs, and back in her bedroom
stripped off the peach satin night-dress, trampling it
beneath her feet. She could have torn it to shreds, as
willingly as she would have torn Hagar had she been at her
mercy just then. Jumping into bed she curled up like an

animal, snatching viciously at the pillow... I'll kill her as well if she doesn't get out of the way, she thought....' But Ruby has another plan. Will it succeed? If you would know you must read next week's long and exciting instalment of this thrilling story. And what girl could resist it? ...

90   Most of the magazines attempt to help readers with their personal worries. The difficulties dealt with in a typical issue of *Family Star* for 26th July 1941 (No. 362), vary in importance from the dilemma of a woman of twenty-six, who is bigamously married and deserted, to the problem of a girl who is advised that she is just an 'old man's darling'. A possible query on abortion – 'it is illegal to do what you would like to. I regret I cannot help you' – is followed by one on how to get a boy – 'learn to dance ... don't consider picking up a young man: that's not how to find a nice one.'

100 A man inquires what he shall do about a fiancée who reads his letters to her pals at work. 'Hopeful, Glasgow' is told that she is quite right to refuse to go with a man if she does not like him and other people receive advice on evacuation, on slimming, and on the support of a parent.

    Anna Maritza in *Secrets and Flame* for 20th September (No. 464), links her personal counsel with the solutions offered by the stars. 'Lonely Brown Eyes' is advised, 'This young man is well suited to you ... The marriage stars enter your horoscope in a few months time': and another girl is

110 urged to go into one of the Services where she may meet the man of her heart – who enters her horoscope within the next two years. 'Anxious Sixteen' is told that there is no sign that anything will come of her present friendship with a boy.

    It is alarming to think that girls really base their actions on such advice, or on the ordinary luck-of-the-week predictions of Madam Sunya, Pama the Indian Seer, and the other astrological experts of these magazines. The girls probably take the actual 'star' forecasts less seriously than

120 older women, but there is no doubt that the correspondence columns of these magazines are among the most important and carefully read parts of the papers. Though it is difficult

188

to say whether all, or most of the queries, are genuine, some of them certainly are real problems which confront real people. They are, moreover, the problems of quite young people. That you constantly find as an answer such advice as 'you are too young to go out with boys', or 'wait a year or so', or 'much too young to be going with a boy', shows both the youthfulness of a good many of the readers and at
130 least some sense of responsibility on the part of those whose business includes the publication of papers of this type.

The letters, as always, are rather pathetic and show where the difficulties and thoughts of the readers lie. The match-box maker of fifteen, with her boy friend of sixteen, her two nights at the pictures and her most cherished possession still an old doll, searches *Silver Star* to see how other, rather older people cope with the problems of sex that are being so constantly brought to her attention now that she is a member of the adult world of workers. How can she get to
140 know the things that older girls know? *Silver Star*, if she is lucky, may give her some information. What social code ought she to follow? What line shall she take in the following dilemma? 'I am only fifteen, but I have been going out with a boy who is eighteen. I love him dearly, but when he took another girl home, she said he told her that he only takes me out to please his pal. When I asked him about it he laughed and said not to listen to tales.' Such difficulties are one of the chief reasons for the popularity of these magazines.

150 The correspondence pages, with their personal problems, are the only realistic part of the papers. The stories themselves provide a fairy-tale world in which these same problems are presented in a much more highly-coloured way, and where good, bad and indifferent, is the all-absorbing theme. *Her Way to Keep His Love, His Brother Stole His Girl, The First Man She Met,* and *The Night She Would Never Forget* are titles that are patterned to catch the eye and which appear with minor variations at the head of nearly every tale.
160 Love comes to heroines who, in the main, are people in

189

fairly humble circumstances, girls with whom the readers can identify themselves. *The Oracle* for 27th September 1941 brings love to a shop girl, an ex-dancer in the Cafe Mena in Cairo, a munition worker, a factory girl, and an innocent (though suspected guilty) young wife. This love comes, however, against a highly glamorous background, a world apart from the tenement house in Gas Street where the reader herself probably has to live. She is transported to the Grand Hotel, to an expensive furnished flat in London,
170 to a lido beneath the snow-capped mountains of Switzerland or to a spot where desert stars look down upon the harem of the Azra Kahn. People in this world still go abroad for their holidays. They drive round Europe in 'luxurious and speedy cars': they have smart maidservants in frilly organdie caps and aprons who open doors to rooms where there is an 'air of almost too much richness'. Expensive clothes occupy a very important place in the picture, and we hear much of silk brocade pyjamas, fox furs, 'faultlessly cut lounge suits of pale grey' and 'simple fragments of satiny
180 material that pass for swimsuits'. The air is heavy with the dream-world longings of young people who come from homes where money is hard to come by. Such tales strengthen girls' convictions that they would be bound to have a good time and be happy if only they could be rich.

The ills that beset the course of true love are almost invariably due to a wicked rival, sometimes to a misunderstanding; but never to a bad social system. Apart from personal problems, the difficulties that people have to face day by day are rarely mentioned, so that the world that is
190 presented is oddly false. Heroines are often left suddenly penniless by the caprice of a relation or the machinations of a rival, but they do not have to struggle with low wages, nor unemployment, nor bad lodgings nor even with the fact that their men are away in the Forces. Two years of war have influenced these magazines extraordinarily little; Canadian soldiers, minesweepers, land girls, are now beginning to appear in the tales, but there is no indication at all that the world in which the readers are living is a world that is

fighting for its life. It is important to remember that these
200 are not merely *some* of a number of books and papers that
hundreds of thousands of the young read, but the only
reading of any kind whatsoever for many girls.

The tales are exciting. You long to get to next week's
instalment. The excitement that they provide however has a
sinister twist and does not offer the straightforward appeal
to use one's wits that an ordinary detective story provides.
Unpleasant people and situations are the very stuff of the
tales, which are weighted with sordidness and harshness.
Love 'comes', but it comes in a sea of jealousy, scandal,
210 revenge, lying, guilty secrets, murder, bigamy, and seduc-
tion. The police and the courts – 'Sarah will swing for this'
– are frequently mentioned: and murder (for domestic
reasons) is a constant theme, not a casual incident. All this
bitterness and sordidness, and the absence of any real
greatness in the characters or the situations, means that the
excitement which the stories undoubtedly provoke is an
unsatisfactory one. Such tales provide only an unprofitable
escape for young people.

Girls think they will have a happy time with these
220 'books'. They want desperately to know what 'love' is, and
the publishers, knowing their young clients, cater for this
demand. What they provide, however, are stories of sex and
sentimentality, not of love. 'The kisses, the love stuff', are
thrown at the readers. Every page is sickly with them. Only
very immature people or girls whose tastes have begun to be
perverted could endure constant repetition of this kind of
description: 'Glyn Curtis was the only man who could
make her heart throb with longing – the longing to be taken
in to his arms, to feel his lips upon hers. Not lightly,
230 caressingly as he had kissed her before, but –!'

It boils down to this. The girls know that the world
which *Red Star Weekly* presents is quite unlike the real
world: but they hope that perhaps some of all this glamour
may come their way. It is just possible that the boss's son
may ask them to marry him, or a pilot officer may invite
them to his father's country mansion next week-end. They

are desperately anxious for adventure and they hope for an easier life than that which their mothers have led. Their very proper desire to know more about the new world of love
240 and sex is played upon by these magazines which feed them with such second rate food. Moreover they are fed forcibly because poor homes do not make for anything but slipshod, easy reading. The little shop on the corner, the elder sister's *Oracle* brought back from the works, and the table drawer stuffed with battered back numbers of these magazines are the handy, and therefore powerful, reading influence to which the girl is subjected. If she were reading other matter as well, they would be relatively unimportant, but since generally she is not doing so, they are immensely important.
250 As A. J. Jenkinson says, 'It is likely that the social and human values underlying them are shallow, opportunist, and ill-thought out. They . . . are tending to stabilise popular feeling and insight at low levels.' There is no greatness about the people or the events of the false world which makes any appeal to the idealism which is one of the lovely gifts of adolescence. If the food is low-grade it is only too likely that the mental and spiritual quality of the consumer will be the same.

5

DOMESTIC AND URBAN ENGLANDS

INTRODUCTION

In this chapter we turn our attention to the idea and the reality of home through a sequence of material offering accounts of domestic and urban England. 'Homes Fit for Heroes' was a major element of the wider programme of social reconstruction embarked upon at the end of the First World War. This slogan was not, however, simply about providing adequate housing for returning servicemen. Implicit in it was the idea that a return to the normality of established gender and familial roles would secure and restore stability in the wake of the upheavals of war. Moreover, army recruitment in both the Boer and the First World War had revealed appalling standards of ill-health. Adequate housing was seen by all political parties as a first step towards rearing a healthy citizenry and promoting 'national efficiency'. The idea of home was also linked to ideals of Empire through the construction of England as 'the homeland'. Returning servicemen, those serving in the colonies and overseas and those living abroad for whatever reason, might look to England and all it represented as 'home' – the motherland, the place of origin, safety and identity.

Between 1919 and 1939 3,998,000 new houses were built. Every major city saw an expansion of suburban housing round its perimeter or along its arterial roads, and the dream of a house in its own garden became a reality for many families who hitherto had occupied over-crowded and insanitary rooms. The ideal of England as 'home' and 'the English home' as signifying a specific set of domestic values took on new meanings and resonances in the years after the First World War (see Giles 1995). Housing policy and design enshrined beliefs about the ways in which domestic and private life was being reformulated to include the newly enfranchised citizens of a 'modern' England (women and men of the working classes) – those previously excluded from the ideals of English family life. At the same time the Victorian bourgeois family with its apparently stuffy conventions, sexual repression and indulgent senti-mentality gave way to a 'modern' domesticity which valued cheerful efficiency and robust 'common sense'.

Whilst the domestic scene was being transformed there nonetheless remained an anxiety about the nature of the new living conditions which were emerging as new forms of urban organisation were introduced. In the ideology of Englishness the English town or city has never carried the same positive connotations as the English village or countryside. Yet since the middle of the nineteenth century England had been an urban nation: the legacy of the huge demographic shift from rural to urban living – a movement which was virtually at an end by 1900 – was street after street of rapidly built, poorly serviced houses which were subject to few national regulations.

By contrast, the city, in this period, is also reconceptualised as the site of modernity; it is the centre which pulls in exiles and émigrés and which provides the context in which individuals and groups can break from established patterns of culture. The city's impact upon individual subjects is explored in a number of canonical literary works from the period (notably James Joyce's *Ulysses*).[1]

In the non-canonical writing which concerns us in the present work the urban is not viewed in a very positive light: the city is seen to be a mess. The writers whose work features in the following extracts suggest various causes: the fecklessness of its inhabitants; the laissez-faire attitude of council planning committees; the lack of direction from central government. Few writers have many positive suggestions for improving the city and even fewer can see anything positive in the new patterns of urban life emerging throughout our period.

This pervasive gloom about the English city helps to further con-textualise the power of appeals to rural England as the locus of the essential aspects of Englishness: the urban England which is revealed in the passages which follow serves as the Other to the idealised (Imagi-nary) rural valorised in works by Thomas or Davies. In J. B. Priestley's *English Journey* it is the Cotswolds and other relatively undeveloped tracts which receive most praise; when Priestley has anything positive to say about a city it is often undercut by a barbed aside. The same pattern is evident in H. V. Morton's *In Search of England*; the account of Wigan (reprinted here) relies upon the familiar binary opposition – town/country – which informs many of the extracts we have selected.

We have divided the material in this chapter into two subsections. The first, 'The Homes of England', provides material which allows the reader to trace some of the ways in which ideas about domesticity, housing and family were being reformulated. One of the key notions in this reformulation was the idea of a standard of specifically 'English' home-life to which all could aspire; as we have seen, when Britain went to war in 1939 the rhetoric of patriotism in this period drew heavily on the idea of protecting and saving a particular version of home and private life (see chapter 3, War and National Identity).

Ebenezer Howard's *Garden Cities of Tomorrow* was a key text in early twentieth-century housing policy. Howard's original work, published in 1898, was entitled *Tomorrow: A Peaceful Path to Real Reform*, and in it he formulated the concept of the garden city, an ideal in which the best aspects of town and country life were synthesised to provide a socialist-inspired form of community. Howard's principles rested on a combination of land nationalisation and decentralisation, which drew in part from the traditions of a socialism and architecture rooted in English pastoralism and the rural vernacular.

John Buchan's hero, Richard Hannay, finds himself in a suburban villa, the practical manifestation of Howard's ideas. For him this represents not the egalitarian and democratic community Howard envisioned, but a set of values with which he has no empathy. The cosy domesticity of suburbia was frequently attacked for its isolationism and cultural paucity, and in Buchan's extract the reader is invited to share and endorse Hannay's position as outsider, the romantic adventurer who despises the trappings of suburban life. Buchan's use of a suburban respectability which hides deep villainy is paralleled in a number of detective fictions from the period, such as those of Agatha Christie; in both writers one can identify an (often subtle) undermining of the supposed sanctity of the English family home.

'Grantchester' by Rupert Brooke and the extract from Daphne du Maurier's *Rebecca* are expressions of exile from an England which is represented both as a geographical place and, more importantly, as a home. The Old Vicarage and Manderley are located in a rural England, dominated by church and squirearchy. Yet neither Brooke nor du Maurier treats these places with unambiguous acceptance: Manderley was the site of loss, fear and terror, and Brooke treats his own nostalgia for Grantchester with an irony often missing from those who quote him.[2] Nonetheless, both extracts function by drawing on a well-established repertoire of images associated with the English home – the rural landscape and, most particularly, afternoon tea – images which are still being reworked and circulated in the countless tea shops around Britain.

The article by James Laver on 'the English home' is equally criss-crossed with tensions. For Laver, the ideal of suburbia – as promoted by thinkers such as Howard – has failed, and new visions of both housing and the home are required if family life is to continue.

This section concludes with three pieces that serve as a counterpoint to the version of domestic life offered by du Maurier or Brooke but that also build upon the sense that different kinds of home have different and quite crucial effects in shaping the values and aspirations of their inhabitants. We have reprinted an extract from Lord Kennet's 1947 essay on 'Town Life'. Lord Kennet was Minister of Health in Macdonald's National Government of 1931 and responsible for various Housing Acts which were designed to promote slum clearance. In this extract he takes the reader on a tour of the imaginary town of Muddleford in order to characterise the situation in many English towns. Some of Kennet's suggested solutions reveal how the bright ideas of one generation can become the problems of the next: the idea that flats were the solution to urban overcrowding was shared by a generation of planners and architects who gave us the municipal estates of the 1950s and 1960s which became the problem housing of the 1970s and 1980s.

The problem of uncoordinated development which is to the fore in Lord Kennet's account of Muddleford is also central to Osbert Lancaster's satire on *Progress at Pelvis Bay*. Whilst for Lancaster the modern home was a blot on the landscape, Stephen Taylor's essay on 'The Suburban Neurosis' argues that modern housing actually causes mental illness. We offer a substantial extract from Dr Taylor's provocative article in which he argues that jerry-built suburbs and the petty mind-set they foster are sapping the vitality from vast numbers of Englishwomen; for Taylor the new suburbs are 'slums of the mind'.

Our second section, 'Urban Englands', is concerned with the Midlands and the North. It should be pointed out that we have chosen not to cover London and its suburbs in any direct way in this book as the changing patterns of city life in the capital are well documented elsewhere.[3] The Midlands was benefiting economically from the development of new industries but, along with Northern England, also saw its heavy industry going through a terminal decline. Our first extract here is a series of letters on the subject of council housing estates – a feature of urban Britain which is fast vanishing today thanks to Conservative legislation promoting the right to buy but preventing councils from spending the money earned on replenishing the housing stock. The letters are of particular interest in that they are written by tenants and prospective tenants, and as such offer an insight into individual experiences of living on one of the new estates which so many cities were developing as a solution to their stock of nineteenth-century slum housing (see Kennet's 'Muddleford', for example). Our extract from Priestley's *English Journey* offers a characteristically grim perspective on urban England: in his account of 'Rusty Lane', West Bromwich, Priestley echoes Dickens in his condemnation of urban housing in industrial districts.

The baneful effects of industrialism are also central to our extract from D. H. Lawrence's account of 'Nottingham and the Mining Country'. This essay describes the development of the mining village of Eastwood, and in it Lawrence argues that the ugliness of many of our towns has led to a situation in which citizenship, and civic pride, fail to develop. Interestingly Lawrence's standard for comparison – the Italian town of Siena – recalls Lord Kennet's discovery of an Italian model for civic order in the figure of the *podestà*. Both writers thus illustrate the common turn to Roman or Italian models as a register for civilisation in discussions of cities in the period. Lawrence also sounds a characteristic note of contempt for the English suburban and pro-rural mentality: a note which firmly situates this essay in the mainstream of modernism's contempt for middle-England. Like many other avant-garde writers and artists Lawrence wants to see a 'truly urban' culture develop in Britain, but, like more traditional commentators, his standards for such a culture are mostly those of the ancient classical civilisations valorised in grammar-school classics lessons. Lawrence does, to be fair, also suggest that 'a greater scope, a certain splendour, a certain grandeur, and beauty' exists in the cities of contemporary America.

We conclude this section with two accounts from H. V. Morton which are concerned with Northern England. The North is the ultimate Other to the green Southlands in several ways. Firstly, it was in decline economically as its staple industries succumbed to foreign competition, the vagaries of world trade and the shift to modern modes of production on Midlands green field sites. Just as 'darkest London' was the unknown territory for many Victorians, so Darkest Jarrow or Leeds were just as unfamiliar to many Edwardians and Georgians.

Morton's accounts of Leeds's slums – written for the Labour Party – offers a view of a Northern city which is far harsher than the account written in his commercial travel writing. Yet it is a view which would do little to alter Southern preconceptions. Morton's Wigan, however, is strikingly different to that which his contemporary readers may have expected and may also surprise modern readers familiar with the Wigan evoked by Orwell in his later study *The Road to Wigan Pier*.[4] Morton partially debunks the 'Wigan Pier' image 'of dreary streets and stagnant canals and white-faced Wigonians dragging their weary steps along dull streets', but only by celebrating the Council's plans for a mock Tudor high street and the town's links with Arthurian legend. In this make-over it comes as no surprise to discover Wigan's Roman heritage being trotted out along with its Italian gardens and place in the fiction of Walter Scott. What Morton's account of Wigan suggests is how far even Urban England was a country of the mind, and also the extent to which there existed a set of coded markers which a skilled journalist like Morton could deploy in order to characterise a place as distinctively English.

Notes

1 The dynamic relationship between urban experience and modernist aesthetics has been explored by a number of critics. An accessible overview is provided by Malcom Bradbury's essay 'The Cities of Modernism', in Bradbury and McFarlane 1976, pp.96–104. See suggested further reading (in the appendix) for additional material.

2 For example, The Orchard Tearooms at Grantchester quote Brooke's poem in full in their marketing pamphlet.

3 For interesting coverage of the early years of our period see Ford Madox Ford's *The Soul of London* (Ford 1905); Simon Pepper's essays on 'The Garden City' and 'John Laing's Sunnyfields Estate, Mill Hill' (Pepper 1992 and 1992a) are accessible modern accounts of crucial aspects of London's development.

4 Chapters 1 and 4 of Orwell's book are of particular relevance.

THE HOMES OF ENGLAND

52 EBENEZER HOWARD
'Garden Cities'

From *Garden Cities of Tomorrow* (1902)

Ebenezer Howard (1850–1928) was a self-taught man who worked as a clerk in a Parliamentary recorder's office. In 1898 he produced a utopian solution to the problems of urban life in a pamphlet entitled *Tomorrow: A Peaceful Path to Real Reform*. This was republished as *Garden Cities of Tomorrow* in 1902 and translated into many different languages. Working from a principle of co-operative ownership Howard set out plans for a 'social city' which provided many city authorities with a uniquely democratic model for town planning. However, Howard's plans for cities which mixed the best of town and country and brought together a strictly limited cross-section of classes and professions were far more radical than the garden suburbs which sprang up around many British towns in the period.

And this principle of growth – this principle of always preserving a belt of country round our cities would be ever kept in mind till, in course of time, we should have a cluster of cities, not of course arranged in the precise geometrical form of my diagram, but so grouped around a Central City that each inhabitant of the whole group, though in one sense living in a town of small size, would be in reality living in, and would enjoy all the advantages of, a great and most beautiful city; and yet all the fresh delights of the country – field, hedgerow, and woodland – not prim
10 parks and gardens merely – would be within a very few minutes walk or ride.[1] And *because the people in their collective capacity own the land* on which this beautiful group of cities is built, the public buildings, the churches, the schools and universities, the libraries, picture galleries, theatres, would be on a scale of magnificence which no city in the world whose land is in pawn to private individuals can afford.

I have said that rapid railway transit would be realized by those who dwell in this beautiful city or group of cities.
20 Reference to the diagram will show at a glance the main

Nº 5.

— DIAGRAM —

ILLUSTRATING CORRECT PRINCIPLE OF A CITY'S GROWTH — OPEN COUNTRY EVER NEAR AT HAND, AND RAPID COMMUNICATION BETWEEN OFF-SHOOTS.

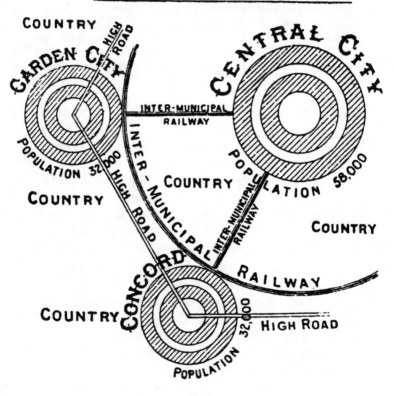

features of its railway system. There is, first, an inter-
municipal railway connecting all the towns of the outer ring
– twenty miles in circumference – so that to get from any
town to its most distant neighbour requires one to cover a
distance of only ten miles, which could be accomplished in,
say, twelve minutes. These trains would not stop between
the towns – means of communication for this purpose being
afforded by electric tramways which traverse the high
roads, of which, it will be seen, there are a number – each
30   town being connected with every other town in the group
by a direct route.

There is also a system of railways by which each town is
placed in direct communication with Central City. The
distance from any town to the heart of Central City is only
three and a quarter miles, and this could be readily covered
in five minutes.

Those who have had experience of the difficulty of
getting from one suburb of London to another will see in a
moment what an enormous advantage those who dwell in
40   such a group of cities as here shown would enjoy, because
they would have a railway *system* and not a railway *chaos* to
serve their ends. The difficulty felt in London is of course
due to want of forethought and pre-arrangement . . . .

But are the people of England to suffer for ever for the
want of foresight of those who little dreamed of the future
development of railways? Surely not. It was in the nature of
things little likely that the first network of railways ever
constructed should conform to true principles; but now,
seeing the enormous progress which has been made in the
50   means of rapid communication, it is high time that we availed
ourselves more fully of those means, and built our cities upon
some such plan as that I have crudely shown. We should then
be, for all purposes of quick communication, nearer to each
other than we are in our crowded cities, while, at the same
time, we should be surrounding ourselves with the most
healthy and the most advantageous conditions.

Some of my friends have suggested that such a scheme of
town clusters is well enough adapted to a new country, but

60 that in an old-settled country, with its towns built, and its
railway 'system' for the most part constructed, it is quite a
different matter. But surely to raise such a point is to
contend, in other words, that the existing wealth forms of
the country are permanent, and are forever to serve as
hindrances to the introduction of better forms: that
crowded, ill-ventilated, unplanned, unwieldy, unhealthy
cities – ulcers on the very face of our beautiful island – are
to stand as barriers to the introduction of towns in which
modern scientific methods and the aims of social reformers
70 may have the fullest scope in which to express themselves.
No, it cannot be: at least, it cannot be for long. What Is may
hinder What Might Be for a while, but cannot stay the tide
of progress. These crowded cities have done their work;
they were the best which a society largely based on
selfishness and rapacity could construct, but they are in the
nature of things entirely unadapted for a society in which
the social side of our nature is demanding a larger share of
recognition – a society where even the very love of self leads
us to insist upon a greater regard for the well-being of our
80 fellows. The large cities of today are scarcely better adapted
for the expression of the fraternal spirit than would a work
on astronomy which taught that the earth was the centre of
the universe be capable of adaptation for use in our schools.
Each generation should build to suit its own needs; and it is
no more in the nature of things that men should continue to
live in old areas because their ancestors lived in them, than
it is that they should cherish the old beliefs which a wider
faith and a more enlarged understanding have outgrown.
The reader is, therefore, earnestly asked not to take it for
90 granted that the large cities in which he may perhaps take a
pardonable pride are necessarily, in their present form, any
more permanent than the stage coach system which was the
subject of so much admiration just at the very moment
when it was about to be supplanted by the railways.[1] The
simple issue to be faced, and faced resolutely, is: Can better
results be obtained by starting on a bold plan on comparatively virgin soil than by attempting to adapt our old cities

to our newer and higher needs? Thus fairly faced, the
question can only be answered in one way; and when that
100 simple fact is well grasped, the social revolution will
speedily commence.

That there is ample land in this country on which such
a cluster as I have here depicted could be constructed with
comparatively small disturbance of vested interests, and,
therefore, with but little need for compensation, will be
obvious to anyone: and, when our first experiment has been
brought to a successful issue, there will be no great
difficulty in acquiring the necessary Parliamentary powers
to purchase the land and carry out the necessary works step
110 by step. County Councils are now seeking larger powers,
and an overburdened Parliament is becoming more and
more anxious to devolve some of its duties upon them. Let
such powers be given more and more freely. Let larger and
yet larger measures of local self-government be granted, and
then all that my diagram depicts – only on a far better plan,
because the result of well-concerted and combined thought
– will be easily attainable.

But it may be said 'Are you not, by thus frankly avowing
the very great danger to the vested interests of this country
120 which your scheme indirectly threatens, arming vested
interests against yourself, and so making any change by
legislation impossible?' I think not. And for three reasons.
First, because those vested interests which are said to be
ranged like a solid phalanx against progress, will, by the force
of circumstances and the current of events, be for once
divided into opposing camps. Secondly, because property
owners, who are very reluctant to yield to threats, such as are
sometimes made against them by Socialists of a certain type,
will be far more ready to make concessions to the logic of
130 events as revealing itself in an undoubted advance of society
to a higher form; and, thirdly, because the largest and most
important, and, in the end, the most influential of all vested
interests – I mean the vested interests of those who work for
their living, whether by hand or brain – will be naturally in
favour of the change when they understand its nature.

Let me deal with these points separately. First, I say vested-property interests will be broken in twain, and will range themselves in opposite camps. This sort of cleavage has occurred before. Thus, in the early days of railway
140 legislation, the vested interests in canals and stage coaches were alarmed, and did all in their power to thwart and hamper what threatened them. But other great vested interests brushed this opposition easily on one side. These interests were chiefly two – capital seeking investment, and land desiring to sell itself. (A third vested interest – namely, labour seeking employment – had then scarcely begun to assert its claims.) And notice now how such a successful experiment as Garden City may easily become will drive into the very bed-rock of vested interests a great
150 wedge, which will split them asunder with irresistible force, and permit the current of legislation to set strongly in a new direction. For what will such an experiment have proved up to the very hilt? Among other things too numerous to mention, it will have proved that far more healthy and economic conditions can be secured on raw uncultivated land (if only that land be held on just conditions) than can be secured on land which is at present of vastly higher market value; and in proving this it will open wide the doors of migration from the old
160 crowded cities with their inflated and artificial rents, back to the land which can be now secured so cheaply. Two tendencies will then display themselves. The first will be a strong tendency for city ground values to fall, the other a less marked tendency for agricultural land to rise.[2] The holders of agricultural land, at least those who are willing to sell – and many of them are even now most anxious to do so – will welcome the extension on an experiment which promises to place English agriculture once again in a position of prosperity: the holders of city lands will,
170 so far as their merely selfish interests prevail, greatly fear it. In this way, landowners throughout the country will be divided into two opposing factions, and the path of land reform – the foundation on which all other reforms

must be built – will be made comparatively easy.

Capital in the same way will be divided into opposite camps. Invested capital – that is, capital sunk in enterprises which society will recognize as belonging to the old order – will take the alarm and fall in value enormously, while, on the other hand, capital seeking investment will welcome an
180 outlet which has long been its sorest need. Invested capital will in its opposition be further weakened by another consideration. Holders of existing forms of capital will strive – even though it be at a great sacrifice – to sell part of their old time-honoured stocks and invest them in new enterprises, on municipally owned land, for they will not wish to 'have all their eggs in one basket'; and thus will the opposing influences of vested property neutralize each other.

But vested property interest will be, as I believe, affected
190 yet more remarkably in another way. The man of wealth, when he is personally attacked and denounced as an enemy of society, is slow to believe in the perfect good faith of those who denounce him, and, when efforts are made to tax him out by the forcible hand of the State, he is apt to use every endeavour, lawful or unlawful, to oppose such efforts, and often with no small measure of success. But the average wealthy man is no more an unmixed compound of self-ishness than the average poor man: and if he sees his houses or lands depreciated in value, not by force, but because
200 those who lived in or upon them have learned how to erect far better homes of their own, and on land held on conditions more advantageous to them, and to surround their children with many advantages which cannot be enjoyed on his estate, he will philosophically bow to the inevitable, and, in his better moments, even welcome a change which will involve him in far greater pecuniary loss than any change in the incidence of taxation is likely to inflict. In every man there is some measure of the reforming instinct; in every man there is some regard for his fellows;
210 and when these natural feelings run athwart his pecuniary interests, then the result is that the spirit of opposition is

inevitably softened, in some degree in all men, while in others it is entirely replaced by a fervent desire for the country's good, even at the sacrifice of many cherished possessions. Thus it is that what will not be yielded to a force from without may readily be granted as the result of an impulse from within.

And now let me deal for a moment with the greatest, the most valuable, and the most permanent of all vested
220 interests – the vested interests of skill, labour, energy, talent, industry. How will these be affected? My answer is, the force which will divide in twain the vested interests of land and capital will unite and consolidate the interests of those who live by work, and will lead them to unite their forces with the holders of agricultural land and of capital seeking investment, to urge upon the State the necessity for the prompt opening up of facilities for the reconstruction of society; and, when the State is slow to act, then to employ voluntary collective efforts similar to those adopted in the
230 Garden City experiment, with such modifications as experience may show to be necessary. Such a task as the construction of a cluster of cities like that represented in our diagram may well inspire all workers with that enthusiasm which unites men, for it will call for the very highest talents of engineers of all kinds, of architects, artists, medical men, experts in sanitation, landscape gardeners, agricultural experts, surveyors, builders, manufacturers, merchants and financiers, organizers of trades unions, friendly and co-operative societies, as well as the very simplest forms of
240 unskilled labour, together with all those forms of lesser skill and talent which lie between. For the vastness of the task which seems to frighten some of my friends, represents, in fact, the very measure of its value to the community, if that task be only undertaken in a worthy spirit and with worthy aims. Work in abundance is, as has been several times urged, one of the greatest needs of today, and no such field of employment has been opened up since civilization began as would be represented by the task which is before us of reconstructing anew the entire external fabric of society,

250 employing, as we build, all the skill and knowledge which
the experience of centuries has taught us. It was 'a large
order' which was presented in the early part of this century
to construct iron highways throughout the length and
breadth of this island, uniting in a vast network all its towns
and cities. But railway enterprise, vast as has been its
influence, touched the life of the people at but few points
compared with the newer call to build home-towns for slum
cities; to plant gardens for crowded courts; to construct
beautiful water-ways in flooded valleys; to establish a
260 scientific system of distribution to take the place of a chaos,
a just system of land tenure for one representing the
selfishness which we hope is passing away; to found
pensions with liberty for our aged poor, now imprisoned in
workhouses; to banish despair and awaken hope in the
breasts of those who have fallen; to silence the harsh voice
of anger, and to awaken the soft notes of brotherliness and
goodwill; to place in strong hands implements of peace and
construction, so that implements of war and destruction
may drop uselessly down. Here is a task which may well
270 unite a vast army of workers to utilize that power, the
present waste of which is the source of half our poverty,
disease, and suffering.

1 See, for instance, the opening chapter of *The Heart of Midlothian* (Sir
Walter Scott).
2 The chief reason for this is that agricultural land as compared with city
land is of vastly larger quantity.

Note

1 Professor Alfred Marshall, in his evidence to the Royal Commission on Imperial
and Local Taxation (1899), suggested a national 'fresh air rate' as a means of
securing country belts around and between towns: 'The central government
should see to it that towns and industrial districts do not continue to increase
without ample provision for that fresh air and wholesome play which are required
to maintain the vigour of the people and their place among nations.... We need
not only to widen our streets and increase the playgrounds in the midst of our
towns. We need also to prevent one town from growing into another, or into a
neighbouring village; we need to keep intermediate stretches of country in dairy
farms, etc., as well as public pleasure grounds.'

53 JOHN BUCHAN
'Fellows like me don't understand ... the folk that live in villas
and suburbs'

From *The Thirty-Nine Steps* (1915)

John Buchan, first Baron Tweedsmuir (1875–1940), the son of a Scottish
minister, was educated at Glasgow and Oxford. Buchan had a distinguished
career culminating in his appointment as Governor General of Canada in 1935.
He wrote over fifty books, including the immensely popular Richard Hannay
stories and other action-packed adventures. *The Thirty-Nine Steps*, notably
filmed by Alfred Hitchcock in 1935, introduces Buchan's hero, the adventure-
loving Richard Hannay. In this excerpt from the climax of the book, Hannay, who
'has travelled about the world', is in search of his German pursuers but is
taken off guard and momentarily paralysed by the trimmings of a middle-
class suburbia he has no understanding of.

A man of my sort, who has travelled about the world in
rough places, gets on perfectly well with two classes, what
you may call the upper and the lower. He understands them
and they understand him. I was at home with herds and
tramps and roadmen, and I was sufficiently at my ease with
people like Sir Walter and the men I had met the night
before. I can't explain why, but it is a fact. But what fellows
like me don't understand is the great comfortable, satisfied
middle-class world, the folk that live in villas and suburbs.
10   He doesn't know how they look at things, he doesn't
understand their conventions, and he is as shy of them as of
a black mamba. When a trim parlour-maid opened the door,
I could hardly find my voice.

I asked for Mr Appleton, and was ushered in. My plan
had been to walk straight into the dining-room, and by a
sudden appearance wake in the men that start of recognition
which would confirm my theory. But when I found myself
in that neat hall the place mastered me. There were the golf
clubs and tennis-rackets, the straw hats and caps, the rows
20   of gloves, the sheaf of walking-sticks, which you will find
in ten thousand British homes. A stack of neatly folded
coats and waterproofs covered the top of an old oak chest;
there was a grandfather clock ticking; and some polished
brass warming-pans on the walls, and a barometer, and a

print of Chiltern winning the St Leger. The place was as orthodox as an Anglican church. When the maid asked me for my name I gave it automatically, and was shown into the smoking-room, on the right side of the hall.

That room was even worse. I hadn't time to examine it,
30 but I could see some framed group photographs above the mantelpiece, and I could have sworn they were English public school or college. I had only one glance, for I managed to pull myself together and go after the maid. But I was too late. She had already entered the dining-room and given my name to her master, and I had missed the chance of seeing how the three took it.

When I walked into the room the old man at the head of the table had risen and turned round to meet me. He was in evening dress – a short coat and black tie, as was the other,
40 whom I called in my own mind the plump one. The third, the dark fellow, wore a blue serge suit and a soft white collar, and the colours of some club or school.

The old man's manner was perfect. 'Mr Hannay?' he said hesitatingly. 'Did you wish to see me? One moment, you fellows, and I'll rejoin you. We had better go to the smoking room.'

Though I hadn't an ounce of confidence in me, I forced myself to play the game. I pulled up a chair and sat down on it.
50 'I think we have met before,' I said, 'and I guess you know my business.'

The light in the room was dim, but so far as I could see their faces, they played the part of mystification very well.

'Maybe, maybe,' said the old man. 'I haven't a very good memory, but I'm afraid you must tell me your errand, sir, for I really don't know it.'

'Well, then,' I said, and all the time I seemed to myself to be talking pure foolishness – 'I have come to tell you that the game's up. I have here a warrant for the arrest of you three gentlemen.'

54 RUPERT BROOKE
'The Old Vicarage, Grantchester'

From *1914 and Other Poems* (1915)

For a biographical note on Brooke, see p.121.

The Old Vicarage, Grantchester
(Café des Westens, Berlin, May 1912)

Just now the lilac is in bloom,
All before my little room;
And in my flower-beds, I think,
Smile the carnation and the pink;
And down the borders, well I know,
The poppy and the pansy blow...
Oh! there the chestnuts, summer through,
Beside the river make for you
A tunnel of green gloom, and sleep
10 Deeply above; and green and deep
The stream mysterious glides beneath,
Green as a dream and deep as death.
– Oh, damn! I know it! and I know
How the May fields all golden show,
And when the day is young and sweet,
Gild gloriously the bare feet
That run to bathe...
    Du lieber Gott!

Here am I, sweating, sick, and hot,
20 And there the shadowed waters fresh
Lean up to embrace the naked flesh.
Temperamentvoll German Jews
Drink beer around; – and *there* the dews
Are soft beneath a morn of gold,
Here tulips bloom as they are told;
Unkempt about those hedges blows
An English unofficial rose;
And there the unregulated sun
Slopes down to rest when day is done,
30 And wakes a vague unpunctual star,

A slippered Hesper; and there are
Meads towards Haslingfield and Coton
Where *das Betreten's* not *verboten*.

ε’ίθε γευοίμην ... would I were
In Grantchester, in Grantchester! –
Some, it may be, can get in touch
With Nature there, or Earth, or such.
And clever modern men have seen
A Faun a-peeping through the green,
40 And felt the Classics were not dead,
To glimpse a Naiad's reedy head,
Or hear the Goat-foot piping low: ...
But these are things I do not know.
I only know that you may lie
Day long and watch the Cambridge sky,
And, flower-lulled in sleepy grass,
Hear the cool lapse of hours pass,
Until the centuries blend and blur
In Grantchester, in Grantchester ...
50 Still in the dawnlit waters cool
His ghostly Lordship swims his pool,
And tries the strokes, essays the tricks,
Long learnt on Hellespont, or Styx.
Dan Chaucer hears his river still
Chatter beneath a phantom mill.
Tennyson notes, with studious eye,
How Cambridge waters hurry by ...
And in that garden, black and white,
Creep whispers through the grass all night
60 And spectral dance, before the dawn,
A hundred Vicars down the lawn;
Curates, long dust, will come and go
On lissom, clerical, printless toe;
And oft between the boughs is seen
The sly shade of a Rural Dean ...
Till, at a shiver in the skies,
Vanishing with Satanic cries,

The prim ecclesiastic rout
Leaves but a startled sleeper-out,
70 Grey heavens, the first bird's drowsy calls,
The falling house that never falls.

God! I will pack, and take a train,
And get me to England once again!
For England's the one land, I know,
Where men with Splendid Hearts may go;
And Cambridgeshire, of all England,
The shire for Men who Understand;
And of *that* district I prefer
The lovely hamlet Grantchester.
80 For Cambridge people rarely smile,
Being urban, squat, and packed with guile;
And Royston men in the far South
Are black and fierce and strange of mouth;
At Over they fling oaths at one,
And worse than oaths at Trumpington,
And Ditton girls are mean and dirty,
And there's none in Harston under thirty,
And folks in Shelford and those parts
Have twisted lips and twisted hearts,
90 And Barton men make Cockney rhymes,
And Coton's full of nameless crimes,
And things are done you'd not believe
At Madingley, on Christmas Eve.
Strong men have run for miles and miles,
When one from Cherry Hinton smiles;
Strong men have blanched, and shot their wives,
Rather than send them to St. Ives;
Strong men have cried like babes, bydam,
To hear what happened at Babraham.
100 But Grantchester! ah, Grantchester!
There's peace and holy quiet there,
Great clouds along pacific skies,
And men and women with straight eyes,
Lithe children lovelier than a dream,

212

A bosky wood, a slumbrous stream,
And little kindly winds that creep
Round twilight corners, half asleep.
In Grantchester their skins are white;
They bathe by day, they bathe by night;
110 The women there do all they ought;
The men observe the Rules of Thought.
They love the Good; they worship Truth;
They laugh uproariously in youth;
(And when they get to feeling old,
They up and shoot themselves, I'm told) . . .

Ah God! to see the branches stir
Across the moon at Grantchester!
To smell the thrilling-sweet and rotten
Unforgettable, unforgotten
120 River-smell, and hear the breeze
Sobbing in the little trees.
Say, do the elm-clumps greatly stand
Still guardians of that holy land?
The chestnuts shade, in reverend dream,
The yet unacademic stream?
Is dawn a secret shy and cold
Anadyomene, silver-gold?
And sunset still a golden sea
From Haslingfield to Madingley?
130 And after, ere the night is born,
Do hares come out about the corn?
Oh, is the water sweet and cool,
Gentle and brown, above the pool?
And laughs the immortal river still
Under the mill, under the mill?
Say, is there Beauty yet to find?
And Certainty? and Quiet kind?
Deep meadows yet, for to forget
The lies, and truths, and pain? . . .
140 Oh!, Stands the Church clock at ten to three?
And is there honey still for tea?

55 DAPHNE DU MAURIER
'Losing Manderley'

From *Rebecca* (1938)

Daphne du Maurier (1907–1989) wrote a number of highly successful novels of which *Rebecca* is probably her best known. Du Maurier specialised in historical and romantic fiction which appealed to those who despised the glamour 'pulp' fiction of women's magazines and sentimental romances. In *Rebecca* a gauche young woman meets and marries the handsome, enigmatic Maximilian de Winter, owner of the West Country estate, Manderley, and whose first wife, Rebecca, died in tragic circumstances. The mysterious circumstances of Rebecca's death, and the heroine's jealousy of her predecessor, are finally resolved in a quasi-tragic ending in which Manderley is destroyed and Maxim's complicity in Rebecca's death forces the couple to live in exile on the Continent. This excerpt comes from the beginning of the novel, which is narrated as a continuous flashback by the second wife. The heroine's account of exile evokes a sense of loss, nostalgia and melancholy which links loss of country with loss of home and social status. The country house, Manderley, becomes the symbolic focus for what has been lost.

We have no secrets now from one another. All things are shared. Granted that our little hotel is dull, and the food indifferent, and that day after day dawns very much the same, yet we would not have it otherwise. We should meet too many of the people he knows in any of the big hotels. We both appreciate simplicity, and we are sometimes bored – well, boredom is a pleasing antidote to fear. We live very much by routine and I – I have developed a genius for reading aloud. The only time I have known him show
10 impatience is when the postman lags, for it means we must wait another day before the arrival of our English mail. We have tried wireless but the noise is such an irritant, and we prefer to store up our excitement; the result of a cricket match played many days ago means much to us.

Oh, the Test matches that have saved us from ennui, the boxing bouts, even the billiard scores. Finals of schoolboy sports, dog racing, strange little competitions in the remoter counties: all these are grist to our hungry mill. Some old copies of the *Field* come my way, and I am transported from
20 this indifferent island to the realities of an English spring. I

read of chalk streams, of the mayfly, of sorrel growing in green meadows, of rooks circling above the woods as they used to do at Manderley. The smell of wet earth comes to me from those thumbed and tattered pages, the sour tang of moorland peat, the feel of soggy moss spattered white in places by a heron's droppings.

Once there was an article on wood pigeons, and as I read it aloud it seemed to me that once again I was in the deep woods at Manderley, with pigeons fluttering above my
30 head. I heard their soft, complacent call, so comfortable and cool on a hot summer's afternoon, and there would be no disturbing of their peace until Jasper came loping through the undergrowth to find me, his damp muzzle questing the ground. Like old ladies caught at their ablutions the pigeons would flutter from their hiding-place, shocked into silly agitation, and, making a monstrous to-do with their wings, streak away from us above the tree-tops and so out of sight and sound. When they were gone a new silence would come upon the place and I – uneasy for no known reason – would
40 realize that the sun no longer wove a pattern on the rustling leaves, that the branches had grown darker, the shadows longer; and back at the house there would be fresh raspberries for tea. I would rise from my bed of bracken then, shaking the feathery dust of last year's leaves from my skirt and whistling to Jasper, set off towards the house, despising myself even as I walked for my hurrying feet, my one swift glance behind.

How strange that an article on wood pigeons could so recall the past and make me falter as I read aloud. It was the
50 grey look on his face that made me stop abruptly, and turn the pages until I found a paragraph on cricket, very practical and dull – Middlesex batting on a dry wicket at the Oval and piling up interminable dreary runs. How I blessed those solid, flannelled figures, for in a few minutes his face had settled back into repose, the colour had returned and he was deriding the Surrey bowling in healthy irritation.

We were saved a retreat into the past, and I had learnt my lesson. Read English news, yes, and English sport, politics,

and pomposity, but in future keep the things that hurt to
60 myself alone. They can be my secret indulgence. Colour and
scent and sound, rain and the lapping of water, even the
mists of autumn and the smell of the flood tide, these are
memories of Manderley that will not be denied. Some
people have a vice of reading Bradshaws. They plan
innumerable journeys across country for the fun of linking
up impossible connexions. My hobby is less tedious, if as
strange. I am a mine of information on the English
countryside. I know the name of every owner of every
British moor, yes – and their tenants too. I know how many
70 grouse are killed, how many partridge, how many head of
deer, I know where trout are rising, and where the salmon
leap. I attend all meets, I follow every run. Even the names
of those who walk hound puppies are familiar to me. The
state of the crops, the price of fat cattle, the mysterious
ailments of swine, I relish them all. A poor pastime,
perhaps, and not a very intellectual one, but I breathe the air
of England as I read, and can face this glittering sky with
greater courage.

The scrubby vineyards and the crumbling stones become
80 things of no account, for if I wish I can give rein to my
imagination, and pick foxgloves and pale campions from a
wet, streaking hedge.

Poor whims of fancy, tender and un-harsh. They are the
enemy to bitterness and regret, and sweeten this exile we
have brought upon ourselves.

Because of them I can enjoy my afternoon, and return,
smiling and refreshed to face the little ritual of our tea. The
order never varies. Two slices of bread and butter each, and
China tea. What a hide-bound couple we must seem,
90 clinging to custom because we did so in England. Here, on
this clean balcony, white and impersonal with centuries of
sun, I think of half past four at Manderley and the table
drawn before the library fire. The door flung open, punctual
to the minute, and the performance, never-varying, of the
laying of the tea, the silver tray, the kettle, the snowy cloth.
While Jasper, his spaniel ears a-droop, feigns indifference to

the arrival of the cakes. That feast was laid before us always, and yet we ate so little.

Those dripping crumpets, I can see them now. Tiny
100 wedges of toast, and piping-hot, floury scones. Sandwiches of unknown nature mysteriously flavoured and quite delectable, and that very special gingerbread. Angel cake, that melted in the mouth, and his rather stodgier companion, bursting with peel and raisins. There was enough food there to keep a starving family for a week. I never knew what happened to it all, and the waste used to worry me sometimes.

56 JAMES LAVER
'Homes and Habits'

From *The Character of England* (1947)

James Laver (1899–1975) is listed in the *DNB* as a 'fashion expert, novelist, dramatist, broadcaster and museum keeper'. Laver taught classes at Camden Town Working Men's College from about 1924, initially in English Literature. From 1926 he introduced life-drawing to the College's art classes. He is the author of *Taste and Fashion* (1937).

The English like to consider that they have a particular sentiment of 'home', a quasi-monopoly of the word itself. They love to point out that even peoples who use the same language employ this term in a different and somehow inadequate manner, as if unconscious of the deeper meanings which we read into it. Thus an American millionaire can be said by the press of his native country to have 'two (or even three) beautiful homes'. But if 'Home is where the heart is', this is obviously impossible. Several houses, yes;
10 several homes, no. Therefore the Americans do not understand what we mean by home. As for the German *Heim*, that belongs to a different order of sentiment, and the French *maison* and the Italian *casa* merely show that the benighted Latins have no word provided by their language for distinguishing a home from a house.

...Home is anything – it may be merely a hole in the

earth – where food can be eaten in common and where the young can find protection. As soon as these two conditions cease to be satisfied a dwelling is a home no more.... The
20 home is in some ways an especially English thing, and all Englishmen have the sentiment of the home, even if fewer and fewer of them possess the thing itself....

We must face the fact that, whether we like it or not, the patriarchal system is over. It was founded (let us face that too) upon the subjection of women. Women are now emancipated to a degree which would have frightened the pioneers of Feminism. They have revolted (wives and domestics alike) against the drudgery of housework. The home, in the old sense, is becoming increasingly impossible.
30 If we persist too long in the effort to maintain it, it is quite possible that the race may die out. We have really reached a crisis in human history beside which the invention of the atom bomb seems unimportant. Can we meet and transcend it, can we turn our technological knowledge to construction instead of destruction, can we expand instead of extinguishing our loyalties? Our English homes and our habits have, in the last thousand years, seen many changes. We are often said to have a genius for compromise. Perhaps it would be kinder to call it a genius for maintaining continuity in the
40 midst of change. This faculty is likely to be put to a severe test in the years that lie immediately ahead. If it survives that, we may yet attain a society in which there is liberty for all – even for the wife and mother; a world in which the sentiment of Home may burn the brighter on a wider altar and in a larger fane.

57 LORD KENNET
'Muddleford'

From *The Character of England* (1947)

Lord Kennett (Edward Hilton Young) (1879–1960), politician and writer. As a young man at Cambridge he was close friends with E. M. Forster, G. M. Trevelyan and the fringes of Bloomsbury. He did not share their pacifism and served in the First World War as a Naval Volunteer; in 1918 he volunteered for the blocking of Zeebrugge and manned a gun turret until his arm was shot away. In Ramsay Macdonald's national government of 1931 he was minister of health and was instrumental in promoting the clearance of slum-housing. He was responsible for the Housing Act of 1935 which, for the first time, laid down enforceable standards regarding accommodation.

Suppose that we are walking from the country towards Muddleford. The first sign that there is a big town coming is that a blackish haze appears on the horizon, with a distant prospect of factory chimneys, and that the grass and trees begin to lose their freshness and to look grimy. We ponder the problem of smoke. Electricity, gas, and the concentration of furnaces at power stations have reduced the size of that problem, but there are the cloud and the grime, and there are the chimneys, some of them making black smoke.
10   We may reflect that there are powers in the law to prevent chimneys from making black smoke; but they are little used. Local authorities are reluctant to enforce them, because it is interfering with industry and costs the factories money. We may have heard it said that there would be little or no black smoke if all stokers were trained to stoke properly, and that enlightened local authorities should have classes to teach them. If so, we have heard a very useful truth, and may think that if all stokers were properly taught, and no one were allowed to stoke without a certificate that he had been
20   taught, local authorities would feel themselves much more free to enforce the law. All but a very little black smoke from factory chimneys would then be mere carelessness. The problem of the domestic hearth would remain. One of the worst features of our obsolete housing is the open fireplaces to burn coal; and there is still a good deal of prejudice against doing without them. The capital cost of converting it all to use gas or electricity would be enormous. It seems as if we must wait for the change to come gradually, with the increase in the supply of electricity and gas, and a fall in
30   their cost. Water-power can make no very substantial contribution in this land of ours until someone finds out how to make water-power plant much more cheaply than it can be made now. Meanwhile let us cherish the hopeful

thoughts of the schools for stokers and the gradual replace-
ment of domestic coal-fires by gas and electricity.

The next sign of the coming town is a railway line, with
a steam locomotive puffing along with a train. We think of
the atmosphere its smoke will be making presently along
the built-up part of the line, and wonder why all railways do
40 not have to adopt the electric haul for the last part of their
journey into large towns. It would be costly, but even in the
matter of expense it would pay in the long run, partly in the
greater convenience and lower cost of running, partly by
attracting traffic to the much pleasanter stations which it
would enable the companies to provide.

Here is a line of pylons striding with us towards the
town. Some people think them an eyesore. But the cost of
buried mains for electricity is so enormous that for the
foreseeable future it is a question of pylons and more
50 electricity or no pylons and much less, but much dearer,
electricity. For myself I prefer pylons and more electricity.
But then I do not dislike the pylons. They have some
beauty; and there is the consoling thought that they do not
permanently affect the landscape. When they go they need
leave no trace behind. We are passing some allotments,
those patches of Mother Earth which give so much pleasure
and peace of mind to some of her children who, but for
them, would not see much of her. We notice the evidence
which they give of our vehement individualism. On each
60 patch there is a separate erection of bits of board and old
tins. It is a shed for the holder's tools. The Allotments
Committee had a plan to provide a row of lockers in a
special structure at the entrance to the allotments. The
lockers would have been neater and more convenient than
the tumble-down sheds on the plots, and they would have
enabled the holders each to have had a bit more ground. But
the holders would have none of them. An Englishman's
house is his castle, and his spade and hoe must have their
castle too. It is part of the pleasure of the allotment. The
70 town itself has stretched out a feeler, and it touches us. Here
are the first of the bungalows. This is the end of a ribbon

which comes coiling from the town far out into the country
and all along the main road. It is 6 o'clock p.m., and the road
is narrowed to half its capacity by many little cars driven up
along the curbs. The authorities ought to have made
accommodation roads parallel to the thoroughfare on both
sides of it; but it would have cost more, and who was to
pay? Here is an odd object to see on the outskirts of a great
town, a windmill. Some enterprising bungalow-dweller has
80 provided himself with his own water-supply from a well;
from which we see that this ribbon was built without any
water supply piped from the town. The authorities ought
either to have laid pipes or not allowed the building. That
is so, too, as to sanitation. There are no sewers. We can see
the earth-closets in the back gardens. These are not uncom-
mon sights. Many authorities are much too weak-kneed
about allowing people to build in areas where there are no
sewers or piped water, and they cannot be laid without
unreasonable cost. It is another instance of feeble planning.
90 We see trees, shrubs, and garden walls and hedges ahead,
and soon we are walking through the town's best residential
suburbs. Here are trim Victorian villas, standing each in its
own garden with a little drive. They were built by the
manufacturers, merchants, and professional men to whom
the town owes much of its prosperity. To be able to afford
to come and live in one of these was the ambition of a
thriving citizen and the reward of his success. There is not
much to be said for the houses. They are solid, roomy, and
comfortable – and nothing more. But their gardens are
100 charming, or were so before the German wars. They were
the pink of neatness and a blaze of flowers. It will be a sad
thing if they with their little glass-houses are never again to
be the homes of the skilful horticulture which was so
pleasant to their owners and the neighbours. It will indeed
be a sad thing altogether if changes in our economy are to
wipe all these villas out of existence. They provided the
town with a green and flowery belt at private expense. If
they must go, the authorities ought to plan the area as park
and open space.

221

110   Leaving the villas behind, we are in the town. We are in
the 'west end', among streets and squares of the town-
houses of the well-to-do. They are tall, thin, Victorian
houses, five or six stories high, with stucco fronts and
porticoes. There are back and front drawing-rooms, steep
stairs, and basements and areas. The servants' rooms are in
the basements or the attics, and there are coal fire-places and
no lifts. What is to become of them? They are caught in the
same draft as the Victorian villas. The incomes have gone
which used to enable people to pay for the many servants
120 needed for them; and, if they had not gone, could servants
be found to accept their inconveniences? If not, is there
nothing for it but to pull them down and build smaller and
more convenient houses, or the more expensive sort of flat,
in their stead? Perhaps that is the ideal, but, like many an
ideal, it is not practicable. With so much else to do we
cannot afford to waste the whole of the big capital value
which they represent. The path of least resistance is already
being marked. By internal alterations they are gradually
being converted into flats. Such flats are not very conveni-
130 ent or economical; hut it is the best we can do. In course of
time, as money becomes available, they will go, and blocks
of flats or smaller houses come in their stead. Not many
tears will be shed over Victorian stucco. But as we penetrate
more deeply towards the centre of the town we find some
streets and squares of Georgian brick; and we notice the
difference. Wherever advertisements allow it the eye is
charmed by their proportions, by the appropriateness of
their use of materials, and by their restrained and harmonious decorations of medallions, wreathed entablatures, and
140 ironwork. Here is some thing worth saving, some beauty to
be taken into account with cheapness and convenience. If
we care about such things we say to our selves perhaps that
at the next municipal election we will write to our candidate
and ask him if he is prepared to have those buildings
scheduled for preservation, and we will tell him that we will
not complain of our small share of the cost. The buildings
get higher, the traffic denser, and we are at the centre of the

town but is it the centre? This town seems to wish only to
disguise the fact that it has a centre. There is a big ganglion
150 of tram and bus lines, a large gentlemen and ladies, and a
huge amorphous front of glass, plaster, nickel-plate, and
print, which is a cinema; and that is all. Black cliffs of office
buildings tower up all round and radiate in dwindling
chasms. A train puffs, audible but unseen. The smoky
cavern of the central station is close by. The indifference we
show to civic centres is significant. Did we think of the
town in which we live as a whole, as a community with a life
of its own and a character of its own, we should think it
natural that its life and character should be expressed and
160 dignified by a fine civic centre. But we do not so think of
our town, or at least not often enough or clearly enough so
we are indifferent to a civic centre. Let London be the
example, which allows the finest site in the world, the centre
of civilisation, to be wasted on the Royal Exchange building, a meaningless lump with a pretentious portico, squalid
with little shops; a building which is useless and purpose-
less, and has no dignity, or beauty, or history. No, our towns
are collections of the separate castles of English men, not
civic units, and it is no doubt that incoherent quality of
170 theirs, and of ours, to which we owe the lack of a dignified
grouping of municipal and central buildings, to express the
town's life and aspirations and to give its citizens a sense
that there is something good in their association together as
citizens, and something to be proud of in their citizenship
of this particular town. Cardiff may serve as an illustration.
It differs in this from other towns. It has a very fine civic
centre, spacious, well laid out, with beautiful and generous
buildings, made pleasant with trees, flowers, sculpture, and
green grass, and, above all, kept clean. The reason for this
180 difference from other towns is to be found in another
difference. During the years of Cardiff's growth into a great
city all the land was in one ownership. The successive
owners, the Lords of Bute, were no doubt not much more
enlightened than the rest of mankind but the fact of their
single ownership enabled the city to develop its centre on a

single plan, free from the clash and drag of many warring
interests and so Cardiff is a fine town, perhaps our finest,
because it had the good luck to have a fortuitous coherence
in its affairs to remedy our native incoherence. Planning was
190 made easy for it. Cardiff suggests a day-dream. The cities of
medieval Italy were often so torn by faction that life therein
was no longer worth living, and a desperate remedy had to
be sought. A city in such case would choose a governor, a
podestà who had no interest in any of the factions and was
commonly a stranger to the city. For the sake of peace and
quiet all the factions swore obedience to his orders, and
while they kept their vows life in the city was worth living
again. Warring interests and jealousies, such as those which
arise between local and central authorities, paralyse plan-
200 ning and development. They do not make town life
intolerable, but they make it not nearly so well worth living
as it might be. One dreams of a golden age when each town
would have a *podestà* for planning and development to
whom all would swear obedience. The town would delegate
by common consent to their *podestà* for planning and
development all powers that could and should be exercised
by the city, and, on their own account, powers equal to
those exercised by the ministry in Whitehall. He would be
for the town in all matters of planning and development
210 both town council, as it were, and the minister, but he
would be the minister localized, near at hand, and serving
the town alone. As long as the citizens kept their vows to
their *podestà*, how the town would advance! But I suppose
it would need an amount of self-restraint and fidelity which
can be found only in dreamland. After these thoughts,
which have come to us on the steps of the grand chromium
cinema which is now the shrine of the Spirit of Muddleford,
let us go on with our walk. Soon it takes us through the
slums. This is the district of wage-earners' houses that was
220 the first gift to Muddleford of the Industrial Revolution,
varied here and there with a few ruinous dwellings which
remain from the eighteenth and even from the seventeenth
century. These mean streets arc true slums. They are not

224

merely inconvenient, monotonous, and ugly. Streets can be that without being slums. The Cromwell road is not a slum. In this district the houses are not only all that, but they are so bad that they are not fit to live in. They are built back to back, in over-narrow streets and courts. They have no gardens or drying-yards. They have no water laid on, and so
230 no bath-rooms or water-closets. A number of houses share a water-tap on a post in the open air and some earth closets at the end of the yard. Round the closets the earth is soaked with sewage. The rooms are too few, too small, and too low. The window panes are broken, the doors are off their hinges, the woodwork has been hacked away for firewood, the paint is gone, the roofs leak, and there are bugs and dry rot. Some of the most horrid dens are built against railway arches. Everybody knows that the district is an outrage against humanity, and as a matter of fact it would have been
240 got rid of by now but for the German wars. But here it is, and it is not only in Muddleford. The Spirit of even that backward city must weep when she looks at it and thinks that in these houses may have been born sailors of the little ships, soldiers of the Eighth Army, or airmen of the Battle of Britain. No doubt in course of time the slums which we have will go. It will be for future generations to realize that slums, like weeds in a garden, soon grow again after a good weeding, unless the gardener keeps his hoe ready for them. They are a big problem but a simple one, and will be solved
250 before long. For this stage of our civilization a much more complicated problem awaits us in the next, and bigger, district just beyond the slums. This is the district of wage-earners' dwellings built in the first half of the nineteenth century. It is the largest and most populous part of the town. On the whole it is not insanitary or unhealthy; but its long, monotonous streets of dreary, ugly, little houses are hopelessly lacking in all the amenities which they should not and need not lack. They are stupidly laid out, stupidly built, and, above all, they are overcrowded. Not a tiro
260 amongst town planners or architects but could now plan and build houses incomparably better. These houses are

innumerable, and obsolete. They are the legacy of stupidity
in the past. That past has left us a troublesome inheritance
indeed in remedying its mistakes. It has left our towns with
these great cores of badly planned, badly designed, and
overcrowded wage earners' dwellings, which are over-
crowded because they are badly planned and designed.
Fully to appreciate the nature and extent of the problem we
must walk on again through two districts which lie next
270 beyond. The very next district is the factory area. We will
try not to think any more about the smoke, about which we
have already had our rueful thoughts. We will cast no more
than a look at the heaps of slag, cinders, and rubbish, the
unkempt and unclean look of the majority of the buildings,
the horrid patches of waste land, and the general look of dirt
and untidiness; and we will do no more than remind
ourselves that there is no reason why a factory area should
look like the Valley of the Shadow of Death, and the muddy
circle in the Inferno, and the black desert of Gobi. Good
280 examples have been given that factories can be made to look
bright and decent, in green and seemly settings, and that
furnaces need not prevent it. There are Port Sunlight,
Bournville, and even the Bath Road. In most cases it needs
only goodwill on the part of the management and the local
authority to enforce tidiness. Widnes and Runcorn and such
chemical cities, and the homes of the blast furnaces, where
grass will not grow, these are harder nuts to crack: but even
there much can be done at reasonable cost by mere tidiness
and cleanliness. After that look round, what we have to
290 note, as a part of Muddleford's general problem, is that this
factory area is next the area of wage-earners' houses. They
must live near their work. If they do not it is bad for them,
in loss of leisure and energy, and bad for the industry, in the
cost of transport. When we have noticed that, let us walk on
through the next district. What a change! This is the Town
Council's pet housing estate, newly developed on the
outskirts of the town. It does Muddleford great credit.
Pretty, convenient little houses in pretty little gardens are
well grouped about pretty little centres, with a few shops

300 and a good inn, an institute and a cinema. All is as it should
be, and the district is spreading fast into the country, on a
good plan. Obviously the city fathers are putting any
amount of energy into it. Now we can fit together the parts
of the town's problem. It has a few remaining slums. It has
a very large central area of obsolete and congested wage-
earners' dwellings. It has a fine modern housing estate,
much smaller than the obsolete congested area, and growing
away from the factories, so that it grows less convenient for
its inhabitants. It is devoting all its energies to the extension
310 of the nice new housing estate on the outskirts, and doing
nothing about the obsolete and congested central area.

58 OSBERT LANCASTER
'English is the only language that has a word for "home"'

From *Progress at Pelvis Bay* (1936)

Osbert Lancaster (1908–1986), cartoonist and illustrator, worked for the
Architectural Review, London Transport and the *Daily Express*. *Progress at
Pelvis Bay* satirised the laissez-faire approach to town planning and is critical
of manifestations of modernity. We have taken a short extract from chapter
7, 'Domestic Architecture and Housing'.

Of a slightly different type, though almost contemporary, is
'Osborne' [p.228]. This dignified and comfortable old house
is one of those erected on what were then the outskirts of the
town when Pelvis Bay first became popular as a place of
retirement for the military and professional classes. A great
feature of these houses are the large park-like gardens and
impressive entrance gates. The ideal of those who developed
this section of the town, and one which it must be admitted
was faithfully realized, was 'rus in urbe'. This particular house
10 was for long the residence of Admiral Sir Carraway Hawks-
moor, afterwards first Viscount Honduras. However comfortable and pleasing as many of these houses are, they have
only to be compared to some of the modern labour-saving
villas put up since the war in order to realize what enormous
strides domestic architecture has made in recent years.

'Osborne'

'Craigweil'

These charming houses, of which 'Craigweil,' the residence of the Mayor, Councillor Busfun, illustrated [left], is a typical example, are not only magnificently planned and fitted with every modern labour-saving device, but are also
20 possessed of those qualities of quaintness and cosiness which are so notably absent from some of the more recent examples of the so-called 'modern' architecture. Moreover, they have been especially designed to harmonize with the beautiful landscape of the downs on which they have recently been erected in large numbers; for despite its willingness to give every encouragement to justifiable commercial enterprise, the Council is never forgetful of its duties as a custodian of rural amenities.

The best example of this praiseworthy anxiety on the
30 part of the council for the preservation of that rustic beauty with which the immediate neighbourhood of Pelvis Bay is so singularly blessed, is perhaps to be found in the new housing estate on the west cliff. Here the greatest care has been taken to avoid all suspicion of urban monotony and the utmost variety of architecture has therefore been encouraged. Belvedere Avenue, the street illustrated [below], was one of the first to be completed, and already well over

half the houses are occupied. A striking tribute to the council's policy of insisting on the erection of dwellings
40 with an individual character of their own and turning a deaf ear to all those cranks and so-called Modernists who are so constantly urging the merits of vast stream-lined, undecorated blocks of flats or rather tenements; despite the fact that they are likely to have little appeal to a people whose proud boast it is that 'An Englishman's Home is his Castle'. Do they realize, one wonders, when they try to foist these continental barracks on us, that English is the only language that has a word for 'home'?

59 DR STEPHEN TAYLOR
'The Suburban Neurosis'

From the *Lancet* (1938)

Dr Stephen Taylor was Senior Resident Medical Officer at the Royal Free Hospital.

Those whose duty it is to deal with the 'poor teaching cases' in the medical out-patient departments of the great London hospitals soon find that most of their patients fall into a few large but not very clear-cut groups. First come the menopausal osteo-arthritics, with or without hypertension and early signs of congestive failure. Then there are the chronic bronchitics and patients with long-standing indigestion, in whom no definite lesions, beyond a few bronchi or a little tenderness, can be discovered. Finally, there are the greater
10 concourse of neurotics, some well hospitalised and saturated with the not very efficacious mixtures of their more organic friends, other, less regular visitors as a rule, scarcely to be distinguished from the early stages of Graves disease.

After four years of such work, I have gained the impression that among the neurotics, there has been a decline of the simple old 'bottle-of-medicine' loving patients, their places being taken by less poverty stricken young women with anxiety states, the majority of whom present a definite clinical picture with a uniform back-

20 ground. It is my aim here to describe that picture – not in
academic terms, but in the words of the patients themselves
– and to throw a little light on that background. I hope to
show that environment plays no less a part in the production of what I venture to call 'the suburban neurosis', than
it does in the production of physical disease.

Clinical Picture

Mrs Everyman is 28 or 30 years old. She and her dress are
clean but there is a slovenly look about her. She has given
up the permanent wave she was so proud of when she was
engaged. Her clothes, always respectable and never as smart
30 as those young hussies who work in the biscuit factory, are,
like her furniture, getting rather shabby. They hang on her
rather as a covering than as something to be worn and made
the most of. She is pale but not anaemic. Her haemoglobin
is 86 per cent. She has left the child outside in the waiting
room. As she sits down I notice that her hands are shaking.

    'I've been to my own doctor,' she begins, 'but he gave me
a bottle of medicine and told me it was nerves. I wasn't
satisfied, so I've come to see you. It can't be nerves, doctor;
I feel such a ...' Then follows the principal symptom. Here
40 are a few of them: –

Lump in my throat that goes up and down or round and
round.
Trembling all over, and I jump at the slightest noise.
Continuous gnawing, nagging headache.
Pain in my back which runs up and down.
My stomach swells up terribly.
Nasty taste in my mouth.
So short of breath when I hurry.
Terrible buzzing in my ears.
50 I can't sleep at night.
I'm getting ever so thin ...
And so on.

    Whatever the principal symptom, several of the others

are certain to be there as subsidiaries.

On examination, there is a definite but variable tremor, a definite but variable tachycardia, pendulous flabby breasts, poor abdominal muscles, very brisk reflexes, and nothing else. Watched over two months, she will gain or lose a pound. She will show no exophtalmos, no goitre, and
60 neither hyper nor hypotension.

All too often at the top of her notes will be written 'N.' or 'HYS.'; she will receive perhaps a bottle of Mist. Pot. Brom. Co.; she will be referred on to the junior assistant, who will in due course write 'Rep.' on her treatment sheet – and she will be forgotten.

The True History

Her parents were respectable and kept themselves to themselves. After school, she went to a shorthand college, and from there to a business house in Brixton. All day she added up figures, on the train she skimmed the *Daily*
70 *Peepshow*, three times a week she went to the cinema, and such mind as school had developed withered and retrogressed. Then love, in the shape of Mr Everyman, came along. He, too, was a clerk in the Brixton business house. And the Boss, who knew enough of human nature to agree with Bacon – 'He that hath wife and children hath given hostages to fortune; for they are impediments to great enterprises, either of virtue or mischief' – liked to see his young men married.

So, after two years of saving, and those lovely walks
80 around Box Hill at the week-ends, they took the plunge into a small semi-detached hire-purchase villa on the wonderful new Everysuburb estate, adjacent to one of our great new by-passes and only twenty minutes from the station. The estate was Mr Jerrybuilder's fifth successful venture in the property market. By this time he had thoroughly mastered the technique of using the cheapest unseasoned timber, the lightest breeze brick, and the smartest bathroom fittings.

All their savings went on the first instalments on the
90 house and furniture. Mr Everyman was an inexperienced
lover and the physical side of marriage shocked and rather
disappointed his wife. After a year of rather unsatisfactory
birth control, during which the thrill of a 'home of her own'
had worn off, they decide to risk a baby. In due course baby
came, and for about a year and a half kept Mrs Everyman's
hands pretty full. Then things began to slacken up. She
developed a routine for doing the housework quickly. She
had to think a little about the shopping, but the cooking she
did almost blindly. The *Peepshow* didn't take long to read,
100 and the wireless was always the same old stuff. They hadn't
been able to get away for a holiday as they had hoped; baby
cost more than they bargained for. Hubby had started to
grumble at her. Then baby had been a bit fretful lately. She
couldn't understand it. She'd been so careful with him. He
couldn't have picked up anything. She hadn't let him mix
with other children.

One day there had dropped through her letter box a
circular. It was sent out by the local doctors, and it was all
about cancer. It said cancer did not hurt at first, and if you
110 took it early it was all right. 'Took it early.' That meant an
operation. It was bad enough when baby came, but an
operation! Then she remembered that pain in her back.
She'd noticed it at first when she was doing the housework,
and she thought she must have strained herself. But it had
stayed on. Cancer didn't hurt *at first*. Her back was hurting.
What if it were? And she was losing weight, too. Hadn't
hubby said she wasn't as nice to cuddle as she used to be?
What if she did get ill? Not cancer, but something she had
to go to hospital with. Baby would have to go to her
120 mother's, and *she* didn't want him. And hubby's cousin
would have to come and look after him. That woman! She
had never liked her – didn't trust her really. The way she
looked at men. Just as though she wanted to eat them.

Suppose hubby should lose his job – or get ill. Then
what? They'd fall behind with the instalments. Then they'd
take the furniture. And perhaps they'd have to live in rooms

– or take a lodger. Perhaps they couldn't get one. You never
saw notices up in Acacia-row with 'Bed and Breakfast. Gent
preferred' on them, like you did in London. What would
130 the neighbours say?

If only she'd someone to talk to. Somehow she couldn't
tell hubby. He'd say she was just being silly. They'd been
there three years and she only knew three people on the
estate. There were the neighbours, but you couldn't call
them neighbourly. And that Mrs Smith in Paradise-avenue,
who'd asked her round to tea. Then, when she found she
couldn't play cards, she'd not asked her any more. The
curate had called once, when hubby was at work. Quite a
nice young chap. He'd asked her to come to the Church
140 social. But hubby had said no. And anyhow, you couldn't
believe in religion much nowadays. Not with the news-
papers, and all this war, and gas-masks for babies.

Then hubby did get ill – neuritis. Sciatica, the doctor
called it, and they'd had to get a plaster for it, and she'd been
so busy she didn't know what to do. Her pain hadn't been
so bad then. In fact, she'd forgotten about it altogether.
She'd been sleeping better, too. None of that horrid sex
business either. She'd just cuddled up close to him and
known it was all right. The boss had been decent about it,
150 and they'd managed the money somehow, and in six weeks
the doctor said he could go back to work.

Then the pain started all over again, worse than ever; she
couldn't stick it. The house was getting her down. If only they
could move to a little flat somewhere, with real live people all
around. When would the instalments finish? Only twenty-
one years, Mr. Jerrybuilder had said. 1956 – Oh God!

After weeks and weeks of it, she'd plucked up courage
and gone to the doctor, and he'd said it was nerves! Nerves
– what had she got to be nervous about? Why, when hubby
160 was bad, she'd been as right as rain. But there it was, nag,
nag, nag. She'd take something, that's what she'd do. Or put
her head in a gas-oven. No that was too horrible. She
couldn't face that. She'd try the hospital instead.

And so at last to 'minor medical out-patients' – and me.

Aetiology

Let me translate this miserable little story into medical jargon. The deep seated aetiological factors of the suburban neurosis are, no doubt, extremely complex. The stomach which swells represents perhaps an unconscious urge to further motherhood, the sleepless nights a longing for a full
170 sex life. Existence in the suburbs is such that the self-preserving, race-preserving and herd instincts can be neither adequately satisfied nor sublimated. The barriers to satisfaction and sublimation are the superficial or 'trigger' causes of the condition, while the symptoms – pathological anxiety, somatic manifestations, failure of conation, and failure of affect – represent a side-tracking of frustrated emotional energy.

The superficial causes are as follows: –

1. *Boredom*, occasioned by –
180   (a) *Lack of friends* – Few who have not worked or lived in the suburbs can realise the intense loneliness of their unhappy inhabitants. There is no common meeting ground like the pub and the street of the slum dwellers, and the golf and tennis club of the middle classes. There is no community of interest such as is found in the village. Lack of individual enterprise, shyness, and bashfulness prevent calling, and the striking up of friendships. It is respectable to keep oneself to oneself. The Englishman's home is
190   still his castle, but for the Englishwoman too often her gaol.
  (b) *Not enough to do* – As long as the housework, the baby or the sick husband keep the young wife busy, all is fairly satisfactory. But once these cease to occupy her she is left with time on her hands, and she starts to think, a process for which she is unadapted.
  (c) *Not enough to think about* – At school she was not taught to use her brain for her own amusement. Since then, all the stimuli reaching her not very adequate
200   cerebrum have been designed to inhibit rather than

235

stimulate thought. The papers she reads and the films she sees are all of the 'flash-in-the-pan' wish fulfilment variety. The wireless, of necessity, dare not be provoking. She has no knowledge of what books to read, nor how to set about getting them. The wisdom of the world, if she did but know it, is waiting for her on the station bookstall, at sixpence a time.

2. *Anxiety* – Anxiety is of two great kinds – justifiable and unjustifiable. To be anxious in an aeroplane is still justifiable. To be anxious in a railway train is not. This dogmatic statement requires qualification. A Solomon Islander riding in his first train would be justifiably anxious. Justifiable anxiety may vanish or become unjustifiable in the face of knowledge and experience. Unjustifiable anxiety is pathological, and is ready to attach itself to the most commonplace events. It is, of course, a psychoneurotic symptom.

The patient suffering from the suburban neurosis shows both kinds of anxiety, though unjustifiable anxiety is symptomatic rather than causative. Our patient is justifiably anxious about –

(a) *Money and the house* – Her little family is not merely living in a hand to mouth way. It has taken on commitments which tie it for the next twenty-one years. By the time the payments on the house and the furniture are completed, the value of both will be very much less than the amount paid for them. In fact, they may be actually unrealisable. Prolonged sickness or the loss of a job on the part of the wage earner may mean the loss of such savings as the instalments paid represent, the break-up of the home, and the disappearance of 'respectability'. Further, if the house should prove unsuitable or unsatisfactory – as it probably will – the chances of getting out are extremely remote.

(b) *Another baby* – The safest forms of birth control are physically the least satisfactory. But even if the safest forms are used, there is always the possibility of an

240 accident, and another child would just push the family budget over to the wrong side. This fear is extremely common in the one-child family.

3. *A false set of values* – The suburban woman has made a fetish of her home. She is aiming at the kind of lifestyle successfully led by people to whom books, theatres and things of intellect matter. To them, home is a necessary part of life, but only part. To her, because she does not see the rest, the home looks like everything, and she wonders why it does not bring her the happiness it appears to bring to them.

250 The other set of values she is offered is that of the *Daily Peepshow* and the weekly cinema. In both, she sees continuous 'tempests of emotion' – uncouth marriages of elderly clergymen to young parishioners, torsos daily discovered in trunks, romantic love triumphing over New York's press men, and plumbers mad rich beyond dreams by Saturday's football pools. One cannot blame her for expecting at least a little of other people's thrills. But there *is* no thrill in Everysuburb....

Treatment and Prophylaxis

If it were possible to establish on each new estate a team of
260 psycho-analysts, the suburban neurotics might learn to see themselves as they are, and carry on and even reconstruct their unsatisfactory lives without developing symptoms. It is hard, however, to imagine a more inverted way of doing good – or, for that matter, a more costly one.

The treatment of the individual case is beset with difficulties. It calls for enthusiasm and perseverance. At the start a complete physical examination, followed by unqualified reassurance is essential. One must attempt to reawaken interest in life. A club of some kind, or a pub, is a great help,
270 but all too often neither is available, or the pub is by unwritten law for men only. A carefully graded reading list is perhaps more use than a bottle of medicine. Another

baby, rather than a new wireless, if it can be afforded, may effect a permanent cure. If the house can be disposed of, a flat near a few friends may work wonders. But all to often one finds oneself up against a deadlock of unpleasant and hopeless reality. The psychological out-patient department is in most hospitals already over-crowded, so one attempts a very superficial analysis. Gross physical difficulties in the
280 sex life are straightened out, but the neurosis persists. And as long as life offers the suburban woman so little to live for, so long will she continue to pluck up her courage and add to the numbers in our out patient waiting halls.

We have, I fear, let matters go too far in the jerry-building, ribbon-development line to institute an entirely satisfactory prophylaxis. We have allowed the slum which stunted the body to be replaced by a slum which stunts the mind. Perhaps, like a pack of cards, these rotten little houses will in due course collapse. Perhaps, when the children
290 grow up, they will break down the barriers which separate family from family. But even this hope may prove false. Instead, the child may see through the values of its family and come to despise it. Or its over-proud parents may push it into a job for which it is intellectually unqualified – and one more neurotic will be launched on its way.

Meanwhile our best plan is, I think, to establish on these new estates social non-religious clubs, catering for all possible interests. Under one roof one would like to see a swimming bath and gymnasium, a cafeteria, a day-nursery,
300 the public library, and reading, smoking and games rooms – something not unlike the Pioneer Health Centre in Peckham, without perhaps such a positive emphasis on health as the main motive of life. Such a club would give the suppressed herd instinct of the unhappy inhabitants of Everysuburb estate a chance to express itself. And in a corporate life, affect and conation would find new outlets. It has been suggested that these new communities will only develop a true corporate sense with some revival of individual local leadership, analogous to the old village squire-
310 archy. Perhaps the success of the totalitarian states with

their lower middle classes is due to just such a reassertion of the 'Leader Principle'.

The prevention of the suburban neurosis, then, is in the hands of the social workers and politicians. And if they require a purely selfish stimulus, one would remind them that, in the latent feelings and strivings of the new mental slum-dwellers, there is waiting a most hopeful field for the teachers of new, and possibly dangerous, political ideologies.

URBAN ENGLANDS:
THE MIDLANDS AND THE NORTH
60 ANONYMOUS
Correspondence on housing estates

From the *Birmingham Mail* (1931)

'Municipal Housing', *20 July 1931*
Sir, – Is it too much to ask that, in the erection of their latest municipal estates, the Housing Committee may be induced to give more consideration to the allocation of the houses?

As a prospective tenant of the Weoley Hill estate, I am rather concerned as to what I have heard (and seen during an inspection of the site) of the type of tenant that is expecting to flock to this estate in large numbers on its completion.

10   I am no snob (on a rental of 15s. 7d. per week!), but personal knowledge of other estates and reports of friends living on or having doings with same are in agreement that the great drawback of accepting a house under the council is the tremendous possibility of undesirable neighbours, to put it mildly. If one attempts to keep to oneself, the neighbours try to 'make it hot for you', and there are many ways of making unpleasantness. It is, indeed, bad for anyone with young children – there is little privacy in municipal back gardens – and they are bound to hear very
20   unsuitable language, and hearing, so often imitate.

The Estates Committee make many and strict enquiries

into all our circumstances before enrolling us on the register, and their visitors can adequately sum up the type of folk with whom they deal. Surely it should not be impossible, therefore, for people who have some regard for the decencies of life to be granted the privilege of living beside one another, and not, as so often happens, be thrust among persons of vastly different manners and tastes.

30 From every quarter one hears such stories of unpleasant surroundings that one hesitates to accept a tenancy when offered.

CAVEAT EMPTOR

'Housing Estates', 22 July 1931
Sir, – I agree with all your correspondent, 'Caveat Emptor', says in his very comprehensive letter, for I have had these conditions to put up with for the past five years.

I have been particularly unfortunate in my neighbours, having the type you mention either side, also opposite, which has made my life almost unbearable, being one of the kind who try to keep myself and children, of whom I have three, as tidy and well dressed as far as means allow.

10 I have asked the Estates Department for an exchange, but am met with the reply that I cannot change into another non-parlour, and they haven't a parlour type at present, so I have to stay here, as I cannot afford to buy, which is my only alternative.

Surely there should be someone put in charge who can tell the one type from the other.

We are told that the decent people are mixed to help lift the others who don't care.

FRANKLY FED UP

'Municipal Houses', 23 July 1931
Sir, – I am glad to see 'Caveat Emptor's' letter. We are tenants of a municipal house. We have four young children, eldest ten years, youngest two years. Our children are snubbed by a neighbour with one child. If they play in the back they must play with boots off and mouths closed. If they play in the street they are spoken to by another neighbour with one child. We keep ourselves to ourselves

and then find all kinds of scandal is said about us.

Houses should be let to tenants with two or more children, not one; these latter should live in flats. My husband, with many more fathers, fought in 1914 for his country.

RESERVED TENANT

'Municipal Housing', 24 July 1931

Sir, – I quite agree with 'Caveat Emptor', and feel I should like to state my own case.

I registered for a parlour house, but three years ago was offered a smaller non-parlour and owing to conditions then prevailing, was compelled to accept it in the hope of getting an exchange. Had I known the class of people I was going to be thrust amongst, I think I should have suffered rooms a little longer until I could have obtained what I registered for.

I know these people have got to have houses to live in, but why not put them all together, not scatter them amongst decent living and respectable folk.

I think it quite time the Estate Committee showed a bit of discretion in this direction.

ANOTHER SUFFERER

Sir, – 'Caveat Emptor' is quite right in all he says. If you have children your life is one long misery, and only too true do they imitate the language they hear.

Yes, if you are peace-loving, you do have it 'made hot for you' in more ways than one. Worst of all are the constant jeers, but, thank heaven, the tenants are not all the same; if they were there would be a few more mothers driven to desperation.

Those in rooms have my sympathy, but my advice to those giving up a pre-war home is to think twice. I have had hardships, sorrow, hunger, but never have I been so unhappy as since becoming a municipal tenant.

HADSOME

Sir, – I should like to endorse what 'Caveat Emptor' says with regard to some of the tenants of municipal houses.

Whereas his observations are based on prospective tenants, I am a tenant with over 12 months experience, during which period I have become completely convinced as to the futility of indiscriminate mixing whereby the Estates Committee hope to make decent citizens out of most undesirable types, to the perpetual annoyance and humiliation of decent-minded clean-living people, who, by sheer force of
10 circumstances, find themselves bound to accept tenancy of a municipal house.

Quite apart from the unspeakable gossip, which one has to ignore, it is most heart-breaking to one who has a keen interest in the beauty of his home and garden, to find litter and filth of all kinds continually strewn about – chip-potato papers and empty beer bottles thrown defiantly into one's front garden, merely because it has the appearance of being well-kept (at considerable expense and hours of labour), privet plant pulled up in one garden and thrown in to the
20 next (or stolen), fences and gates chalked with obscene words, to say nothing of thefts from back gardens.

Recently, one woman said she was 'fed up' because there were no drunken brawls and fights, so she was going back to the slums, where she 'could have a scrap any night'. Such are the people (and they are by no means few) whom decent, respectable folk are expected to influence in the matter of good citizenship.

TENANT

61 J. B. PRIESTLEY
'Rusty Lane, West Bromwich'

From *English Journey* (1934)

For a note on Priestley and on *English Journey*, see p.26.

My second day there was a Sunday, and in foul weather. Sometimes the raw fog dripped; sometimes the cold rain steamed; but throughout it was thick and wet and chilled. I lunched in one of the smaller towns with a man in the metal trade. There were several Black Country business men

there, large hearty fellows, sturdy eaters and drinkers. There
had been a sudden flurry of business in the metal trade, and
my friend was going back to his office and warehouse in
West Bromwich after lunch. I went with him, and on the
10 way was shown, among other things, the last dairy farm in
the district. It stood there surrounded for miles by the grim
paraphernalia of industrialism; I had only a glimpse of it, a
solitary surviving farmhouse in the wet fog, with a few
ghostly fields on either side. My friend's warehouse was in
– shall we say? – 'Rusty Lane', West Bromwich. He keeps
sheets of steel there, and no doubt any place is good enough
to keep sheets of steel in; but I do not think I could let even
a sheet of steel stay long in Rusty Lane. I have never seen
such a picture of grimy desolation as that street offered me.
20 If you put it, brick for brick, into a novel, people would not
accept it, would condemn you as a caricaturist and talk
about Dickens. The whole neighbourhood is mean and
squalid, but this particular street seemed the worst of all. It
would not matter very much – though it would matter – if
only metal were kept there; but it happens that people live
there, children are born there and grow up there. I saw some
of them. I was being shown one of the warehouses, where
steel plates were stacked in the chill gloom, and we heard a
bang and rattle on the roof. The boys, it seems, were
30 throwing stones again. They were always throwing stones
on that roof. We went out to find them, but only found
three frightened little girls, who looked at us with round
eyes in wet smudgy faces. No, they hadn't done it, the boys
had done it, and the boys had just run away. Where they
could run to, I cannot imagine. They need not have run
away for me, because I could not blame them if they threw
stones and stones and smashed every pane of glass for miles.
Nobody can blame them if they grow up to smash
everything that can be smashed. There ought to be no more
40 of those lunches and dinners, at which political and financial
and industrial gentlemen congratulate one another, until
something is done about Rusty Lane and West Bromwich.
While they still exist in their present foul shape, it is idle to

congratulate ourselves about anything. They make the whole pomp of government here a miserable farce. The Crown, Lords and Commons are the Crown, Lords and Commons of Rusty Lane, West Bromwich. In the heart of the great empire on which the sun never sets, in the land of hope and glory, Mother of the Free, is Rusty Lane, West
50 Bromwich. What do they know of England who only England know? The answer must be Rusty Lane, West Bromwich. And if there is another economic conference, let it meet there, in one of the warehouses, and be fed with bread and margarine and slabs of brawn. The delegates have seen one England, Mayfair in the season. Let them see another England next time, West Bromwich out of the season. Out of all seasons except the winter of our discontent.

62 D. H. LAWRENCE
'Nottingham and the Mining Country'

From the *New Adelphi* (1930)

For a biographical note on Lawrence, see p.31.

Now Eastwood occupies a lovely position on a hilltop, with the steep slope towards Derbyshire and the long slope towards Nottingham. They put up a new church, which stands fine and commanding, even if it has no real form, looking across the awful Erewash Valley at the church of Heanor, similarly commanding, away on a hill beyond. What opportunities, what opportunities! These mining villages *might* have been like the lovely hill-towns of Italy, shapely and fascinating. And what happened?
10   Most of the little rows of dwellings of the old-style miners were pulled down, and dull little shops began to rise along the Nottingham Road, while on the down-slope of the north side the company erected what is still known as the New Buildings, or the Square. These New Buildings consist of two great hollow squares of dwellings planked down on the rough slope of the hill, little four-room houses with the 'front' looking outward into the grim, blank street,

and the 'back', with a tiny square brick yard, a low wall, and
a w.c. and ash-pit, looking into the desert of the square,
20 hard, uneven, jolting black earth tilting rather steeply down,
with these little back yards all round, and openings at the
corners. The squares were quite big, and absolutely desert,
save for the posts for clothes lines, and people passing,
children playing on the hard earth. and they were shut in
like a barracks enclosure, very strange.

Even fifty years ago the squares were unpopular. It was
'common' to live in the Square. It was a little less common
to live in the Breach, which consisted of six blocks of rather
more pretentious dwellings erected by the company in the
30 valley below, two rows of three blocks, with an alley
between. And it was most 'common', most degraded of all
to live in Dakins Row, two rows of the old dwellings, very
old, black four-roomed little places, that stood on the hill
again, not far from the Square.

So the place started. Down the steep street between the
squares, Scargill Street, the Wesleyans' chapel was put up and
I was born in the little corner shop just above. Across the
other side of the Square the miners themselves built the big,
barn-like Primitive Methodist chapel. Along the hill-top ran
40 the Nottingham Road, with its scrappy, ugly mid-Victorian
shops. The little market-place, with a superb outlook, ended
the village on the Derbyshire side, and was just here left bare,
with the Sun Inn on one side, the chemist across, with the gilt
pestle-and-mortar, and a shop at the other corner, the corner
of Alfreton Road and Nottingham Road.

In this queer jumble of the old England and the new, I
came into consciousness. As I remember, little local spec-
ulators already began to straggle dwellings in rows, always
in rows, across the fields: nasty red-brick, flat-faced dwell-
50 ings with dark slate roofs. The bay-window period only
began when I was a child. But most of the country was
untouched. There must be three or four hundred company
houses in the squares and the streets that surround the
squares, like a great barracks wall. There must be sixty or
eighty company houses in the Breach. The old Dakins Row

will have thirty to forty little holes. Then counting the old
cottages and rows left with their old gardens down the lanes
and along the twitchells, and even in the midst of Nottingham Road itself there were houses enough for the popula-
60   tion, there was no need for much building. And not much
building went on when I was small.

We lived in the Breach, in a corner house. A field-path
came down under a great hawthorn hedge. On the other
side was the brook, with the old sheep-bridge going over
into the meadows. The hawthorn hedge by the brook had
grown tall as tall trees, and we used to bathe from there in
the dipping hole, where the sheep were dipped, just near the
fall from the old mill-dam, where the water rushed. The mill
only ceased grinding the local corn when I was a child. And
70   my father, who always worked in Brinsley pit, and who
always got up at five o'clock, if not at four, would set off in
the dawn across the fields at Coney Grey, and hunt for
mushrooms in the long grass, or perhaps pick up a skulking
rabbit, which he would bring home at evening inside the
lining of his pit-coat. . . .

The real tragedy of England, as I see it, is the tragedy of
ugliness. The country is so lovely: the man-made England
is so vile. I know that the ordinary collier, when I was a boy,
had a peculiar sense of beauty, coming from his intuitive and
80   instinctive consciousness which was awakened down pit.
And the fact that he met with just cold ugliness and raw
materialism when he came up into daylight, and particularly
when he came to the Square or the Breach, and to his own
table, killed something in him, and in a sense spoiled him as
a man. The woman almost invariably nagged about material
things. She was taught to do it; she was encouraged to do it.
It was a mother's business to see that her sons 'got on', and
it was the man's business to provide the money. In my
father's generation, with the old wild England behind them,
90   and the lack of education, the man was not beaten down.
But in my generation, the boys I went to school with,
colliers now, have all been beaten down, what with the din-
din-dinning of Board Schools, books, cinemas, clergymen,

the whole national and human consciousness hammering on the fact of material prosperity above all things.

The men are beaten down, there is prosperity for a time, in their defeat – and then disaster looms ahead. The root of all disaster is disheartenment. And men are disheartened. The men of England, the colliers in particular, are dis-
100 heartened. They have been betrayed and beaten.

Now though perhaps nobody knew it, it was ugliness which betrayed the spirit of man, in the nineteenth century. The great crime which the moneyed classes and promoters of industry committed in the palmy Victorian days was the condemning of the workers to ugliness, ugliness, ugliness: meanness and formless and ugly surroundings, ugly ideals, ugly religion, ugly hope, ugly love, ugly clothes, ugly furniture, ugly houses, ugly relationship between workers and employers. The human soul needs actual beauty even
110 more than bread. The middle classes jeer at the colliers for buying pianos – but what is the piano, often as not, but a blind reaching out for beauty? To the woman it is a possession and a piece of furniture and something to feel superior about. But see the elderly colliers trying to learn to play, see them listening with queer alert faces to their daughter's execution of *The Maiden's Prayer*, and you will see a blind, unsatisfied craving for beauty. It is far more deep in the men than in the women. The women want show. The men want beauty, and still want it.

120   If the company, instead of building those sordid and hideous Squares, then, when they had that lovely site to play with there on the hill top: if they had put a tall column in the middle of the small market-place, and run three parts of a circle of arcade round the pleasant space, where people could stroll or sit, and with the handsome houses behind. If they had made big, substantial houses, in apartments of five and six rooms and with handsome entrances. If above all, they had encouraged song and dancing – for the miners still sang and danced – and provided handsome space for these.
130 If only they had encouraged some form of beauty in dress, some form of beauty in interior life – furniture, decoration.

If they had given prizes for the handsomest chair or table, the loveliest scarf, the most charming room that the men or women could make. If only they had done this, there would never have been an industrial problem. The industrial problem arises from the base forcing of all human energy into a competition of mere acquisition. You may say the working man would not have accepted such a form of life: the Englishman's home is his castle, etc. etc. – 'my own little
140 home'. But if you can hear every word the next-door-people say, there's not much castle. And if you can see everybody in the square if they go to the w.c.! And if your one desire is to get out of the 'castle' and your 'own little home' – well, there's not much to be said for it. Anyhow it's only the woman who idolizes 'her own little home' – and it's always the woman at her worst, her most greedy, most possessive, most mean. There's nothing to be said for the 'little home' any more: a great scrabble of ugly pettiness over the face of the land.

150   As a matter of fact, till 1800 the English people were strictly a rural people – very rural. England has had towns for centuries, but they have never been real towns, only clusters of village streets. Never the real *urbs*. The English character has failed to develop the real *urban* side of a man, the civic side. Siena is a bit of a place, but it is a real city, with citizens intimately connected with the city. Nottingham is a vast place sprawling towards a million, and it is nothing more than an amorphous agglomeration. There *is* no Nottingham, in the sense that there is Siena. The English-
160 man is stupidly undeveloped, as a citizen. And it is partly due to his 'little home' stunt, and partly to his acceptance of hopeless paltriness in his surrounding. The new cities of America are much more genuine cities, in the Roman sense, than is London or Manchester. Edinburgh used to be more of a true city than any town England ever produced.

   That silly little individualism of 'the Englishman's home is his castle' and 'my own little home' is out of date. It would work almost up to 1800, when every Englishman was still a villager, and a cottager. But the industrial system

170 has brought a great change. The Englishman still likes to think of himself as a 'cottager' – 'my home, my garden'. But it is puerile. Even the farm labourer today is psychologically a town-bird. The English are town-birds through and through, to-day, as the inevitable result of their complete industrialisation. Yet they don't know how to build a city, how to think of one, or how to live in one. They are all suburban, pseudo-cottagy, and not one of them knows how to be truly urban – the citizens as the Romans were citizens – or the Athenians – or even the Parisians, till the war came.

180   And this is because we have frustrated that instinct of community which would make us unite in pride and dignity in the bigger gesture of the citizen, not the cottager. The great city means beauty, dignity, and a certain splendour. This is the side of the Englishman that has been thwarted and shockingly betrayed. England is a mean and petty scrabble of paltry dwellings called 'homes'. I believe in their heart of hearts all Englishmen loathe their little homes – but not the women. What we want is a bigger gesture, a greater scope, a certain splendour, a certain grandeur, and beauty,

190 big beauty. The American does far better than we, in this.

    And the promoter of industry, a hundred years ago, dared to perpetrate the ugliness of my native village. And still more monstrous, promoters of industry to-day are scrabbling over the face of England with miles and square miles of red-brick 'homes', like horrible scabs. And the men inside these little red rat-traps get more and more helpless, being more and more humiliated, more and more dissatisfied, like trapped rats. Only the meaner sort of women go on loving the little home which is no more than a rat-trap

200 to her man.

    Do away with it all, then. At no matter what cost, start in to alter it. Never mind about wages and industrial squabbling. Turn the attention elsewhere. Pull down my native village to the last brick. Plan a nucleus. Fix the focus. Make a handsome gesture of radiation from the focus. And then put up big buildings, handsome, that sweep to a civic centre. And furnish them with beauty. And make an

absolute clean start. Do it place by place. Make a new
England. Away with little homes. Away with scrabbling
210 pettiness and paltriness. Look at the contours of the land,
and build up from these, with a sufficient nobility. The
English may be mentally or spiritually developed. But as
citizens of splendid cities they are more ignominious than
rabbits. And they nag, nag, nag all the time about politics
and wages and all that like mean narrow housewives.

63 H. V. MORTON
'What I Saw in the Slums'

From Labour Party pamphlet (1933)

For a biographical note on Morton, see p.81.

I took one glance at Leeds and felt like bolting in terror
from the place. Reformers of this town who are interested
in slum problems have my deepest sympathy.

Where are they to begin? If you gave them all the gold
reserves in the Bank of England, I can still imagine them
standing in an hypnotic trance for years. The magnitude of
the problem is terrifying because, to be quite frank, the
whole of Leeds should be scrapped and rebuilt.

It is as archaic as Stephenson's 'Rocket', to which period
10   it belongs. When a man looks at Leeds he realises what a
blessing a really big fire can be to a city. The Fire of London,
which history books call 'a terrible disaster', was one of the
finest things that ever happened to the Metropolis.

It was a huge accidental slum clearance. It came just after
the Great Plague, when the huddled streets of the old city
were like bits of modern Liverpool! The fire swept them all
away, with their filth and their disease.

The 'most horrid, malicious, bloody flame' – a chronicler
of the time described it – did more in a few hours than all
20   the Parliaments ever elected could have done.

Four hundred streets, 13,200 houses, eighty-nine churches and all the public buildings went up in a glorious
bonfire, while Charles II and the Duke of York tried to stop

the good work by blowing up houses with gunpowder.

One looks at Leeds and thinks with envy of this lovely fire!

The problem of Leeds is the problem of the back-to-backs. This revolting type of house has dominated the architectural history of Leeds. Long after other cities were 30 ashamed of it, Leeds continued to build it, so that you have regular vintage years of back-to-backs.

They are not scattered timidly about the place as in Birmingham, Liverpool and Manchester. Leeds is a town of back-to-backs.

For the benefit of those lucky enough not to understand what I mean, I must explain that the back-to-back system was invented in the bad old days with the object of packing the population on a principle since adopted by sardine salesmen.

40 Imagine that two rows of normal houses whose back gardens meet become telescoped so that the gardens disappear, and you have, rather roughly, the back-to-back.

There is no through draught in these houses. The long rows face each other bleakly across a few yards of paved street.

The conveniences, known vaguely but politely to house-agents as 'usual offices', are crammed away in odd corners of the rows; dustbins are openings in a wall not far from the living room window, and the lavatories are in a side 50 passage.

But these are good back-to-backs. The older ones are built in rows of eight with 'usual offices' erected in a small space between each block.

In 1920 there were 72,000 of these awful houses in Leeds, and only 12,000 were given a fairly clean bill of health by the Coalition Government's Unhealthy Areas Committee.

So you can imagine what Leeds is like.

At the present moment, Leeds has gazed with horror at itself and formulated a five-year plan which hopes to pull 60 down 400 back-to-backs a year. So that if Leeds sticks nobly to its resolve the town should begin to look a little more healthy in about 180 years.

It is estimated that about 350,000 of our unfortunate fellow countrymen are at the moment living in Leeds in the squalor of the 19th century.

The worst back-to-backs number about 33,000. Even the Coalition report said that 'it is difficult to suggest any method of dealing with them satisfactorily short of complete clearance'.

70 They stand seventy and eighty to the acre! The jerry builders of a century ago used rotten brick. They also forgot a damp course! They knew or cared nothing for the fresh air.

The average two-room back-to-back was a superficial area of 350 feet compared with the minimum of 620 feet ordained by the 1930 Act. In a word, Leeds is the creation of the big commercial booms of the 19th century, when no one cared for anything but profit and exploitation. It is a nasty, dirty old money box.

80 If any public man of Ancient Greece or Rome – empires which made no bones about slavery – could see Leeds he would simply refuse to believe it. He would fling his toga over his head and cry:

'Oh, that I should have witnessed the evidence of such selfishness.' For the ancients, even if they did sometimes feed their mullet with slaves, were very proud of their cities.

I hope you are grateful to me for sparing you miserable glimpses into the interior of these slums. I could tell the
90 same dreary story of poverty and overcrowding. I could describe the same overworked women longing for, but quite hopeless about, a decent place in which to bring up the children.

But I must say this about Leeds. Its slums are the cleanest I have seen. A perfect passion for cleanliness obsesses the women of Leeds. They scrub the back-to-backs until I marvel that there is anything left of them.

Thousands of horrid doorsteps, worn as thin as wafers in the centre, are whitened or raddled. Every time a door
100 opens you see a woman cleaning something.

What wasted energy it is! If one could only wave a wand and give these earnest housewives something worth the cleaning!

It is interesting, but part of the general tragedy of our housing problem, that 33 per cent of the members of the building trade in Leeds are unemployed. These men who should all be working overtime are drawing State relief! The yards are full of bricks, the sheds are full of timber, and a town whose houses have outlived their function waits to be
110 remade.

'And unless we are very careful', said a building trades expert, 'we shall soon see something almost worse than demolition. I mean the building of the slums of to-morrow. If the Government finances the building societies we shall get the jerry builder at work. Lack of capital has kept him out. Finance him and we have the old cut-throat race of the speculator.

'We shall be building down to price and not up to standard. In other words, we shall be repeating in 1933 the
120 history of 1833 and piling up exactly the same problems for the people of 2033.'

As I left Leeds I felt that my impression of the place has been perfectly expressed by Omar Khayyam: –

> O love. Could'st thou and I with Fate conspire
> To wreck this sorry scheme of things entire,
> Might not we shatter it to bits and then
> Re-mould it nearer to the heart's desire.

64 H. V. MORTON
'Wigan'

From *In Search of England* (1927)

For a biographical note on Morton, see p.81.

Wigan, were it not inhabited by a race of sturdy and rather tough Lancashire folk, would be the most self-conscious town in England. For years it has suffered from a joke. The words 'Wigan Pier' spoken by a comedian on a music-hall stage are sufficient to make an audience howl with laughter, and the ease with which the name works on the sensibilities of an audience is probably, in some measure, responsible for the great success of this joke.

10   Wigan, to millions of people who have never seen and never will see the town, represents the apex of the world's pyramid of gloom. So serious has the Wigan joke become that the go-ahead Corporation, who are full of local pride, take what steps they can to counteract it; but the silly old joke goes on! Certain Wigonians of high commercial standing believe that this joke delays the prosperity of Wigan, which not only affords rich sites for new factories, but also offers all the necessary conditions for manufacture, such as good transport, labour, and coal, so to speak, laid on in normal times.

20   Now, I had been in Wigan just ten minutes when I saw that there is no joke! Wigan is a spa compared with towns like Wednesbury, in the Black Country, and with certain of the Staffordshire pottery towns. I admit frankly that I, too, shared the common idea of Wigan. I admit that I came here to write an impression of unrelieved gloom – of dreary streets and stagnant canals and white-faced Wigonians dragging their weary steps along dull streets haunted by the horror of the place in which they are condemned to live.

This is nonsense. I would not mind spending a holiday in

30   Wigan – a short one.

'This town has been badly libelled,' I said to a man who was standing in the main street.

'I'm reet glad to hear thee say that!' he cried warmly. 'I've lived in Wigan all my life, and wish for no better town.'

He beamed on me. He offered to show me the chief glories of Wigan. I told him that I wanted to find them for myself. Still he beamed on me! They all do this in Wigan if you go up and say frankly that the town has a certain attraction.

40   Wigan's swift reaction to praise is rather pathetic.

Now, when you enter Wigan expecting the worst, it is

254

surprising to find a place which still bears all the signs of an old-fashioned country town. Its wide main street meanders down a hill in a casual, leisurely way. Along this street are many modern half-timbered buildings. The Corporation of Wigan has made a rule that buildings on the main streets must be rebuilt in the Tudor style, so that in twenty years or so there will not be a more original or better-looking manufacturing town in the north of England.

50   During an hour's walk round Wigan I discovered many things. Wigan was made by the Romans. They called it Coccium, which I think, is a much funnier name. Perhaps the Legions went into fits of laughter when any one said 'Coccium' in Roman Britain! All that remains of Coccium is a Roman altar, which I found built into the north window bay of the tower of the fine but much-restored fourteenth century church.

King Arthur knew Wigan! It is famed as the scene of some of his most glorious exploits.

60   Beyond the Market Square I entered a park of about thirty acres. In it were Italian gardens and an ornamental lake. In slandered Wigan I found one of the few good war memorials I have seen in England, and also the largest open market-place outside Nottingham.

But no one could tell me the meaning of the word Wigan. So I went to the Town Clerk.

'The derivation is obscure,' he said. 'It is Saxon, of course, for we are very old. The Wigan motto is "Ancient and Loyal", you know. I believe that the word Wigan means

70 "the rowan trees near the Church".'

'And this,' I said, 'is the name that rocks a thousand stalls!'

'Yes,' he replied, 'the Wigan joke has gone too far. It is surprising what a joke can do to a town. It can spread an entirely false idea. Now just let me take you to the outskirts of Wigan, and you will agree that few manufacturing towns are surrounded by such rustic scenery...'

We went round Wigan. Before we had left the town we smelt hay. Wigan is surrounded by fields which rise on the

80   north towards Duxberry Hall, the only American pilgrimage in this part of the world, where the doughty Miles Standish was probably born. On the main road we came to the scene of Wigan's most cherished legend: a rough stone cross.

'That,' explained the Town Clerk, 'is Mabs Cross. It is mentioned in Walter Scott's *The Betrothed*. The story is that while Sir William Bradshaigh, a knight of Wigan, was away on the Crusades his wife Mabel, believing him to have been killed, married a Welsh knight. Sir William came home

90   suddenly, discovered what had happened, and killed the Welsh knight, for which he was outlawed for one year. His wife Mabel was publicly shamed. Her confessor imposed this penalty: that once every week she must walk, bare legged and barefoot to Mabs Cross. I believe it all ended happily, and that husband and wife came together again!'

Within five minutes of notorious Wigan we were in the depth of the country. On either side were fields in which men were making hay; old bridges spanned streams; there were high hedges, delicious little woods, and valleys.

'This is all Wigan!' said the Town Clerk with a smile.

APPENDIX

SUGGESTED ACTIVITIES AND FURTHER READING

In compiling this book we have assumed that it will be used in a number of teaching contexts. Though its chapters and sections on particular topics can be readily slotted into existing courses on the period's literary, cultural or social history, we use it as a course reader on a first-year cultural and critical studies course on national identity, supplementing the extracts by work on period texts and other media and by appropriate field trips. We have written the introductory material with a student audience in mind and have selected further reading which is both accessible and reliable in its coverage of debates.

Parts of this book have been incorporated in other teaching contexts. For example, material from chapter 4, Culture and Englishness, has been used in literature teaching to deepen students' understanding of the reception of modernist fiction. Other sections might be used to con-textualise First World War poetry; to provide a context for the re-evaluation of the use of the discourse of rurality in the work of E. M. Forster and D. H. Lawrence; or to broaden students' engagement with the class politics of many Edwardian fictions. In history and women's studies courses we have used material featured here as the focus for seminars on domesticity and on housing, for work on perceptions of suburbia and for work on mass culture.

In compiling the book we envisaged that the chapter 1, The Ideas and Ideals of Englishness, would be a point of departure for work on national identity. To this end we purposely included a series of short accounts which can be engaged with as assertions about and perspectives on national characteristics that students can test against their own sense of the constitutive factors of national identity. Debates generated by this material can be used to open up the subject to students and allow a sense of ownership and involvement in the topic to emerge. This chapter also includes some more substantial pieces which make a good basis for small-group discussions and provide material which can be used to generate a set of (in part competing) accounts of Englishness. These can then be tested and re-evaluated in the context of the slightly narrower debates which are focused upon in the remaining chapters.

Each chapter is prefaced by a short introduction to the debates in the area and to the pieces we have included. As we hope that this book will be used as a teaching text we felt it might be helpful if we included in this appendix a few suggestions for further discussion and related seminar work. Clearly there are many more ways in which this book might be used than those suggested by our own questions and suggestions for further work. Questions and topics vary in complexity and scope – some being suitable for small-group work, some for whole-group discussions, some as small-scale independent learning projects, and others simply as guides or goads to further study. We have purposely offered more questions on the first chapter as we envisaged this as providing the foundation for later work.

We also include in this appendix a number of suggestions for further reading, often of quite short pieces, which allow students to pursue debates and interests for themselves.

In the lists of further reading, the place of publication is London unless otherwise stated. Where two dates are given, the first is the text's original publication date, the second the date of publication of the edition we have used.

1 THE IDEAS AND IDEALS OF ENGLISHNESS

Activities

1 In the first extract from *Howards End* E. M. Forster describes a specific landscape. Which aspects are perceived by him as representative of England and why? Can you identify other examples of the use of landscape in any of the extracts? In what ways are these examples similar to or dissimilar from Forster's?
2 Arnold Bennett suggests that there are certain personality characteristics which are specifically English. What are they? Do any of the other writers in this chapter consider Englishness as a form of

personality, and how does this echo or question Bennett's formulation?

3 Do the views expressed in these extracts seem representative or are there significant omissions? For example, all but one of the writers cited are male. How do women feature in the versions of Englishness offered? Equally, how are different social classes or races featured?

4 Note any references or allusions to England's past or to English literature and culture in the past. Do common themes emerge?

5 Find out more about the lives and beliefs of one or more of the following writers, and the historical events at the time they were writing: E. M. Forster; Ford Madox Ford; Arnold Bennett; Wyndham Lewis; D. H. Lawrence; W. H. Davies; T. S. Eliot. Are there any connections between each writer's life, the historical moment and the form and content of his writing?

6 Which aspects of English life and culture seem cause for concern and what kind of solutions are offered?

7 Find out more about the conflicts and anxieties of the Edwardian period (1900–1914) and consider how these relate to the concerns expressed by C. F. G. Masterman. You might also consider E. M. Forster's *Howards End* in this context. How and why do these writers construct a discourse around ideas of 'England' and 'Englishness'?

8 Ernest Barker edited *The Character of England* in 1947. Find out more about the immediate post-war period. Are there any ways in which Barker reworks or reuses images or ideas from either C. F. G. Masterman or Ford Madox Ford? Do certain ideas about the English 'character' tend to recur?

9 Taking Phillip Gibbs's essay as a starting point, find out more about the role of radio broadcasting in the transmission of national ideals. You might also explore other media of the period: documentary films such as *Night Mail* (1936) and commercial films such as *South Riding* (1938), *The Thirty-Nine Steps* (1935) and *Love on the Dole* (1940), which promote versions of England that focus on social cohesiveness; and David Lean's *Brief Encounter* (1945), made at the end of the Second World War, which valorises English reticence and restraint.

10 Reference to the 'Englishman' is pervasive in all these extracts but England itself is frequently referred to by use of the female pronoun. Identify examples of this and consider the effect on (a) the reader's concept of England and English character; (b) the versions of masculinity and femininity offered in the various extracts; and (c) the male or female reader of the period, and the male or female reader of the 1990s.

11 Consider carefully who is being addressed by the various articles. Do the writers address themselves to a like-minded readership, and what might this be? Do they set out to challenge preconceptions of a certain group in society? What is the tone; how are readers addressed? Are certain reading positions suppressed or excluded? For example, how might Irish, Scottish or Welsh readers read these texts; are working class and female readers included amongst those addressed?

Selected further reading

Anderson, Benedict (1983) *Imagined Communities* (Verso)

Bennett, Arnold (1908/1983) *The Old Wives' Tale* (Harmondsworth, Penguin)

Briggs, Asa (1961) *The History of Broadcasting in the United Kingdom*

Colls, R. and Dodds, P. (1986) *Englishness: Politics and Culture: 1880–1920* (Croom Helm)

Curran, J. and Porter, V. (eds) (1983) *British Cinema History* (Weidenfeld & Nicolson)

Eliot, T. S. (1948) *Notes Towards the Definition of Culture* (Faber)

Forster, E. M. (1910/1985) *Howards End* (Harmondsworth, Penguin)

Hobsbawm, E. J. (1990) *Nations and Nationalism since 1780*, esp. chapter 5 (Canto)

Light, Alison (1991) *Forever England: Femininity, Literature and Conservatism between the Wars*, Introduction/Afterword (Routledge)

Porter, Roy (ed.) (1992) *Myths of the English* (Cambridge, Polity)

Samuel, Raphael (ed.) (1989) *Patriotism: The Making and Unmaking of British National Identity: Volume 1: History and Politics, Volume 2: Minorities and Outsiders, Volume 3: National Fictions* (Routledge)

Smith, Anthony (1991) *National Identity* (Harmondsworth, Penguin)

Stevenson, John (1984) *British Society 1914–1945* (Harmondsworth, Penguin)

Wiener, M. (1981) *English Culture and the Decline of the Industrial Spirit* (Cambridge University Press)

2 VERSIONS OF RURAL ENGLAND

Activities

1 Read through the extracts by J. B. Priestley, H. V. Morton and Stanley Baldwin: identify what the key features of English identity are for each writer.

2 Compare and contrast Edward Thomas's and H. V. Morton's accounts of tramps, paying particular attention to the use of language and mode of characterisation.

   (a) In each case ask yourself: are the tramps in any way threatening or perceived as dangerous by the writer?

   (b) Find some coverage of modern travellers (CD-ROMs of back issues of *The Times* and the *Guardian* are accessible sources): compare and contrast the attitudes of your contemporary sources with those of Thomas and Edmund Blunden.

3 Consider how the discourse of pastoralism and the evocation of rural England is used today – in the marketing of Laura Ashley, in home-furnishing catalogues, in the marketing of Winnie-the-Pooh products, in films like *Maurice* and *Howards End*, in tourist board advertising, etc.

4 Examine the language used to describe the relationship between

people and their environment: is the human presence part of the natural world or disruptive of it? You might like to compare Edward Thomas's account of 'The Village' with H. V. Morton's description of rural England.

5 Compare the retrospective accounts of the individuals interviewed by Paul Thompson (see Selected further reading below) with those on offer here: what similarities and differences emerge in the perspective on rural England? How do you account for these?

6 Compare a period evocation of England in fiction of the period (e.g. the extracts from E. M. Forster's *Howards End* reprinted in chapter 1) with those featured here: how far does the fiction deploy rural England to construct a version of national identity?

Selected further reading

Period accounts

The *Batsford* guides, Methuen's *Companion* series on the English counties and Arthur Mee's *King's England* series are widely available in libraries and could be used to provide access to period material on your own county. Other texts worth examining for an overview include: C. Bradley-Ford *et al.* (1935) *The Legacy of England: An Illustrated Survey of the Works of Man in the English Country* (Batsford); H. J. Massingham, H. E. Bates, H. Batsford *et al.* (1939) *The English Countryside: A Survey of its Chief Features* (Batsford); and J. B. Priestley (ed.) (1939) *Our Nation's Heritage* (Dent).

Generally available accounts of rural England which might be suitable as the basis for case studies include Edward Thomas's 1932 account of *The South Country* (1982, Dent), and the works of Mary Webb, of which her 1924 *Precious Bane* (Cape) is perhaps the best known. These are alternatives to the more familiar evocations to be found in Flora Thompson's *Lark Rise* (1939), *Over to Candleford* (1941) and *Candleford Green* (1943) (all Oxford University Press; published by OUP in 1945 in one volume as *Lark Rise to Candleford*).

Modern accounts

Rural England has received extensive coverage in literary and historical works on the period. The following are offered as useful starting points for further reading. They are generally short enough to be used for teaching purposes as suggested, reading in conjunction with the material in this chapter.

Crowther, M. A. (1992) 'The Tramp', in Roy Porter (ed.) *Myths of the English* (Cambridge, Polity), pp.91–113

Howkins, Alun (1986) 'The Discovery of Rural England', in R. Colls and P. Dodds (eds) *Englishness: Politics and Culture 1880–1920* (Croom Helm), pp.62–88

Thompson, Paul (1977) *The Edwardians: The Re-Making of British Society* (Harmondsworth, Penguin): chapter 3, 'Country and Town', pp. 43–56; chapter 8, 'The Borderline: Peter Henry' (Shetland Crofting Family), pp.115–121; chapter 10, 'Working Class: The Semi-Skilled: Fred Mills' (a labourer), pp.149–156

Williams, Raymond (1973) *The Country and the City* (Paladin), especially chapter 1

3 WAR AND NATIONAL IDENTITY

Activities

1 Explore further the ways in which First World War poetry challenged or reinforced the patriotic ideals represented so explicitly in the Ernest Raymond extract.

2 Find out more about public schools in the early twentieth century and the kinds of ideals and education they offered. Consider the role of the public school in constructing certain versions of national identity.

3 Explore attitudes to the First World War in the 1920s and 1930s. Try to link the changing climate of opinion about the war and imperialism to ideas about England and Englishness.

4 Taking Virginia Woolf's ideas on the relationship between women and national identity, find out how women responded to the First World War and, later, to the Second World War. Are there differences which can be explained by reference to gender?

5 Consider the ways in which left-wing writers and commentators attempted to capture a form of Englishness which was socially inclusive in 1940, and think about how and why this combined so successfully with Churchillian nationalism.

6 Look, if you can, at some of the films mentioned and consider how they construct versions of Englishness.

7 During the Falklands War of 1982 the *Sun* attempted to appropriate Churchillian rhetoric for the Conservative government with headlines like 'Our Darkest Hour'. Consider the ways in which 1940 has become a cultural myth expressing certain specifically national values which have since been lost. Think about how 1940 can be read from both a right-wing, nationalist position and from a left-wing, social democratic position. Which elements would each position articulate if attempting to evoke the spirit of 1940 today?

Selected further reading

Brittain, Vera (1933) *Testament of Youth* (Gollancz)

Bushaway, Bob 'Name Upon Name: The Great War and Remembrance', in Roy Porter (ed.) (1992) *Myths of the English* (Cambridge, Polity), pp.136–167

Calder, Angus (1969/71) *The People's War: Britain 1939–1945* (Panther)

Fussell, P. (1977) *The Great War and Modern Memory* (Oxford University Press)

APPENDIX

Higonnet, M. R., et al. (eds.) (1987) *Behind the Lines: Gender and the Two World Wars* (New Haven, Conn., Yale University Press)

Mangan, J. A. (1981) *Athleticism in the Victorian and Edwardian Public School: The Emergence and Consolidation of an Ideology* (Cambridge University Press)

Samuel, R. (ed.) (1989) *Patriotism: The Making and Unmaking of British National Identity: Volume 1: History and Politics, Volume 2: Minorities and Outsiders, Volume 3: National Fictions* (Routledge)

Wright, D. G. (1978) 'The Great War, Government Propaganda and English "Men of Letters": 1914–1916', *Literature and History*, 4, no. 7 (Spring), pp.70–100

4 CULTURE AND ENGLISHNESS

Activities

1 Find out about the English Association and the development of English studies. How is the former reflected in the Newbolt Report? (See Baldick 1983, Doyle 1982 and 1986, or Palmer 1965.) How do the experiences of women and working-class people square with the aims for adult education set out by the Report (see material from Rowbottom 1983 and Howarth and Curthoys 1987) in the extracts featured here?

2 Read a modernist short story, such as Katherine Mansfield's 'The Wind Blows'(Mansfield 1920/1962): how far is it comparable with Pont's satire of the genre? What were the characteristic features of the modernist short story? (See Head 1992.)

3 Find out about Bloomsbury (see material in Bell 1968 or Edel 1979): how far does Frank Swinnerton paint an accurate picture? You might also like to consider how far E. M. Forster's Schlegel sisters (in *Howards End*) – share the patronising attitudes to the lower classes ascribed by Swinnerton to Bloomsbury: how far is *Howards End* a satire of Bloomsbury and how far a celebration?

4 Find pictures by Steer or by Brabazon and compare them with works by Monet or Pissarro: can you find any evidence to support or reject James Bone's accusation that the British painting is merely decorative and lacks ideas? (See material in Flint 1984 and Bullen 1988 for period reactions; see Tillyard 1988 and Farr 1978 for overviews.)

5 Explore further the debates about mass culture which generated so much concern in the period. (See Hoggart's retrospective account of the 1930s in Hoggart 1958.)

6 Examine the extracts from George Orwell and Pearl Jephcott and try to identify the ways in which ideologies of gender are functioning.

Selected further reading

Functions for English

Baldick, Chris (1983) *The Social Mission of English Criticism: 1848–1932* (Oxford University Press)

Doyle, Brian (1989) *English and Englishness* (Routledge) (See in particular chapter 1, 'English Literature and Cultural Identities', pp.17–40.)

Howarth, Janet and Curthoys, Mark (1987) 'The Political Economy of Women's Higher Education in Late Nineteenth and Early Twentieth Century Britain', *Historical Research*, 60, no. 142 (June), pp.208–231

Palmer, D. J. (1965) *The Rise of English Studies* (Oxford University Press)

Rowbottom, Sheila (1983) 'Travellers in a Strange Country: Responses of Working-Class students to the University Extension Movement: 1873–1910', in *Dreams and Dilemmas: Collected Writings* (Virago), pp.267–305

Soffer, Reba N. (1987) 'The Modern University and National Values 1850–1930', *Historical Research*, 60, no. 142 (June), pp.166–187

Reactions to cultural change

Bell, Quentin (1968) *Bloomsbury* (Hogarth)

Bloom, Clive (ed.) (1993) *Literature and Culture in Modern Britain: 1900–1929* (Longman)

Bullen, J. B. (1988) *Post-Impressionists in England* (Routledge)

Edel, Leon (1979) *Bloomsbury: A House of Lions* (Harmondsworth, Penguin)

Farr, Dennis (1978) *English Art: 1870–1940* (Oxford, Clarendon)

Flint, Kate (1984) *Impressionists in England* (Routledge)

Head, Dominic (1992) *The Modernist Short Story* (Cambridge University Press)

Tillyard, Stella (1988) *The Impact of Modernism: The Visual Arts in England* (Routledge)

Sport

McKibbin, Ross (1990) 'Work and Hobbies in Britain: 1880–1950', in *The Ideologies of Class: Social Relations in Britain 1880–1950* (Oxford University Press), pp.139–166

Mangan, J. A. (1981) *Athleticism in the Victorian and Edwardian Public School: The Emergence and Consolidation of an Ideology* (Cambridge University Press)

Mason, Tony (1980) *Association Football and English Society: 1863–1915* (Brighton, Harvester)

Popular culture and everyday life

Barker, Martin (1989) *Comics: Ideology: Power and the Critics* (Manchester University Press)

Bourke, Joanna (1993) *Working Class Cultures in Britain: 1890–1960* (Routledge)

Briggs, Asa (1972) *Mass Entertainment: The Origins of a Modern Industry* (Oxford University Press)

Cockburn, C. (1972) *Bestseller: The Books that Everyone Read 1900–1940* (Sidgwick & Jackson)

Cross, Gary (1990) *Worktowners at Blackpool* (Routledge)

Sabin, Roger (1993) *Adult Comics: An Introduction* (Routledge)

Willis, Susan (1991) *A Primer for Daily Life* (Routledge)

5 DOMESTIC AND URBAN ENGLANDS

Activities

1   Find out more about the Garden City Movement and consider how it embodied ideals about English landscape and rural life.

2   Think about the links between citizenship and home ownership. To what extent is the idea of belonging to society tied to ownership of property? How has this been embodied in civil and political emancipation? Were certain groups excluded from citizenship in the past and how was the idea of home used as a means by which such groups might be incorporated?

3   Explore the idea of England as 'the homeland'. To whom might this concept appeal, how was it orchestrated and what have been the effects?

4   Compare Lord Kennet's Muddleford with the other towns featured in this chapter: what features distinguish the towns? What features do they have in common. Can you identify regional differences?

5   Identify and discuss the operation of the following oppositions in the pieces featured in this chapter: past–present; rural–urban; Roman/ Italian–English.

6   Compare D. H. Lawrence's view of Eastwood with his fictional perspectives on the mining community in *Sons and Lovers* or *Women in Love*.

7   For D. H. Lawrence the urban English are 'like mean narrow house-wives': for Dr Stephen Taylor 'The Englishman's home is still his castle, but for the Englishwoman too often her gaol.' Critically evaluate the tension between masculinity and femininity in these two extracts.

Selected further reading

The Homes of England

Beddoe, Deirdre (1989) *Back to Home and Duty: Women between the Wars: 1918–1939* (Virago)

Burnett, John (1973) *A Social History of Housing* (Newton Abbot, David & Charles)

Giles, Judy (1995) *Women: Identity and Private Life: 1900–1950* (Macmillan)

Oliver, P., Davis, I. and Bentley, I. (1981) *Dunroamin': The Suburban Semi and its Enemies* (Barry & Jenkins)

Service, A. (1977) *Edwardian Architecture: A Handbook to Building Design in Britain 1890–1914* (Thames & Hudson)

Swenarton, M. (1981) *Homes Fit For Heroes: The Politics and Architecture of Early State Housing in Britain* (Heinemann)

The Modernist City

Accessible coverage of the significance of the city for modernism is to be found in the following works. These will helpfully disrupt the predominantly negative sense of the city likely to be gleaned from the extracts featured in this section.

Bradbury, Malcolm and MacFarlane, James (eds) (1976) *Modernism: 1890–1930* (Harmondsworth, Penguin). Chapter 3, 'The Geography of Modernism', offers full coverage

Butler, Christopher (1994) *Early Modernism: Literature, Music and Painting in Europe: 1900–1916* (Cambridge University Press). Excellent chapter on 'The City'

Williams, Raymond (1989) 'Metropolitan Perceptions and the Emergence of the Avant Garde', in *The Politics of Modernism* ed. T. Pinkney (Verso)

BIBLIOGRAPHY

Place of publication is London unless otherwise stated. Where two dates are given, the first is the text's original publication date, the second the date of publication of the edition we have used.

Primary sources

Baldwin, Stanley (1926) *On England* (Phillip Allan), pp.1–9

Barker, Ernest (1947) 'An Attempt at Perspective', in Ernest Barker (ed.) *The Character of England* (Oxford, Clarendon), pp.563–570

Bennett, Arnold (1908/1983) *The Old Wives' Tale* (Harmondsworth, Penguin), p.512

Birmingham Mail (1931) Correspondence, 20 July p.163, 22 July p.168, 23 July p.169, 24 July pp.162–170

Blunden, Edward (1932) *The Face of England*, in J. B. Priestley (ed.) (1939) *Our Nation's Heritage* (Dent), pp.122–126

Bone, James (1913/1988) 'The Tendencies of Modern Art', *Edinburgh Review*, April 1913, pp.420–434; reprinted in J. B. Bullen (ed.) (1988) *Post-Impressionists in England* (Routledge), pp.433–447

Brooke, Rupert (1915) *1914 and Other Poems* (Sidgwick & Jackson), **28** pp.15, 59–63

Buchan, John (1915/1993) *The Thirty-Nine Steps* (Ware, Herts., Wordsworth Editions), pp.108–109

Calder, A. and Sheridan, D. (eds) (1984) *Speak for Yourself: A Mass Observation Anthology: 1937–49* (Cape), pp.113–114

Cardus, Neville (1931) *Good Days* (Cape), pp.80–93

Churchill, Randolph S. (ed.) (1941) *Into Battle: War Speeches by Right Hon. Winston S. Churchill* (Cassell), p p.208, 222–223

Davies, W. H. (1939), in J. B. Priestley (ed.) *Our Nation's Heritage* (Dent), p.150

du Maurier, Daphne (1938) *Rebecca* (Gollancz), pp.8–12

Eade, Charles (ed.) (1945) *Victory: War Speeches by Right Hon. Winston S. Churchill* (Cassell), pp.129, 139–141

Eliot, T. S. (1948) *Notes Towards the Definition of Culture* (Faber), p.51

Ford, Ford Madox (1907) *The Spirit of the People*, in Sondra J. Stang (ed.) (1986) *The Ford Madox Ford Reader* (Carcanet), pp.293–298. Original source: Ford Madox Hueffer (1907) *England and the English* (New York, McClure Phillips), pp.334–341

Forster, E. M. (1910/1985) *Howards End* (Harmondsworth, Penguin), pp.170–171, 362–363

—— (1983) *Selected Letters of E. M. Forster: Volume 1: 1879–1920* eds Mary Lago and P. N. Furbank (Collins), pp.253–254

Gibbs, Phillip (1935) *England Speaks* (Heinemann), pp.3–4, 23–36

Holtby, Winifred (1937) *Letters to a Friend*, eds Alice Holtby and Jean McWilliam (Collins), pp.34–35

Howard, Ebenezer (1902/1946) *Garden Cities of Tomorrow* (Faber), chapter 12 'Social Cities', pp.142–150

Jephcott, Pearl (1943) *Girls Growing Up* (Faber), chapter 5 'Leisure', pp.98–111

Kennett, Lord (1947) 'Town Life in England', in Ernest Barker (ed.) *The Character of England* (Oxford, Clarendon), chapter 21, pp.434–441

Lancaster, Osbert (1936) *Progress at Pelvis Bay* (John Murray), chapter 7 'Domestic Architecture and Housing', pp.46–49

Laver, James (1947) 'Homes and Habits', in Ernest Barker (ed.) *The Character of England* (Oxford, Clarendon), chapter 23, pp.462, 479–480

Lawrence, D. H. (1930/1971) 'Nottingham and the Mining Country', *New Adelphi* (June–August 1930), reprinted in *A Selection from Phoenix*, ed. A. A. H. Inglis (Harmondsworth, Penguin), pp.103–111

—— (1932/1981) *The Letters of D. H. Lawrence*, ed. G. Zytaruk and J. T. Boulton (Cambridge University Press), pp.46–47, 431–432

Lewis, Wyndham (1939/1991) *The Hitler Cult*, in *The Essential Wyndham Lewis*, ed. Julian Symons (Vintage), pp.127–130

Masterman, C. F. G. (1909) *The Condition of England* (Methuen), chapter 1 'The Spirit of the People', pp.1–18

Mee, Arthur (ed.) (no date) 'Ourselves and the Nation', *The Children's Encyclopaedia* (Educational Book Company Ltd) vol. 9, chapter 52, pp.6373–6376

Ministry of Information (1940/1982) *Documentary Newsletter*, pp.5–7, reprinted in Open University A309: *Documents 1918–1970* (Milton Keynes, Open University Press)

Morrison, Herbert (1943) *Looking Ahead: Wartime Speeches by the Right Hon. Herbert Morrison* (Hodder & Stoughton), pp.11–13

Morton, H. V. (1927) *In Search of England* (Methuen), pp.vii–xi, pp.187–190, 234–236

—— (1933) *What I Saw in the Slums*, article reprinted from the *Daily Herald*, in Labour Party Pamphlet VII, 'A City of "Back to Backs"'

Newbolt Committee (1921) *The Teaching of English in England: Being the report of the Departmental Committee appointed by the President of the Board of Education to inquire into the position of English in the Educational System of England* (HMSO), Introduction, pp.21–23, chapter 8, pp.252–260

Orwell, George (1947/1968) 'Boys' Weeklies', in *The Collected Letters, Essays and Journalism of George Orwell: Volume I: An Age Like This: 1920–1940* (Secker & Warburg), pp.460–485

Pont (1938/1988) *The British Character: Studied and Revealed by Pont* (Salisbury, Element Books), chapter 5 'Domestic', p.58

Priestley, J. B. (1934) *English Journey* (Heinemann), pp.114–115, 179–186, 265–268, 389–390, 397–406

Priestley, J. B. (1968) *All England Listened: The Wartime Broadcasts of J. B. Priestley* (New York, Chilmark Press), pp.51–58

Raymond, Ernest (1922) *Tell England: A Study in a Generation* (Cassell), pp.318–320

Robertson-Scott, J. W. (1925) *England's Green and Pleasant Land: The Truth Attempted* (Harmondsworth, Penguin), chapter 25 'What the Awakened Parson Saw', pp.153–158

Sackville-West, Vita (1947) 'The Outdoor Life', in Ernest Barker (ed.) *The Character of England*, chapter 20, pp.410–411

Sassoon, Siegfried (1962) 'Memorial Tablet' in *Georgian Poetry*, ed. J. Reeves (Harmondsworth, Penguin)

Sheridan, D. (ed.) (1990) *Wartime Women* (Mandarin), pp.232–234

Struther, Jan (1939/1989) *Mrs Miniver* (Virago), pp.115–116, 122–123

Swinnerton, Frank (1935/1938) *The Georgian Literary Scene: A Panorama* (revised edition) (Hutchinson), chapter 13 'Bloomsbury', pp.353–358

Taylor, Stephen (1938) 'The Suburban Neurosis', *Lancet*, 26 March, pp.759–761

Thomas, Edward (1906) *The Heart of England* (Dent), pp.102–115

—— (1981) *The Collected Poems of Edward Thomas*, ed. R. G. Thomas (Oxford University Press), pp.325–327

Thomas, J. H. (1920) *When Labour Rules* (Jonathan Cape), pp.20–21

Woolf, Virginia (1938/1991) *Three Guineas* (Hogarth), pp.122–126

Other period sources

This lists those works which space did not permit us to include and those which we have found helpful in teaching contexts.

Bell, Clive (1928) *Civilisation* (Harmondsworth, Penguin)

Bradley-Ford, C. *et al.* (1935) *The Legacy of England: An Illustrated Survey of the Works of Man in the English Country* (Batsford)

Brittain, Vera (1933) *Testament of Youth* (Gollancz)

Delafield, E. M. (1930/1984) *The Diary of a Provincial Lady* (Virago)

Firth, C. H. (1909) *The School of English Language and Literature: A Contribution to the History of Oxford Studies* (Oxford University Press)

Ford, Ford Madox (1905) *The Soul of London* (Alston Rivers)

—— (1907) *England and the English* (New York, McClure) (One-volume edition of *The Soul of London*, *The Heart of the Country* and *The Spirit of the People*)

Grahame, Kenneth (1908) *The Wind in the Willows* (Chatto)

Graves, Robert and Hodge, Alan (1940/1991) *The Long Weekend: A Social History of Great Britain: 1918–1939*, (Cardinal)

Greenwood, Walter (1933) *Love on the Dole* (Harmondsworth, Penguin)

Herford, C. H. (1910) 'The Bearing of English Studies upon the National Life', *English Association Leaflet*, no. 16 (June) (Oxford)

Macdonell, A. G. (1933) *England, Their England* (Macmillan)

Mansfield, Katherine (1920/1962) *Bliss and Other Stories* (Harmondsworth, Penguin)

Massingham, H. J., Bates, H. E., Batsford, H. *et al.* (1939) *The English Countryside: A Survey of Its Chief Features* (Batsford)

Milne, A. A. (1926) *Winnie-the-Pooh* (Methuen)

Ministry of Information (1940/1982) 'Commentary of the film *London (Britain) Can Take It*', *Documentary Newsletter*, November 1940, pp.6–7, reprinted in Open University *A309 Documents 1918–1970* (Milton Keynes, Open University Press)

Newbolt, Sir H. (1928) 'The Idea of an English Association', *English Association Pamphlet*, No. 70 (July)

Orwell, George (1937) *The Road to Wigan Pier* (Gollancz)

—— (1945/1968) 'Poetry and the Microphone', in *The Collected Essays, Journalism and Letters of George Orwell: Volume 2: My Country Right or Left: 1940–1943* (Secker & Warburg), pp.329–336

—— (1945a/1968) 'The English People', in *The Collected Essays, Journalism and Letters of George Orwell: Volume 3: As I Please: 1943–1945* (Secker & Warburg), pp.1–37

Potter, Stephen (1937) *The Muse in Chains: A Study in Education* (Cape)

Priestley, J. B. (ed.) (1939) *Our Nation's Heritage* (Dent)

Thomas, Edward (1932/1982) *The South Country* (Dent)

Thompson, Flora (1939) *Lark Rise* (Oxford University Press)

—— (1941) *Over to Candleford* (Oxford University Press)

—— (1943) *Candleford Green* (Oxford University Press)

—— (1945) *Lark Rise to Candleford* (Oxford University Press)

Webb, Mary (1924) *Precious Bane* (Cape)

Yorke, F. R. S. (1944) *The Modern House in England* (Architectural Press/ Aberdeen University Press)

Other works

Addison, P. (1977) *The Road to 1945* (Pimlico)

Anderson, Benedict (1983) *Imagined Communities* (Verso)

Baldick, Chris (1983) *The Social Mission of English Criticism: 1848–1932* (Oxford University Press)

Balfour, M. (1979) *Propaganda in War 1939–1945* (Routledge)

Barker, Martin (1989) *Comics: Ideology: Power and the Critics* (Manchester University Press)

Batchelor, John (1982) *The Edwardian Novelists* (Duckworth)

Beddoe, Deirdre (1989) *Back to Home and Duty: Women between the Wars: 1918–1939* (Pandora)

Bell, Michael (ed.) (1980) *The Context of English Literature: 1900–1930* (Methuen)

Bell, Quentin (1968) *Bloomsbury* (Hogarth)

—— (1972) *Virginia Woolf: A Biography* (2 vols.) (Hogarth)

Beloff, M. (1984) *Wars and Welfare: Britain 1914–1945* (Edward Arnold)

Biddiss, Michael (1977) *The Age of the Masses: Ideas and Society in Europe since 1870* (Harmondsworth, Penguin)

Bloom, Clive (ed.) (1993) *Literature and Culture in Modern Britain: 1900–1929* (Longman)

Boyce, D. G. (1986) 'The Marginal Britons: The Irish', in R. Colls and P. Dodds (eds) *Englishness: Politics and Culture 1880–1920* (Croom Helm), pp.230–253

Bourke, Joanna (1993) *Working Class Cultures in Britain: 1890–1960* (Routledge)

Bradbury, Malcolm and McFarlane, James (eds) (1976) *Modernism: 1890–1930* (Harmondsworth, Penguin)

Brantlinger, Patrick (1988) *Rule of Darkness: British Literature and Imperialism: 1830–1914* (Ithaca, NY, Cornell University Press)

Briggs, Asa (1961) *The History of Broadcasting in the United Kingdom* (Oxford University Press)

—— (1972) *Mass Entertainment: The Origins of a Modern Industry* (Oxford University Press)

Brooker, Peter and Widdowson, Peter (1986) 'A Literature for England', in R. Colls and P. Dodds (eds) *Englishness: Politics and Culture 1880–1920* (Croom Helm), pp.116–163

Bullen, J. B. (ed.) (1988) *Post-Impressionists in England* (Routledge)

Burnett, John (1973) *A Social History of Housing* (Newton Abbot, David & Charles)

—— (1976) *Useful Toil: Autobiographies of Working People from the 1820s to the 1920s* (Allen Lane)

Bushaway, Bob (1992) 'Name upon Name: The Great War and Remembrance', in Roy Porter (ed.) *Myths of the English* (Cambridge, Polity), pp.136–167

Butler, Christopher (1994) *Early Modernism: Literature, Music and Painting in Europe: 1900–1916* (Cambridge University Press)

Calder, Angus (1969/1971) *The People's War: Britain 1939–1945* (Panther)

Cameron, James (1980) *Memory Lane: A Photographic Album of Daily Life in Britain 1930–1953* (Dent)

Chant, C. (ed.) (1989) *Science, Technology and Everyday Life: 1870–1950* (Routledge)

Clarke, J., Crichter, C. and Johnson, R. (eds) (1979) *Working Class Culture: Studies in History and Theory* (Hutchinson)

Cockburn, C. (1972) *Bestseller: The Books that Everyone Read 1900–1940* (Sidgwick & Jackson)

Colls, R. (1986) 'Englishness and the Political Culture', in R. Colls and P. Dodds (eds) *Englishness: Politics and Culture 1880–1920* (Croom Helm), pp.29–61

Colls, R. and Dodds, P. (eds) (1986) *Englishness: Politics and Culture 1880–1920* (Croom Helm)

Cross, Gary (1990) *Worktowners at Blackpool* (Routledge)

Crowther, M. A. (1992) 'The Tramp', in Roy Porter (ed.) *Myths of the English* (Cambridge, Polity), pp.91–113

Cunningham, Hugh (1986) 'The Conservative Party and Patriotism', in R.

Colls and P. Dodds (eds) *Englishness: Politics and Culture 1880–1920* (Croom Helm), pp.283–307

—— (1989) 'The Language of Patriotism', in Raphael Samuel (ed.) *Patriotism: The Making and Unmaking of British National Identity: Volume 1: History and Politics* (Routledge), pp.57–89

Curran, J. and Porter, V. (eds) (1983) *British Cinema History* (Weidenfeld & Nicolson)

Doyle, Brian (1982) 'The Hidden History of English Studies', in P. Widdowson (ed.) *Re-Reading English* (Methuen), pp.17–31

—— (1986) 'The Invention of English', in R. Colls and P. Dodds (eds) *Englishness: Politics and Culture 1880–1920* (Croom Helm), pp.89–115

—— (1989) *English and Englishness* (Routledge)

Dyhouse, C. (1989) *Feminism and the Family in England: 1880–1939* (Oxford, Basil Blackwell)

Eagleton, Terry (1984) *The Function of Criticism from 'The Spectator' to Post-Structuralism* (Verso)

Edel, Leon (1979) *Bloomsbury: A House of Lions* (Harmondsworth, Penguin)

Eliot, Valerie (ed.) (1990) *The Collected Letters of T. S. Eliot: Volume 1: 1898–1920* (Harcourt Brace Jovanovitch)

Farr, Dennis (1978) *English Art: 1870–1940* (Oxford, Clarendon)

Flint, Kate (1984) *Impressionists in England* (Routledge & Kegan Paul)

Ford, Boris (ed.) (1992) *Early 20th Century Britain* (Cambridge University Press)

Freedon, M. (1986) *Liberalism Divided: 1914–1939* (Oxford University Press)

Fussell, P. (1977) *The Great War and Modern Memory* (Oxford University Press)

Gervais, David (1993) *Literary Englands: Versions of 'Englishness' in Modern Writing* (Cambridge University Press)

Giles, Judy (1995) *Women: Identity and Private Life: 1900–1950* (Macmillan)

Gittins, D. (1982) *Fair Sex: Family Size and Structure 1900–1939* (Hutchinson)

Glucksman, M. (1990) *Women Assemble: Women Workers and the New Industries in Inter-War Britain* (Routledge)

Gott, Richard (1989) 'Little Englanders', in Raphael Samuel (ed.) *Patriotism: The Making and Unmaking of British National Identity: Volume 1: History and Politics* (Routledge), pp.90–109

Grainger, J. (1986) *Patriotisms: Britain 1900–1939* (Routledge & Kegan Paul)

Gross, John (1969) *The Rise and Fall of the Man of Letters: Aspects of Literary Life since 1800* (Harmondsworth, Penguin)

Harrison, Charles and Wood, Paul (1992) *Art in Theory: 1900–1990: An Anthology of Changing Ideas* (Oxford, Basil Blackwell)

Head, Dominic (1992) *The Modernist Short Story* (Cambridge University Press)

Heyck, Thomas W. (1987) 'The Idea of a University in Britain, 1870–1970', *History of European Ideas*, 8, no. 2, pp.205–219

Higonnet, M. R., *et al.* (eds) (1987) *Behind the Lines: Gender and the Two World Wars* (New Haven, Conn., Yale University Press)

Hobsbawm, E. J. (1990) *Nations and Nationalism since 1780* (Canto)

Hoggart, Richard (1958) *The Uses of Literacy* (Harmondsworth, Penguin)

Hopkin, D. (1970) 'Domestic Censorship in Britain in the First World War', *Journal of Contemporary History*, 5, no. 4, pp.151–169

Howarth, Janet and Curthoys, Mark (1987) 'The Political Economy of Women's Higher Education in Late Nineteenth and Early Twentieth Century Britain', *Historical Research*, 60, no. 142 (June), pp.208–231

Howkins, Alun (1986) 'The Discovery of Rural England', R. Colls and P. Dodds (eds) *Englishness: Politics and Culture 1880–1920* (Croom Helm), pp.62–88

Hunt, L. (ed.) (1989) *The New Cultural History* (Berkley, Calif., University of California Press)

Hunter, Jefferson (1982) *Edwardian Fiction* (Cambridge, Mass., Yale University Press)

Karl, Frederic (1985) *Modern and Modernism: The Sovereignty of the Artist 1885–1925* (New York, Athenaeum)

Keating, Peter (1989) *The Haunted Study: A Social History of the English Novel: 1875–1914* (Secker & Warburg)

Keith, W. J. (1975) *The Rural Tradition: William Cobbett, Gilbert White and Other Non-fictional Prose Writers of the English Countryside* (Brighton, Harvester)

Kelsall, Malcom (1992) *The Great Good Place: The Country House and English Literature* (Brighton, Harvester)

Laybourn, K. (1990) *Britain on the Breadline: A Social and Economic History of Britain Between the Wars* (Alan Sutton)

Light, Alison (1991) *Forever England: Femininity, Literature and Conservatism between the Wars* (Routledge)

Longmate, Norman (1981) *The Home Front: An Anthology: 1938–41* (Chatto & Windus)

Mackay, Jane and Thane, Pat (1986) 'The Englishwoman', in R. Colls and P. Dodds (eds) *Englishness: Politics and Culture 1880–1920* (Croom Helm), pp.191–229

Mangan, J. A. (1981) *Athleticism in the Victorian and Edwardian Public School: The Emergence and Consolidation of an Ideology* (Cambridge University Press)

Marwick, A. (1965) *The Deluge: British Society in the First World War* (Macmillan)

Mason, Tony (1980) *Association Football and English Society: 1863–1915* (Brighton, Harvester)

McAleer, J. (1993) *Popular Reading and Publishing in Britain: 1914–1950* (Oxford, Clarendon)

McKibbin, Ross (1990) 'Work and Hobbies in Britain: 1880–1950', in *The Ideologies of Class: Social Relations in Britain 1880–1950* (Oxford University Press), pp.139–166

Miles, P. and Smith, M. (1987) *Cinema, Literature and Society* (Croom Helm)

Morris, William (1891) *News from Nowhere* (Longman)

Mowatt, Charles Loch (1954/1984) *Britain between the Wars: 1918–1940* (Cambridge University Press)

Oliver, P., Davis, I. and Bentley, I. (1981) *Dunroamin': The Suburban Semi and its Enemies* (Barry & Jenkins)

Orel, Harold (1992) *Popular Fiction in England: 1914–1918* (Brighton, Harvester)

Oxford Companion to English Literature (1985) eds M. Drabble and J. Stringer (Oxford University Press)

Palmer, D. J. (1965) *The Rise of English Studies* (Oxford University Press)

Pelling, Henry (1960) *Modern Britain: 1885–1955* (Harmondsworth, Penguin)

Pepper, Simon (1992) 'The Garden City', in Boris Ford (ed.) *Early 20th Century Britain* (Cambridge University Press), pp.295–305

—— (1992a) 'John Laing's Sunnyfields Estate, Mill Hill' in Boris Ford (ed.) *Early 20th Century Britain* (Cambridge University Press), pp.101–115

Pollard, S. (1983) *The Development of the British Economy 1914–1980* (Edward Arnold)

Porter, Roy (ed.) (1992) *Myths of the English* (Cambridge, Polity)

Priestley, J. B. (1973) *The English* (Heinemann)

Pronay, N. (1972) 'British Newsreels in the 1930's: Their Policies and Impact', *History*, 57, no. 189, pp.63–72

Raitt, Suzanne (1993) *Vita and Virginia: The Work and Friendship of V. Sackville-West and Virginia Woolf* (Oxford, Clarendon)

Ramsay, J. G. (1993) *England, This England: In the Steps of J. B. Priestley* (Sinclair Stevenson)

Read, Herbert (1974) *A Concise History of Modern Painting* (Thames & Hudson)

Reid, Fred (1980) 'The disintegration of Liberalism, 1895–1931', in Michael Bell (ed.) *The Context of English Literature: 1900–1930* (Methuen), pp.94–125

Roberts, R. (1973) *The Classic Slum: Salford Life in the First Quarter of the Century* (Harmondsworth, Penguin)

Rowbottom, Sheila (1983) 'Travellers in a Strange Country: Responses of Working-Class Students to the University Extension Movement: 1873–1910', in *Dreams and Dilemmas: Collected Writings* (Virago), pp.267–305

Rowntree, B. S. (1902) *Poverty: A Study of Town Life* (Macmillan)

—— (1941) *Poverty and Progress: A Second Social Survey of York* (Longman)

Said, Edward (1993) *Culture and Imperialism* (Chatto & Windus)

Sabin, Roger (1993) *Adult Comics: An Introduction* (Routledge)

Samuel, Raphael (1975) *Rural Life and Labour* (Routledge & Kegan Paul)

—— (ed.) (1989) *Patriotism: The Making and Unmaking of British National Identity: Volume 1: History and Politics* (Routledge)

—— (ed.) (1989a) *Patriotism: The Making and Unmaking of British National Identity: Volume 2: Minorities and Outsiders* (Routledge)

—— (ed.) (1989b) *Patriotism: The Making and Unmaking of British National Identity: Volume 3: National Fictions* (Routledge)

Service, A. (1977) *Edwardian Architecture: A Handbook to Building Design in Britain 1890–1914* (Thames & Hudson)

Sheridan, D. (1984) 'Mass Observing the British', *History Today*, 34 (July), pp.42–46

Smith, Anthony (1991) *National Identity* (Harmondsworth, Penguin)

Smith, Dennis (1986) 'Englishness and the Liberal Inheritance after 1886', in R. Colls and P. Dodds (eds) *Englishness: Politics and Culture 1880–1920* (Croom Helm), pp.254–282

Soffer, Reba N. (1987) 'The Modern University and National Values 1850–1930', *Historical Research*, 60, no. 142 (June), pp.166–187

Spiering, M. (1992) *Englishness: Foreigners and Images of National Identity in Post-war Literature* (Studia Imagolgica 5) (Amsterdam and Atlanta, Editions Rodopi)

Stevenson, J. and Cook, C. (1979) *The Slump: Society and Politics during the Depression* (Quartet Books)

Stevenson, John (1984) *British Society 1914–45* (Harmondsworth, Penguin)

Summers, Anne (1989) 'Edwardian Militarism', in Raphael Samuel (ed.) *Patriotism: The Making and Unmaking of British National Identity: Volume 1: History and Politics* (Routledge), pp.236–256

Swenarton, M. (1981) *Homes Fit For Heroes: The Politics and Architecture of Early State Housing in Britain* (Heinemann)

Taylor, P. (1979) 'Daughters and Mothers – Maids and Mistresses: Domestic Service between the Wars', in J. Clarke, C. Crichter and R. Johnson (eds) *Working Class Culture: Studies in History and Theory* (Hutchinson)

Thompson, Paul (1977) *The Edwardians: The Re-Making of British Society* (Harmondsworth, Penguin)

Thomson, David (1981) *England in the Twentieth Century: 1914–1979* (Harmondsworth, Penguin)

Tillyard, Stella (1988) *The Impact of Modernism: The Visual Arts in England* (Routledge)

Trotter, David (1993) *The English Novel in History* (Routledge)

Waites, Bernard (1976) 'The Language and Imagery of Class in Early Twentieth Century England (circa 1900–1925)', *Literature and History*, 4, no. 4 (Autumn), pp.30–55

——— (1976a) 'The Effect of the First World War on Class and Status in England: 1910–1920', *Journal of Contemporary History*, 11, no. 1, pp.27–48

Ward, S. (ed.) (1992) *The Garden City: Past, Present and Future* (E & F. N. Spon)

Webber, G. (1986) *The Ideology of the British Right 1918–1939* (New York, St Martin's Press)

Widdowson, P. (ed.) (1982) *Re-Reading English* (Methuen)

Wiener, M. (1981) *English Culture and the Decline of the Industrial Spirit* (Cambridge University Press)

Williams, Raymond (1958/1961) *Culture and Society: 1780–1950* (Harmondsworth, Penguin)

——— (1961) *The Long Revolution* (Harmondsworth, Penguin)

——— (1970) *The English Novel from Dickens to Lawrence* (Hogarth Press)

——— (1973) *The Country and the City* (Paladin)

——— (1981) *Culture* (Fontana)

——— (1989) *The Politics of Modernism*, ed. T. Pinkney (Verso)

Willis, Susan (1991) *A Primer for Daily Life* (Routledge)

Wright, D. G. (1978) 'The Great War, Government Propaganda and English Men of Letters: 1914–1916', *Literature and History*, 4, no. 7 (Spring), pp.70–104

Yeo, Stephen (1986) 'Socialism, The State and Some Oppositional Englishness', in R. Colls and P. Dodds (eds) *Englishness: Politics and Culture 1880–1920* (Croom Helm), pp.308–389

INDEX

Page numbers in bold denote biographical details of the author.